NF

GW00500287

IN THE CITY

IN THE CITY

BRIAN WIDLAKE

ff

faber and faber

LONDON · BOSTON

First published in 1986 by
Faber and Faber Limited
3 Queen Square London WC1N 3AU
Photoset by Parker Typesetting Service, Leicester
Printed in Great Britain by
Mackays of Chatham, Kent

British Library Cataloguing in Publication Data
Widlake, Brian
In the City.
1. Financial institutions—England—London
I. Title
332.1'09421'2   HG186.G7
ISBN 0-571-13516-1

CONTENTS

The Markets and money flows
in London's financial system

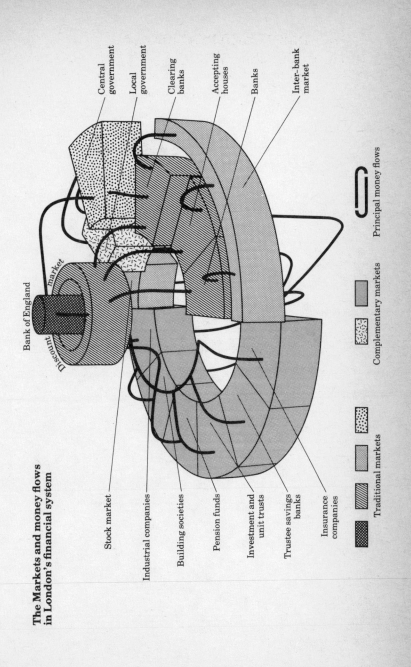

Central government

Local government

Clearing banks

Accepting houses

Banks

Inter-bank market

Bank of England

Discount market

Stock market

Industrial companies

Building societies

Pension funds

Investment and unit trusts

Trustee savings banks

Insurance companies

Traditional markets

Complementary markets

Principal money flows

THE SQUARE MILE

The City of London may cover an area of a square mile, but it is certainly not a square. Looked at from the air, the City is the shape of a helmet, with Liverpool Street station an excrescence on the back of the head. The whole of its southern edge is lapped by the Thames. Its eastern limit is marked by the Port of London Authority, Fenchurch Street station and Aldgate. The western flank is bounded incongruously by the Inns of Court and the Fleet Street press – incongruously because neither can be said to be part of the City. To the north of Fleet Street there are Hatton Garden, for diamonds, the meat markets of Smithfield, and Bart's Hospital. North-east of Smithfield there is the Barbican, now an expensive, unattractive area of tall, grey apartment blocks, which have done nothing to enhance the City's limited architectural appeal. Only Sir Christopher Wren left an enduring mark on the City, with St Paul's Cathedral, fifty-one churches and the Monument. Even Sir John Soane's Bank of England, which superseded George Sampson's original building, was rebuilt in the 1930s.

The Overseas Presence

Much has happened to this landscape in the last twenty years. Physically, it has undergone random change – the kind of change that architects and planners devise when they run out of space. The City can expand sideways no longer; it has to be upwards. Almost every month a new building takes shape, eventually to poke a finger of steel and glass into the sky above the City of Wren, Soane and Sir William Tite. Since the 1960s there has been a burst of vigorous expansion as the City invested in its home ground regardless of cost. The big institutions have poured millions of pounds into new office blocks, many of them hideous, in order to accommodate the increasing demand for financial services. The overseas presence is growing all the time. American, German, French, Swiss and Italian banks are commonplace; the Arabs are much in evidence.

NatWest and Canary Wharf

No building typifies more the process of expansion than the National Westminster Bank's new building at 25 Old Broad Street. It looks as if it should be the head office, but it is not – the bank prefers Lothbury, a few yards from the Bank of England. The new premises dwarf the lofty Colditz of the Stock Exchange, a product of the early seventies, and shrink to nothing the glass box of the Hongkong Banking Group in Bishopsgate. The building is composed of superlatives. At 600 feet, it is the highest in Britain and the second tallest in Europe. It took nine years to build, has fifty-two floors and from the top it is possible to see six counties. The cost ran to £98 million – testimony, if any were needed, that the banks have an immensely strong grip on the country's economic life.

But the development of Canary Wharf in London's Dockland will dwarf that by far. It will be a City in itself – proof, if any were needed, that the financial revolution taking place in the Square Mile is already going well beyond the City's traditional boundaries.

2

INTRODUCTION

The City of London has always been a formidable place, embracing within its famous square mile (and sometimes outside it) a concentration of financial power that until recent years had no equal. It is the only highly populated area in Britain I can think of where a stranger can feel truly lonely: the passing traffic of men, messengers and secretaries bears no relation to the busy thoroughfares of London's West End or those of our provincial cities, where almost anyone can perceive and understand what it is that other people are doing.

Privacy and Enigma

The City is quite different. Men in silk hats and expensive suits drift along the pavements, apparently without purpose. Others, like the White Rabbit, scurry from building to building, consulting their watches to see that they are in time for whatever they are supposed to be in time for. Rolls-Royces glide up Cornhill or along Moorgate, their occupants addressing themselves to their cigars or balance sheets or, just as likely, the racing pages. The City has its own police force, Lord Mayor and livery companies. It has a restrained panoply and contained ceremony of its own, which rarely reach the light of day (once or twice a year, perhaps, with the Lord Mayor's Show and the Lord Mayor's Banquet) or come under anything so vulgar as the searchlight of public interest. Privacy and enigma are what it lives by. A stranger can roam its streets and learn nothing. It has a tiny resident population (just under 5,000) but a working population of tens of thousands, most of whom understand only a small fraction of what it does or how it does it. On the surface, it is impenetrable and complex, distant and isolated, encompassing a different breed of humanity, which earns its livelihood from the practice of arcane mysteries. In short, there is no other place like it on earth.

Change

Why, then, bother to write a book about it? It has been done before. Walter Bagehot, the first editor of *The Economist*, studied the money markets in his classic *Lombard Street* and subsequently he has been followed by others who have broadened the scope of that early City analysis. There is, however, a compelling precedent for writing such a book now. The people who walk down Lombard Street, or potter through Change Alley, or who can be seen emerging from the Royal Exchange dressed improbably in blazers are undergoing the most radical change in the City's history. The young men in blazers are a small part of that change – they work in the new financial futures market, an idea imported from America, which has already put down firm roots in the City.

The Big Bang

But no more than a stone's throw from their market – up the road in Old Broad Street, the home of the Stock Exchange – there are stockbrokers and jobbers who for the first time in their lives, indeed for the first time in centuries, are having to throw all their cherished practices and traditions out of the window to confront the biggest challenge the City has ever had to contend with. And not merely brokers and jobbers, but clearing banks, merchant banks, discount houses and our major investment institutions – they are all being fanned by a wind of change that, by the end of 1986, the year of the 'Big Bang', will have altered the stable, old-fashioned structure of the City beyond recognition.

Even now, most of the old alliances have dropped away to be replaced by new ones. The cosy demarcation between jobbers and brokers has all but disappeared. Firms that once worked alone, and were proud of their independence, their contacts and their individualism, now find themselves obliged to join forces with groups that are alien by nature, psychology and practice. They have not done it from choice but from necessity. When the basic structure of a great market changes, the instinct for survival tends to take precedence. When the pressure of reform is too urgent to resist, old habits are quickly buried and new fashions adopted. The banks are putting up millions of pounds for a slice of the action and a large part of the major risk the changes involve – something they would never have considered a few years ago. The Americans and the Swiss, too, have been buying broking firms, talent and skills. The hunt for people with the capacity to make profits, to serve new markets and masters, has become a ruthless chase in which the cheque book has been talking more persuasively than words or promises. Only the City could invent the 'golden hello' to compete with the golden handshake.

Agnostics and Believers

What makes this process of rapid, radical change even more exciting is that no one knows what or where it will lead to. The idea that it will benefit the serious investor, or the man in the street with just a few hundred pounds to spend, is still a hazy one. Certainly, the abolition of restrictive practices in the Stock Exchange, which is how the whole process began under Mrs Thatcher's Government, should lead to more competition among the new market makers who will be vying with each other to get more business. Whether that will feed through to the investor's pocket in the shape of more competitive prices and better service is quite another matter. There are wise men in the City – cautious, prudent; many would say unrealistic – who will have no part of this revolution, who are already predicting that it will lead to a savage bloodbath in which some of the new conglomerates will have their throats cut by tougher, bigger and shrewder competitors with deeper pockets and more determination. The investor, they say, will be simply a hapless spectator on the sidelines; he will be assailed by market makers with promises of profit without knowing what he is really getting or at what real cost. He will be in a strange new world desperately getting to grips with itself after centuries of gradual, painstaking evolution, which has always been the City's preferred style.

Winners and Losers

In that context, the years ahead are not going to be dull or stable. There will be crashes and failures. Already there are brokers who cannot find a niche for themselves in the City's brave new world and who are fading from the scene. Inevitably, they will be followed by others who will find that the heat in the kitchen is too hot. The days of padded, secure and handsomely paid jobs are shortening by the month to be replaced by a new environment where risk, uncertainty and fierce competition are the brute facts of City life but where the rewards will be perversely larger than they were before.

The City revolution is the prime reason for writing this book now. In it, I have attempted to plot the process and course of change, to chart the new alliances and suggest where they might be going in a restructured market. At this stage, one can reasonably say that the architecture of the new City is in place, but that the bricks and mortar and the size and shape of the buildings that will emerge from the revolution are still shadowy. As I have suggested earlier, the 'Big Bang' of 1986 will produce shock waves that are likely to reduce some of the architecture to rubble. It will be a few years yet before we are able to see what is still standing, whether it adorns or disfigures the landscape, and whether, after the traumatic destruction of tradition and practice, something has been created which is of real benefit.

The City's Markets

That is one reason why I wrote this book. Another is that the City is too important not to be understood. Its ramifications and influence are extensive and its fingers probe deeply into our personal lives. Whether they like it or not, people who have bank accounts are indissolubly tied to the banking parlours of Lombard Street and not, as they might imagine, to their local bank manager. The contents of their modest deposit accounts are already far away in the money markets earning valuable interest for their banks or providing someone else with the means to finance a factory or build an office block. Their money is always working and there are people in the City whose sole job is to make it work. Anyone who has a mortgage knows what an impact interest rates have on family finances. But these rates are not thought up or devised by the local banks: they are merely a link in a long chain that extends back through the high street to the banks' head offices to the discount houses to Threadneedle Street. It is there that the Bank of England manipulates the money supply to take into account such factors as the exchange rate of sterling and the government's economic policy. It is the Bank that determines the price of money and the cost of loans. For money is not an isolated commodity: like wheat or barley, whose price is dependent on good or bad harvests, it is volatile. It can be cheap one week, expensive the next. Its price is an important factor in determining how much investment goes into the economy, which in turn can determine the rate of growth, its effect on jobs, the price employers pay for their labour and the amount of goods they choose to produce.

Money Touches Everything

In one way or another, everything the City does is concerned with money although its constituent markets do not immediately give that impression. The Baltic Exchange, the clearing

7

house for people who want to charter ships to carry their goods, concerns itself with the rates for that shipping and the availability of ships to do the job. But money eventually changes hands. The insurance market gets involved, too, because shipping has to be insured and so do the goods that the ships carry. That has to be paid for. It may well be that the ship owner has to be paid in dollars and not sterling, in which case a British exporter will have to acquire the dollars through the foreign-exchange market. And behind the exporter and the ship owner there will be the banks – the clearing and merchant banks – who will often have to provide the finance to make the deal possible. What happens in one market, therefore, invariably involves other markets; they interact with each other. I have tried to explain these institutions and how they work because there is nothing we buy that does not involve the City of London : it oils the wheels of trade, industry and finance on one level and on another it arranges our credit-card transactions, our overdraft limits and, to a large extent, our patterns of living and expenditure. It is far less remote than we care to imagine and sometimes much too close for comfort. Some of these markets are older than the Bank of England itself; others are babies that have been born in the last few years and are now useful additions to a growing family of markets.

Fraud, Regulation, Tradition

But the City's influence is not always as benign as it would like us to believe, nor are its institutions as perfect as it often claims. Fraud, for example, is as old as mankind and its vigour is undiminished. It has struck the Lloyd's insurance market with depressing frequency in the last ten years and the sums involved, together with the damage it has done to Lloyd's reputation and the fortunes of individual underwriters, are breathtaking. It says something for the resilience of the backwoodsmen in Lloyd's that they have fought change tooth and nail and have resisted what efforts there have been to reduce malpractice with the grim determination of General Custer at his last stand at Little

Bighorn. In time, no doubt, these clansmen will be routed by the Indians but while they can muster a rifle between them they are going to make a fight of it. Fraud has touched the Stock Exchange, too, the commodity markets and even the banks. It poses tough problems for the regulators, who up to now have preferred self-regulation to the statutory kind that could be imposed by Parliament. It is a battle they may well lose. The City revolution is already throwing up a host of question marks, not the least of which is how to deal with conflicts of interest – a polite way of referring to groups of people who by the nature of their business can take advantage of other groups of people, generally investors, to line their own pockets. But it is only one of many problems, some of which I have set out in this book. One way or another, the City is going to have its considerable capacity for innovation and flexibility tested to the full and what is happening now is its sternest examination yet. But it would be pleasant to think that beneath the gilded crust of a very rich cake investors will emerge from the lower layers and get a coating, however thin, of some of the cream. It can be scarcely before time.

THE BANKS

THE BANK OF ENGLAND

Ask anyone outside the City what the Bank of England does and the answer would probably be that it issues the notes we carry around in our pockets. That is true, but it is a very small part of the Bank's pervasive role in the country's financial policy. Apart from the Governor, Robin Leigh-Pemberton, its officials and directors are virtually unknown except to the City itself and even then often in the vaguest way. They do not have the high profiles that the local managers of Barclays or NatWest enjoy in their high streets or leafy suburbs. Yet they mix freely with the chairmen of the clearing banks, who lend an attentive ear to what they have to say, and they wine and dine with senior brokers, merchant bankers and the people who run the discount houses. They range widely over a small patch, but it is a patch that includes the other central banks around the world, the International Monetary Fund, the Bank for International Settlements, the World Bank and a handful of other financial institutions that influence the international monetary scene.

The City's Core Institution

Put as baldly as that, the Bank appears to comprise no more than a handful of monetary technicians who discuss international finance at an arcane level in distant and pleasant financial centres. Yet the Bank of England is the core institution of the City. From its large, almost triangular bastion in Threadneedle Street its tentacles of influence and persuasion spread through the banking system, the money markets and the City's securities industry. Almost everything of a financial nature is monitored by the Bank. Its powers are formidable; its influence scarcely perceptible to the outsiders; its discretion total – except in those well-publicized instances when the Bank has disagreed openly with the Treasury on matters of economic interpretation. In the last three years, however, it has become a much more open institution, actively stirring the City into making the biggest structural changes in its history.

Ambiguity

But the Bank has always had an ambiguous relationship with government. In its early history, the ambiguity arose from the privileges conferred upon it by politicians, in return for which governments expected, and generally received, financial help and support from the Bank in some form or other. However, the relationship has not always been easy. There were often disagreements; politicians were never much less than suspicious of the Bank's motives, imputing to it – often wrongly – a preference for profit rather than the national interest. That is a common complaint about great and powerful financial institutions – whether it concerns banks investing in South Africa or the provision of funds for industry – and it continued, in the case of the Bank, right up to 1946 when it was nationalized by Attlee's Labour Government. Even now, the Bank is sometimes regarded, inside and outside government, as an institution that tries to pursue a role independent of its political masters. In part, this perception arises from the fact that the Bank is the hub of our financial markets and very few people can grasp what these markets do, even less how the Bank relates to them. It is attractive, therefore, to assume that the Bank can play a dark and sometimes malign role in our economic and financial affairs, without realizing that most of its work is technical and that its skills, whether they are applied to funding the government's expenditure requirements or restructuring the City, are not duplicated in the Treasury or in other government departments.

In this sense, the Bank is unique. A politician may think he can get to grips with the National Health Service or the problems of defence, but what he cannot do is tell the Bank how to get its hands on a large international loan to help the country's economy or guide it on how it should influence interest rates in the money market. Central-banking techniques, and the way central bankers relate to each other, are not subjects that can be acquired quickly at a two-day seminar run by a business school.

Central Bank and Bankers' Bank

Again, the breadth of the institution is somewhat daunting. It is not only the central bank of the country, it is also the bankers' bank where all the other banks keep accounts. It controls the money markets and through them the amount of liquidity there is in the banking system: the Bank implements the government's monetary policy through the financial 'instruments' at its disposal. It is also the agent of the government's policy on the sterling exchange rate as against other currencies. The Bank has other functions as well: the supervision of the banking system and the conduct of the City's markets among them.

League of Gentlemen

None of this occurred through any planning or foresight. When the Bank was founded in 1694 the name 'England' was entirely fortuitous. Even its founders – men of the utmost *gravitas* heavily endowed with self-esteem – had no idea then that the country's first public bank was to assume such importance in the nation's affairs. But its foundation was a necessity. The Goldsmith bankers, who had virtually taken over the banking system from the Lombard firms (they had disappeared in a morass of bankruptcies), had been badly treated by the Crown. Charles II, who owed them the best part of £1 million, had put a 'stop' on interest payments on part of this loan, and although the Goldsmiths eventually recouped their money the government's credit and standing did not recover. The reign of the Stuarts was characterized by a very low credit rating and being bankers to royalty was more a millstone than a profitable privilege.

The Need for a Public Bank

When William of Orange came to the throne, his main concern was to safeguard the country's interests against the French. He was desperately short of money – government debt by this time was grossly inflated – and there was a general recognition that there was a need for a public bank. Ever since Cromwell and the Commonwealth, during which government borrowing had soared, there had been a constant debate about some rationalization of the banking system, which, at that time, was a loose confederation of merchants who accepted deposits at interest and used many of the banking instruments we know today. However, there were no banks as such, places where people could deposit their money, get paid interest and withdraw cash on demand.

Although the system was efficient, if cumbersome, any government in the market to finance wars, and loaded with debt, was an obvious candidate for a bank that would help to finance these expensive and tedious obligations. William Paterson, a Scot and a City liveryman, came up with the idea of the Bank of England. Paterson was an imaginative man who tended to 'come up' with things. He came up, for example, with an idea to colonize the eastern province of Panama, Darien, with Scottish emigrants – an unmitigated disaster that inflicted on the wretched colonists an appalling climate they could not cope with.

Although he is now seen as either overrated or a crank, Paterson at least was an 'ideas man' and it is unlikely that the Bank would have been founded when it was without his initiative. The Scot's scheme had the full backing of Charles Montagu, the Chancellor of the Exchequer, who saw in it a political and financial expedient that suited the government down to the ground. For the privilege of banking status, the Bank's initial capital of £1.2 million was to be lent to the government immediately in return for a 'perpetual fund of interest' of £100,000 a year.

The Early Directors

The Bank's first Court of Directors reflected the City's obsession with respectability and affluence. Sir John Houblon was elected the first Governor. He was a rich merchant and a Lord Mayor of the City; so was Sir Thomas Abney, another Director. Sir William Hedges was an old East India Company hand, a former Governor of Bengal, who stood for the mayoralty of the City but was never elected. Houblon's brother James was on the original Court and so was Abraham Houblon, another brother. Paterson was also a Director for a short time. Sir Gilbert Heathcote, a founding Director of the Bank and a Lord Mayor as well, was rich but noted for his meanness. Alexander Pope, in his *Moral Essays*, had no time for him: 'The grave Sir Gilbert holds it for a rule/That every man in want is knave or fool.' Heathcote complained to his local parson about the burial fees for his brother – a few shillings – and, not surprisingly, died the richest commoner in England, worth some £700,000.

The first Court had twenty-six Directors, including the Governor and his Deputy, a merchant called Michael Godfrey who was killed a year later in the Flanders trenches. By that time the Bank had decided to set up an agency in Antwerp to coin money for paying the troops in Flanders and Godfrey was one of the Directors appointed to 'methodize the same'. When they arrived at Namur, which was besieged by William, the King invited them to dinner in his tent and afterwards they inspected the trenches. Godfrey was killed by an enemy cannonball, the first and last Director to be killed in this way while going about his business. But he had already managed to publish a pamphlet, *A Short Account of the Bank of England*, although he could not have been overburdened with material since the Bank had been in existence for only a year.

The Bank's Symbol

On their election, the Directors swore they would be 'indifferent and equall to all manner of persons' and promised to do their best for the Bank. The Bank chose Britannia as its symbol. Britannia had been modelled by Frances Stewart, Duchess of Richmond, at Charles II's insistence in 1667. It was not surprising – the King was besotted with the young beauty. She was originally bare-legged, but her shapeliness was soon covered up and the Royal Mint, which belonged to the King and had nothing to do with the Bank, used her on its designs for its copper halfpennies and farthings. The Bank followed the farthing design, but made some alterations: a bank of money, or coins, was introduced by her feet, and her shield bore only the Cross of St George and not the combined crosses of England and Scotland. The Bank's Britannia carried a spear, not a trident, and this was the most important difference between the two. The bank of money disappeared for a long period during the eighteenth and nineteenth centuries when for some reason successive artists mistook it for a beehive.

Customers and Methods

The Bank quickly settled down to its major task, which was how the banking business was to be carried out. Initially, it employed exactly the same system as the Goldsmith bankers. People who deposited money with the Bank would have the choice of three methods 'and none other'. They could receive 'running cash notes' payable on demand, either in whole or in part; part payments would be endorsed on the notes. They could keep a 'book of paper' in which deposits and payments would be entered by the Bank. Or they could draw notes on the Bank to the extent of their deposits, which the Bank would then 'accept'. In fact, these methods were the forerunners of the banknote, the passbook and the cheque. The trouble was that customers could use only one of the methods at any one time, although they could change it if they gave notice to the Court. The system was hopelessly cumbersome and time-consuming and the Bank soon changed to customer accounts, which kept a running record of all their transactions.

The Bank's First Home

There was also some additional housekeeping to do – namely, where to put the Bank. Apparently the Royal Exchange was out of the question, so the Bank took an 11-year lease – later extended to 40 years – on the hall of the Grocers' Company, in which it accommodated thirty-six people, but not its porters and watchmen. It was from here that the Bank had to deal with the demands of the government, which were not inconsiderable. The original capital of the Bank (£1.2 million) had been authorized for the war against France. It had been subscribed within six months and was quickly handed out to the Army and Navy, but the Navy took the bulk of the funds – it was already a large industry in the process of technological improvements. But the main problem was to pay the Army in the Flanders trenches. Not long after Godfrey's death by cannon, the Bank set up a complex network of agents throughout Europe – most of the Continent was allied against the French anyway – who used foreign banks and merchants to help them in their funding operation for the armed forces.

The Bank's Enemies

Between 1694 and 1720, the year the South Sea Bubble burst, the Bank became firmly involved in the financial life of the country, but not always as smoothly as the Directors would have liked. In 1695, it survived a petition to Parliament from City merchants and traders, which said that the Bank was 'ruinous and destructive to trade in general' and that it was interested only in anything advantageous to itself. William Paterson, who was still a member of the Bank's Court, emerged in a new guise – as the promoter of a rival bank, curiously called the Orphans' Fund. It was not the act of a gentleman. The Court said Paterson had broken his trust as a Director. Paterson voluntarily sacked himself.

Competition

But there was more competition in the offing. This was the idea of land banks, whose assets would be based on land and money. It appealed to Tory landowners, who would back any scheme that extracted from their land the capital they frequently needed. The Bank was against it, of course, but the notion had some powerful backing and the establishment of the land bank received the Royal Assent in April 1696. Two months later, subscription lists were opened. (The King, so it was said, was a subscriber.) It was a dismal failure, but the fact that it had been supported by the government had not done the standing or the credit of the Bank much good.

Privilege

The government's awareness that it had bungled the land bank affair gave it a new perception of the Bank of England's role. In 1696, the Commons endorsed the Bank's pre-eminence in the country's financial life by conferring upon it an extraordinary privilege: it passed an Act that excluded any other organization from competing with it for the next five years. The importance of the Bank's own notes was also recognized – the death penalty for anyone who forged them. While they were not yet the King's money, they were getting close to it.

There was another side to the privilege, of course: namely, the government's eagerness to raise the value of its tallies, which were already heavily discounted. The Bank absorbed the lot, thereby increasing its capital in the short term, and offered them for public subscription with the Treasury buying them back as redemptions fell due. The Bank received 8 per cent on the tallies and the whole debt of rather more than £1 million was written off in eleven years. The parsimonious Gilbert Heathcote, a Bank Director, reputedly made £60,000.

The Tories Try to Take over the Bank

The work of the Bank at this time was carried on by a staff of less than a hundred. Outside the Court of Directors, all of whom enjoyed social and financial distinction, the clerks who worked in 'the House', as it is called, were a varied bunch of people. There were no age limits to employment. For two centuries at least, many of the clerks had business interests outside the Bank. 'Holy-dayes' numbered around forty, so there was opportunity for commercial activities on the side. A number of people actually lived in the Bank. There were five members of the staff, servants, who lived in, along with the gate porter who, in 1697, was fitted out with a 'crimson clothe lined with orange and a large Bamboo cane with a silver head'. The uniform is still worn today by the porter on duty at the gate. Over some thirty years at Grocers' Hall there were additions of nightwatchmen, messengers and doorkeepers. At night the watchmen were armed and worked in pairs, both inside the Bank and outside in the yard and garden.

In 1710, the Bank needed more than its staff to protect its premises. The Bank was a creature of the Whigs, in tune with the Party's policy of supporting those who dissented from the Established Church. It was a policy that alarmed High Tory churchmen, among them Dr Henry Sacheverell. Sacheverell preached two sermons in his most intemperate language and was subsequently impeached in the House of Lords for 'malicious, scandalous and seditious libels, highly reflecting upon Her Majesty and Her Government, the late happy revolution, and the Protestant Succession'.

Sacheverell is Impeached

The case led to rioting by Sacheverell's supporters who wrecked the Dissenters' meeting houses and then turned their eyes towards the Bank, a Whig stronghold and supposedly bulging with gold. Squadrons of the Horse Guards had to be mobilized before the mob was dispersed. The Bank was not in any real danger, but the Directors had reason to be alarmed by the wider implications of the Sacheverell affair. Sacheverell was only narrowly impeached and his punishment reflected it: his two sermons were burnt and he was forbidden to preach for three years. The Whigs had not only made a bad tactical error, they now had a churchman on their hands who was touring the country receiving the plaudits of substantial crowds. It was clear that the Tories would cash in on it.

The Bank's Directors were so alarmed by the possibility of a change of government that they relayed their fears to Queen Anne. The Tories were infuriated by the Directors' presumption. But the Bank was proved right. In November 1710 the Tories were returned with a sweeping majority on the back of Sacheverell's impeachment. The Bank now faced an administration hostile to it in every way. Typically, the Directors grovelled with toadying reassurances that they would support the 'Publick Credit and concur in any measures that their Lordships should think proper for that end'. Their Lordships knew a good thing when they saw it and promptly requested a further loan from the Bank for £50,000. It was not refused.

Sacheverell Tries Again

Now it was the Tories' turn to blunder. They did not feel ambivalent about the Bank; they were determined to get control of the Court of Directors. For some reason they thought that Sacheverell, who was enjoying the popularity of a public martyr, could do the job for them. Four months after the Tories were returned, the doctor bought £500 of stock, which entitled him to a vote in the April election of Governors and Directors. He was whistling in the wind. The voting body was the General Court of Proprietors and it could not have been very different in composition from the original one at the Bank's foundation. They came down heavily on the side of the existing Directors, who were all returned after the highest vote ever recorded. The only sop to Sacheverell's failure to oust the Directors was when he sold his stock three years later and made a decent profit.

In that year, 1714, Queen Anne died and George I came to the throne. A few months after his accession there were Jacobite plots in London, which not only included the proclamation of the Pretender as King but the seizure and incineration of the Bank and the assassination of Sir Gilbert Heathcote, who by now was Governor. These plots were all frustrated.

The South Sea Bubble

Six years later the Bank found itself involved in the scandal of the South Sea Bubble, which was on the point of bursting. The affair is described in more detail later, in relation to the Stock Exchange, but what happened is that the Bank was asked by the South Sea Company, now on the point of collapse through an outrageous and crooked speculation, to lend it a hand. The Bank willingly complied. It converted almost £4 million of debt owed to it by the government in exchange for South Sea stock – no doubt tempted by the enormous rate of interest the South Sea directors were offering: no less than 400 per cent. When the Bank opened subscriptions for the stock, money poured through its doors.

The Bank's Role

It was too late. The Sword Blades Bank, the South Sea's main creditor, stopped any further payments to the company, by now convinced that the game was up. The Bank faced a run on its cash and two months after its agreement with the South Sea Company it precipitately revoked it, thereby incurring the blame for the crash. But the Bank did not escape unscathed. It had to call in 25 per cent of the loans it had made on its own stock and went down on its knees to get debtors to return the remainder. It also called in advances made to the East India Company and other corporations. Customers were offered interest-bearing

notes, with 90-day maturity, in return for ordinary notes
and cash. By the end of the year it was in the clear again and
its stock stood well above par. The Bank, in effect, had
ditched the South Sea. This seems to be borne out by the
subsequent litigation between the Bank and the company
when the Bank was ordered to pay some recompense.

Sir Theodore Janssen, who was a Director of the Bank and
the South Sea Company did not come out of the affair with
clean hands. Indeed, the Bank's participation must to some
extent have been prompted by him since he had a foot in
both camps. Together with the governors, directors and officials of the South Sea Company he was brought before the
Bar of the House of Commons and, like them, ordered to
forfeit his estates. But he was luckier than most – he was
allowed to keep £50,000. His parliamentary career, however, was ruined. He was expelled from the House of Commons, where he represented Yarmouth. The league of
gentlemen, which founded the Bank, was otherwise intact.

Domestic Matters and Fraud at the Bank

What kind of business was the Bank doing at this time?
First, there was government business. Under the terms of
its renewed Charter, which gave it a clear run until 1733,
the Bank was allowed to double its authorized capital to
£4.4 million. It agreed to advance £400,000 to the government, which meant that the State's indebtedness to the
Bank was now £1.6 million at 6 per cent – revised from the
old arrangement of £1.2 million at 8 per cent, the deal
struck when the Bank was founded. But apart from helping
to finance the National Debt, the Bank had also been managing part of the Debt as well – the tallies and so on. It also
acted as receiving agent for the State Lotteries of 1710 and
the two subsequent years. In other words, its closeness to
the government meant that it was not only becoming a
public institution, but was on the road to becoming banker
to the nation.

For the domestic customer the process of withdrawing

THE BANK OF ENGLAND

cash from the bank was still an arduous process, involving
several ledgers, some form-filling, authorization and eventually payment. The piece of paper he presented to the teller
was known as a 'drawn note', the precursor of the cheque,
and the paper itself was chequered. The notes he received
were called 'cashier's' or 'running cash notes', embossed
with a Britannia medallion with all the relevant information – such as date and amount – written by hand. Discounting bills of exchange was also an early and important part
of the Bank's business. A bill of exchange was simply an
order addressed by one person (the drawer) to another (the
drawee) to pay a certain sum on a given date to a named
payee, or to the bearer (i.e. the person who was delivering
it). Essentially, it is cashing a bill before it matures, and
when the Bank did this it paid less than the face value of the
bill by discounting it at whatever the prevailing rate was.
The Bank also traded in gold and silver.

Crooked Clerks and a Crooked Governor

There was also trading of another kind going on in the
Bank, but it was under the counter and fraudulent. The
Accountant-General, Sir Edward Northey, noted that the
clerks had been cooking the books and making a quick profit
before they were caught. That was hardly surprising,
bearing in mind the prevailing morality and habits of the
working classes. But no one expected a Governor of the
Bank to play the same game. Humphry Morice, Member of
Parliament for Grampound, had been a Director of the Bank
for fifteen years and Governor from 1727 to 1729. But it was
discovered shortly after his death that he was a crook,
having been 'for Many years before, and until his Death,
reputed to be a Person of great Wealth, and of undoubted
Fairness and Integrity in his Dealings'.

Morice was obviously a conman of distinction and he
couldn't have had a better job behind which to conceal his
talent for fraud – after all, who in the Bank could possibly
suspect the Governor of forging bills that the Bank then
discounted for him? It was a perfect arrangement. Nor was

that all. Morice was not only hopelessly in debt when he died, but the man of 'Fairness and Integrity' had also pillaged a trust fund set up by a maternal uncle for his motherless daughters. They and the wretched Mrs Morice were the heaviest losers in the whole affair. The Bank sued her for their losses – just under £29,000 – but she complained and there was a new trial. Litigation continued right up until her death. Many years later the Bank managed to salvage £12,000 from the mess and then wrote off the balance of £17,000 to profit and loss.

'Consols' and Funding Military Commitments

It must not be thought, however attractive the idea may be, that the Bank was constantly being used as a tool of financial manipulation by unscrupulous Directors and staff. It had a much more serious purpose than that. The post-Morice era saw the Bank deeply involved in a role it was becoming accustomed to: lending to the government to finance its military commitments. It put up £1 million for the war with France and for the suppression of the Jacobite Rebellion, which ended with Culloden Field in April 1746. Shortly afterwards the Bank's capital was increased to very nearly £11 million. Six years later the 3 per cent annuities that had been issued in the reigns of the two Georges were consolidated into one fund and became known as 'Consols'. Annuities, in fact, represented the major part of the government's funding programme for the war with France and they were managed by the Bank. By the time the war ended in 1763 the National Debt had swollen from a mere £27 million thirty-six years earlier to a massive £139 million. If the war had been enormously expensive, it had also had repercussions on the City's trading community, which felt the backlash of some major bankruptcies on the Continent, notably in Hamburg and Amsterdam. Consequently, a number of merchant firms found themselves in financial difficulties and the Bank advanced £1 million to forestall a panic.

The Bank Expands

The Bank's increasing business meant a bigger staff. It was time to move from Grocers' Hall. Some years before Morice became Governor, the Directors had bought a site in Threadneedle Street that consisted of four houses fronting on to the street itself and a house at the back in which Sir John Houblon's widow still lived. It was the beginning of the Bank's colonization of its present island site, which is bounded by Lothbury and Threadneedle Street to the north and south and Bartholomew Lane and Princes Street to the east and west. The new building was not completed until 1733 and the Bank opened for business in June 1734. It occupied about a fifth of the present site and over the next fifty years – as business expanded – the Bank took over the Crown tavern, the Sun Fire office and a couple of other premises to the east, and eventually got permission to build on the site of St Christopher's Church and churchyard, which hugged its western flank. (After the Gordon Riots, the Directors regarded the church as a security risk because the building dominated the Bank.) The Bank also took over the church's glebelands and bought a number of houses surrounding the church. By 1788, when Sir John Soane was appointed architect to enlarge the premises, the Bank occupied the whole of the present 3-acre site.

Soane's Bank is generally considered to be his masterpiece, and one of the finest buildings in Europe, until it was mutilated by Sir Herbert Baker who totally redesigned the building between the two world wars, finishing the project in 1939. Its only virtues, if they can be called that, are that in the process of reconstruction two Roman mosaics were uncovered and restored. Even so, it was a high price to pay for what was a beautiful building. Ironically, Soane himself wanted to rebuild Sir Robert Taylor's impressive and beautiful Court Room, where the Directors meet, but they stopped him from doing it. Baker had it translated, reconstructed, to the Bank's first floor. The room's design and purpose are still much the same as Taylor left it.

More Frauds – Guest and Clutterbuck

The mid-eighteenth century saw some more frauds within
the Bank but not on the scale of Morice. Clerks were not at
all well paid – about £50 a year, which kept them on the
breadline, certainly not much above it. The temptations
must have been enormous and inevitably the more
ingenious succumbed. One clerk, William Guest, designed a
machine that could 'clip' the gold from coin and then make a
new milled edge. The whole purpose of milling edges was to
prevent clipping. He used the Bank's guineas for clipping –
access was easy since he was a teller – and by the time he
was arrested he had managed to collect a bagful of gold
clippings that weighed almost 5 pounds. In those days
people messed about with the King's coinage at their peril.
Guest was taken to Tyburn and hanged.

Fifteen years after the Guest affair, Thomas Clutterbuck
devised a way of defrauding the Bank that involved none of
Guest's ingenuity. Clutterbuck's job was to complete banknotes by writing in the amount and any other details before
these were passed to the cashier for signature and payment.
From there it was a short step to obtaining numbers of
blank forms or notes, filling out the amounts for himself and
forging the signatures. He cashed in almost £6,000 worth of
these and took off for France. The English demanded his
extradition. The French refused but later decided to try him
themselves. Clutterbuck was condemned to the galleys for
life.

Crisis and Bankruptcies

Just how important the Bank of England had become to the
English financial community only seventy years after its
foundation is amply illustrated by the wave of speculation
that hit the country with the end of the Seven Years War
against France in 1763. It led to more than 500 bankruptcies, but they showed that the Bank was up to fulfilling
its obligations in the marketplace. The speculation was triggered by the government's offer of lottery prizes in return
for the conversion of its 4-per-cent annuities into 'Reduced 3

per cents'. All the government was trying to do was reduce the burden of its interest payments. But it gave the annuity holders the idea that they could get something for nothing and a speculative wave swamped the City, hitting particularly the stock of the East India Company. It was not the right moment for the East India since it had heavy political and military commitments in India and it was borrowing heavily from the Bank to meet them. But the Bank decided to pull in its horns and limit the amount of discounting it was doing; if companies could not get their bills discounted it meant they couldn't get their hands on any cash.

In June 1772 the banking house of Neale & Co. in Threadneedle Street went bankrupt when a partner absconded. Another banking house – Glyn and Halifax – stopped payment. The City didn't need any more warning signals; it simply panicked and the panic spread through England and Scotland and over to the Continent, which was also enjoying a period of heavy speculation. Credit looked as if it were about to collapse totally.

The Bank, on the other hand, did remarkably well at this point. Nervous traders decided that the only safe place to put their money was with the Bank and not with the numerous small firms they usually dealt with. As the money poured in, the Bank had to take on extra staff. But if the threat of more bankruptcies was to be stopped the Bank had to lift the restriction on its discounting – which it promptly did. Firms in trouble had to have cash, otherwise they would go under. The East India Company had its back to the wall and its credit position was further squeezed when the Bank asked the company for repayment of its £600,000 debt – hardly the moment to exercise bankerly prudence so far as the East India Company was concerned. The crisis was eventually resolved when the Bank lent the Treasury £1.6 million at 4 per cent to help the company and by 1775 – less than two years after the trouble began – the Bank and the East India Company were on terms again. It was an adroit arrangement by the Bank. Rather than lend directly to the East India Company as a rescue operation, the Bank secured the loan with the Treasury and thereby left the government with the responsibility of bailing out the company while still paying interest on the debt to the Bank.

The Gordon Riots

Politically, however, the Bank at times found itself in absurd predicaments not of its own making. The first and last time that it came physically under siege was occasioned by the Gordon Riots of 1780, masterminded by Lord George Gordon, an unpredictable zealot who was later imprisoned. Gordon had just become President of the Protestant Association, whose purpose was to oppose the Catholic Relief Act, the first of a number of Acts designed to relieve Catholics from the civil and legal restrictions imposed on them from the time of Henry VIII. Gordon, accompanied by thousands of his followers, presented a petition to the Commons. The House delayed consideration of the petition for a week; the crowd became restive and one night, 29 May, destroyed some Catholic chapels. During the following week they burned down Newgate, the King's Bench prison and the New Bridewell. Their numbers swelled by several thousand liberated prisoners, they were now less concerned with Catholic persecution than they were with looting. They launched two attacks on the Bank, which had been garrisoned by the militia, the military and volunteer reinforcements. They were repelled; eight rioters were killed and a large number wounded. Gordon, to give him his due, tried to dissuade the rioters from the steps of the Bank, but they mistook his appeals for encouragement. The riots persuaded the Bank's Directors of the need for vigilance. After that, a military picket was mounted at Threadneedle Street every night for almost 200 years.

William Pitt and Unpaid Dividends

However, ten years later – in 1790 – the Bank entered an awkward political phase with the government, which was to test its authority as banker to the country. There was no ambiguity in its relationship with William Pitt, then Prime

Minister, who knew what he wanted and was determined to get it. He had found that the Bank had more than £500,000 at its disposal in the form of unpaid dividends on government debt. For one reason or another, people had not claimed them. Pitt proposed to take the lot – all, that is, except £50,000. The Bank opposed it. It was not so much a matter of customers suffering from financial amnesia – conveniently presumed by Pitt to be permanent rather than temporary – but many of them had left their dividends in the Bank's hands because they thought they were safer there than anywhere else. The Prime Minister had no such moral qualms.

Realizing that Pitt was not likely to give in, the Bank took the simple course of publishing all the dividends unclaimed up to September 1780. The consequent rush of claimants had the right effect. Pitt was persuaded to change his mind, but not before the Bank had agreed to give the government a 'perpetual loan', free of interest. It was a *quid pro quo*, but at least the Bank had demonstrated its belief in prudentiality and the rights of its customers.

Pitt continued to be a thorn in the side of the Bank. When the Bank proposed an issue of £5 million of Exchequer bills as advances to the merchant and financial community on approved securities, Pitt agreed to the proposal but not to one suggesting that the Bank should handle the fund. He argued that the Bank dealt only in short-term funds and that this was a long-term one that ought to be handled by the Exchequer. But he gave the Bank a sop: it would be represented on the Committee of Administration. These 'commercial' bills provided the liquidity the market needed.

The 'Old Lady'

Just when stability had been restored, there was promptly another bout of financial trouble. It began with a drain of gold from England to France. It was illegal, but when there was money to be made there were plenty of merchants able to evade the regulations. A great deal of gold left the

country because the French revolutionary government had
decided to restore its currency to a metallic base.

Panic

There were two other causes of the gold drain. A loan made
to the Habsburg Emperor of Germany for £4.6 million was
paid partly in gold, and keeping up Britain's military commitments abroad inevitably meant a further outflow of bullion. The public was also nervous, worried about the
possibility of a French invasion. People took their cash and
deposits out of the banks and stuffed them in their mattresses. Added to the drain of gold, the banks were now short
of cash. Consequently the Bank of England's stock of coin
drifted down to little more than £1 million. The Bank drew
the attention of the government to the problem, inquiring
quite properly how long it should continue paying out cash
on demand.

No sooner had it asked the question than there was a
report that a French force had landed in Wales – the kind of
event guaranteed to cause panic and a run on the Bank.
James Gillray's cartoon of that year (1797) depicts the Bank
at bay: 'Political Ravishment or the Old Lady of Threadneedle Street in Danger', a soubriquet that has remained
with the Bank ever since. The government solved the problem by forbidding the Bank to make any further cash payments until Parliament could be consulted. Simultaneously,
the Secretary of the Bank issued a statement reassuring
everyone that the Bank was in the 'most affluent and
prosperous situation'.

The City Helps Out

Quite what the public made of two quite contradictory and
separate assertions – that the Bank was in good shape and
that it could not pay out any money – can be only guessed at,
but it must have been alarmed. The City had no doubt about
where it stood: it knew quite well that if it did not support
the government and the Bank it was likely to be ruined.
Self-interest can be a powerful spur to co-operative action. It

was the shortage of cash that was the problem, and all the leading merchants guaranteed to take banknotes in exchange for debts owing to them; they would make payments to their creditors in the same way. The declaration was signed by more than 4,000 merchants and posted in all the coffee houses.

Cash Problems

However, it did not solve the general shortage of small change. In spite of the Bank's issues of £1 and £2 notes, a £1 note was not much good to someone who bought 5 shillings' worth of goods and wanted 15 shillings in change. The government decided on an ingenious substitute. These were 'pieces of eight', the Spanish dollars that were the spoils of war, large numbers of which lay in the Bank's vaults. The dollars were worth 8 reals each and bore the head of the Spanish monarch; each coin was worth 4 shillings and 6 pence. The head of George III was stamped on the head of the old enemy, occasioning an anonymous couplet: 'The Bank, to make their Spanish dollars pass,/Stamped the head of a fool on the neck of an ass.'

But this makeshift, bastard coin had a bullion content of 4 shillings and 8 pence – 2 pence more than its face value and ideal for melting down. Consequently, the government delayed the issue of the coins for two days while it revalued them to 4 shillings and 9 pence. Meanwhile the Bank was having trouble with its £1 and £2 notes, which were being copiously forged. In 1798 it produced fresh designs and offered the new notes, or cash, in exchange for the old ones. But the currency problem persisted; there was not enough of it for domestic needs. Four years later the Bank decided on a second issue of dollars, the design altered from the previous issue, but then withdrew it: it had found a firm in Birmingham with steam presses powerful enough to obliterate the Spanish design altogether. The Bank of England Five-Shilling Dollar was first issued on 21 May 1798. On one side it bore the King's head and a Latin inscription, on the other a seated Britannia.

The dollars were worth 5 shillings on issue, but the steady rise in the silver price in subsequent years made them worth more than their face value. In 1811 they were revalued to 5 shillings and 6 pence. The Bank also made a supplementary issue of tokens, worth 3 shillings and 1 shilling and 6 pence, made from smaller Spanish coins. But local tradesmen were quick to get in on the act, relieving the general shortage of coin by having their own tokens struck for them. The government put a stop to the practice a year later – it was an infringement of the State's practice of coining its own money.

Income Tax; More Fraud; the Bank Gets a Bad Name; Competition

The State had another prerogative at this time. It was income tax, introduced by Pitt in 1798 to boost the revenues to fight Napoleon. It was not a success. He was no forecaster and the expected revenues from industry and the private taxpayer fell short by £4.6 million. When Pitt resigned in 1801, Henry Addington, his successor, repealed the tax; he had just concluded the long-drawn-out peace negotiations with France. But the tax holiday was extraordinarily brief. In 1802, the year after repeal, England was at war with France again and Addington was obliged to introduce what he tactfully called 'a separate tax on property'. It was at only half Pitt's rate (Pitt's was 10 per cent) and went through Parliament as the Property Duty Act. The Chancellor of the Exchequer, Nicholas Vansittart, repealed it in 1816 – the year after Napoleon's defeat at Waterloo.

But it meant a drop in revenue of £16 million. This was partly cushioned by the increased yield from customs and excise, which was still the mainstay of government revenue. The National Debt, however, stood at £861 million. The Bank made a loan to the government of £3 million at 3 per cent and its capital was increased to just over £14.5 million. The Bank's Directors were also required to hand over to the Exchequer all amounts in excess of £100,000 held by them in unclaimed dividends. Pitt would have approved.

Aslett Tries to Emulate His Boss

A few years earlier the Bank had decided to introduce a system of dual control over its financial systems, designed to ensure that no single person had access to the Bank's purse strings without someone else acting as a check. The Bank had at last concluded that fraud, if not endemic, was a constant worry. The Second Cashier, Robert Aslett, was the cause of their new, if unwelcome, awareness. Aslett was impressed by the fortune that his boss, Abraham Newland, had amassed by speculating in Pitt's loans. Aslett gambled and lost and took to fraud. He abstracted Exchequer bills from the Bank to the value of £200,000 and used them as security to obtain loans. When he was caught Aslett was sent to prison, but later released on condition that he left the country.

'Grand Purveyors to the Gibbet'

When the Bank at last entered the nineteenth century it found itself in an unhappy and ironic confrontation with public opinion. The Bank's £1 and £2 notes were not only easy to forge, they quickly got into circulation. The criminal law of the time specified only one sentence for forgery and that was hanging. Between 1797 and 1829 the best part of 600 people went to the gallows. If the penalty was barbarous, the Bank's Directors did not speak out against it. They became known as 'grand purveyors to the gibbet' and 'priests of Moloch's blood-stained altar'.

Then George Cruikshank, the artist and caricaturist, took a hand in the controversy by designing his 'Bank Restriction Note' of 1818, which probably did more for his reputation than any of his other work. He called it the 'artistic event of his life'. Cruikshank's note – 'not to be Imitated' – depicted a string of male and female bodies hanging from a gibbet, criminals in chains or behind bars and, most savage of all, the Bank's Britannia eating a live infant. The demand for copies was so great that Cruikshank made £700 in a few hours, but the event went to his head: 'I had the satisfaction of knowing', he said, 'that no man or woman was ever hung after this for passing one-pound forged notes ... the final effect of my note was to stop the hanging for all minor offences, and thus has been the means of saving thousands of men and women from being hanged.'

Cruikshank was almost certainly overdoing it. The death penalty for forging notes was not abolished until fourteen years after his famous etching and there is nothing to suppose that people were not hanged between times. But the Bank's Directors remained supine in the face of public outrage. Their 'prudentiality' was evidently deeply qualified and confined to narrow financial horizons.

The Bank's Ambitions Are Frustrated

There was good reason for not wanting to get politically involved. At this stage the Directors had their eyes set on what was their ultimate target, the establishment of the Bank as a proper State institution. In the early part of the nineteenth century the Bank's position was ambiguous: it was a private, profitable concern on the one hand, but on the other it was inextricably bound up with government and the economy. It had begun to show an important feature that characterizes the present Bank of England – the ability to step into the market when the going becomes difficult and restore stability. It had lent to other institutions when they were in trouble and it had acted as an arm of government, though not always with enthusiasm. It was not a State organization, however, any more than it was a private bank – its size and influence took it out of that category. The Directors recognized that and were anxious to see that the Bank retained its financial primacy in the financial community. In other words, they were frightened of competition.

But it was something they could not forestall. After the financial crash of 1825, in which thirty-seven issuing banks were bankrupted, the government held an inquest during which it considered arguments for establishing large joint-stock banks. The government's Country Bankers Act of 1826 created the climate for their establishment: it limited the Bank's monopoly to a radius of 65 miles from London; it liberalized previous legislation, which prohibited any bank from having more than six partners (from now on as many as they liked), and it allowed them to print their own banknotes. On the other hand, the Bank of England could set up branches wherever it liked. It did so straight away: one in Gloucester, two more in the same year at Manchester and Swansea, and in 1827 it established branches at Birmingham, Liverpool and Leeds.

Joint-stock Banks

When the Bank's Charter was extended six years later to 1855, the government decided to allow joint-stock banks in London 'and within sixty-five miles thereof'. The Bank fought it on the grounds that it infringed its existing privilege of exclusive banking, but it lost. However, it did manage to prevent joint-stock banks from issuing their own notes. From the moment the Bill became law, the prospectus for a London joint-stock bank was published – the London and Westminster. By 1844 the City was beginning to brim with banks. In addition to some sixty private banking firms, other joint-stock banks had opened – among them the London Joint Stock Bank, the National Provincial, the Bank of Australasia, the Royal Bank of Australia and the Bank of British North America.

The earlier reforms of 1834, in which the Exchequer was abolished, meant that the Bank increased its role as banker to the government. It received government revenues and credited them to the 'Account of His Majesty's Exchequer'. It was already Registrar of Government Stocks and by now had most of the features of a central bank. Since 1833 its notes were legal tender and the bank held the view that it alone should be responsible for the note circulation. But it did not get total mastery of the note issue until as late as 1921, when the last country bank lost the right to issue notes.

The government by now had taken a very active role in the banking affairs of the country. It extended that role further in the Charter Act of 1844 when it tightened its hold on the Bank itself by insisting that the note issue was to be kept quite separate from the general banking business: there was to be the 'Issue Department' (it still exists today), which would issue notes up to the value of £14 million – this money represented the securities held by the department, mainly in the form of government debt. Notes could be issued for more than this amount only if they were backed by gold coin or gold and silver bullion transferred from the Banking Department.

Three of the Bank's Directors Bankrupted

Many of the financial crises of the mid-nineteenth century were caused either by trade difficulties or by slumps, neither of which could be controlled by England. When the Irish potato crop failed in 1845 and 1846, corn had to be imported as a substitute and paid for in gold. There was a steady drain from the Bank's reserves and Bank Rate was put up twice. The Bank checked the demand for notes by discounting only short-dated bills and limiting the number it accepted. This stopped the outward flow of gold, but nothing could prevent what was happening to wheat, which was plummeting in price as imports were rising, the downward trend being accelerated by the prospect of a good harvest at home. Three of the Bank's Directors – William R. Robinson, the Governor; Sir John Reid and Abel Lewis Gower – were partners of firms that dealt in corn. Their firms failed and the three men were bankrupted. Consequently, they had to resign from the Court of Directors. They were not the only victims. Eleven private and joint-stock banks collapsed, including the Royal Bank of Liverpool. The Stock Exchange crashed and no one would part with hard cash if they had it.

The worldwide slump of 1857, which started in America where 1,500 banks failed, was followed by the collapse of a number of important firms in Britain. There was a run on gold; Bank Rate rose to a record 10 per cent and there was a

shortage of cash as people changed their notes and coins for
gold. Once again the government offered the Bank a Bill of
Indemnity to issue notes above its statutory limit on condition that it did not lower Bank Rate. The country survived,
although it took industry and commerce some time before
they found their feet again.

Overend, Gurney

The history of the Bank of England until 1919 was dominated by England's adherence to the gold standard. There
may be something admirable in a system that allowed customers to trade in banknotes for their equivalent value in
gold, but it had enormous snags and the Bank spent a great
deal of its time dealing with them. The truth is that the
currency was often under attack, either for external or for
domestic reasons. Sometimes domestic crises shook the
banking system far more severely than international factors. Overend, Gurney – the distinguished discount house –
was a case in point.

It was a puzzling business. The firm had been taken over
by young partners who turned it into a conglomerate: grain,
iron-founding, shipping, railways, any speculative business
that they thought had the slightest prospect of success. In
spite of an enormously profitable discount business, they
still had to go to the market to raise capital for their new
conglomerate. It collapsed in 1866 with debts of £9 million.

The day after the failure was known as 'Black Friday'.
Bill brokers, bankers, merchants – anyone, in fact, who was
a creditor of Overend – besieged the Bank for advances and
the Directors lent out almost £4 million. They hoisted Bank
Rate from 6 to 10 per cent. The Bank reserve fell by half and
the government once again said it could issue more notes to
deal with the crisis. As it turned out, this was not necessary.

The 'Baring Crisis'

The next domestic crisis came only four years later and was
effectively much more serious. It was the 'Baring crisis' of
1890. The Chancellor of the Exchequer, George Goschen,

had earlier managed to convert £600 million of National Debt into low-interest-bearing stock, much of which forms the 2½-per-cent Consols quoted on today's Stock Exchange. But it was not attractive to punters who put their money into speculative investments, many of which were in South America. Baring Brothers was heavily committed in that part of the world, whose reputation for political and commercial stability was no better then than it is today. Barings' problem was that it did not have enough liquidity to meet its short-term liabilities and bills.

A City Rescue

The firm had liabilities of £22 million and immediate liquid assets of £15 million. The Chancellor was unwilling to help. That left William Lidderdale, the Bank's Governor, with no alternative but to organize a City rescue. What the City was facing was a financial crisis that dwarfed any previous episodes. By present-day standards it bore comparison with the secondary-banking crisis of 1974. But in just forty-eight hours the guarantee fund Lidderdale opened at the Bank received subscriptions from the City community of rather more than £17 million. Although it was a triumph of crisis management by Lidderdale, there was still a great deal of money at risk in the sense that no one could be sure that Barings' assets could begin to meet the firm's liabilities, which at that time looked to be about £9 million. However, the liquidation of the firm was a total success; none of the guarantors lost a penny and Barings was reconstructed as a joint-stock company and has not looked back since. At a Mansion House dinner in his honour, Lidderdale set out the lesson they had all learned: that it was vital that all banks, not just the Bank of England, should maintain reserves that were adequate for national needs. He could just as well have been talking about 1974, the year of the secondary-banking crisis, or 1985, the year that Johnson Matthey Bankers had to be rescued.

Cunliffe, Ambiguity and Rows with the Treasury

While Lidderdale was an outstanding Governor, it was Walter Cunliffe who raised serious doubts about the relationship the Bank had with government. Until Cunliffe took up the reins at Threadneedle Street at the beginning of World War I, the Bank had enjoyed the support of successive administrations. The relationship had its ambiguities, of course: the Bank had fought competition and it had frequently wanted to do things that the government opposed. Inevitably, there had to be ambiguities and disagreements: the financial authority vested in Threadneedle Street was bound to cause strains with the government when it came to the management of the economy, the National Debt and the banking system. But the strains never reached breaking point, although there were times when they came close to it.

A Gold and Cash Drain

Cunliffe, however, imposed tensions between the Bank and government. These arose from his overbearing and autocratic temperament. He began unpromisingly by telling Lloyd George that the City was totally opposed to Britain's intervention in the war. The view from the City was bleak: there were no financial measures in place to deal with a war and Cunliffe knew that there would be a financial panic. Only four days before Britain declared war on Germany, £1.5 million of gold went abroad. Cunliffe raised Bank Rate from 4 to 8 per cent and the next day he pushed it up to the 'crisis' rate of 10 per cent. It was Saturday, a day when banks still opened regularly, and it was also the day before bank holiday, which meant that everyone was withdrawing cash for their holiday needs. There were queues at the Bank itself, where people were presenting their £5 notes in exchange for gold sovereigns. They could have gone to their own banks, but these were clinging to their gold stocks and referring customers to the Bank. In less than a week, the

Bank's reserves were down to £11 million from £38 million.
The familiar cycle had begun.

Postal Orders Fill the Gap

The Bank issued more notes under the customary letter of
indemnity. Bank advances were not to be made at less than
10-per-cent interest. Lloyd George and his Cabinet decided
to extend the bank holiday, not out of consideration for the
population but to give the government breathing space to
pull itself together. Consequently, the Stock Exchange was
closed, which temporarily eliminated one area of panic. A
month's moratorium on paying bills of exchange was
ordered, thus stopping any immediate outflows of gold. And
postal orders became legal tender to plug the gap in the
shortage of notes.

'Bradburys'

But the Bank did not have the capacity to print the extra
notes it had been authorized to issue. The Treasury
therefore decided to print its own, through Waterlows, the
printers, who managed to get out the first issue in three
days. The notes were smudgy but performed a function.
Signed by Sir John Bradbury, Permanent Secretary to the
Treasury, they became known as 'Bradburys'. Cunliffe and
his Directors did not like the Treasury taking over the note
issue and said so, but it was not until 1928 that they managed to claw back their traditional role.

Surprisingly, there was no further drain of gold. In fact,
most of what had been taken out was returned, relieving the
pressure on the banking system. But debts had to be paid in
gold. Fortunately, the war risks involved in shipments pre-
cluded any immediate drain from the reserves. It worked in
reverse, of course: the gold owing to Britain was less likely
to come in. However, Britain was helped out by the Empire.
The Indian government held more than £3 million of gold at
the Bank and agreed to release it. Canada and South Africa
lent a hand with buying and storage arrangements, so the
net effect was that some of Britain's gold reserves were held

actually outside the country. The total gold reserve amounted to a little more than £43 million.

The Bank returned to its traditional role of managing the hand-to-mouth funding of the war. It also lent to the government. The government's long-term borrowing for World War I, the War Loans, amounted to more than £1.8 billion, added to which there was a variety of short-dated borrowings, such as National War Bonds and War Savings Certificates – the latter to become an established instrument of government funding and public saving.

The Central Bank – at last

All these funding operations were handled by the Bank and its prestige was enormously enhanced. But there was an important addition to its status during this period – one that clearly made it the country's central bank. The Bank of France and the Banca d'Italia opened accounts at the Bank of England. They were quickly followed by the national banks of Switzerland, Belgium, Serbia, Chile, Norway and the Netherlands.

Cunliffe's Rows

No one could doubt that the Bank's pre-eminence was the work of Cunliffe. He had been created Baron early in the war in recognition of the way he had handled the gold and currency problems and his continued administration of the Bank's affairs throughout the war was sure-footed if autocratic. But he lacked finesse. He had a limited personal appeal within the Bank and did not always tell his Directors what he was doing. Ironically, Cunliffe's first major row with the Chancellor, Bonar Law, was because the Governor thought he was being kept in the dark by the Treasury. At the time, he was Chairman of the London Exchange Committee, a body set up to deal with the problems of foreign exchange. Cunliffe complained that the Committee was 'a mere cypher, entirely superseded by Sir Robert Chalmers (a Joint Secretary to the Treasury) and Mr Keynes' (John Maynard Keynes, the economist, later to become a Director of the Bank). Cunliffe was jealous of Keynes's direct access to the Treasury and felt that things were being done behind his back. Cunliffe compounded his anger by saying that in business circles both men were not 'considered to have any knowledge or experience in practical exchange or business problems'. He demanded that they should be sacked. Bonar Law was furious.

Some Trouble with the Treasury

But worse was to come. J. P. Morgan, the Wall Street bankers, had lent the Bank $85 million; it also had another loan to the Treasury outstanding. Morgan demanded prompt repayment of both. Cunliffe instructed Ottawa to pay £17.5 million of the Bank's gold there to Morgan. It was then that Cunliffe learned that the Treasury's representative in America was also drawing gold from Ottawa. The Governor told the Treasury man that he could keep what he had drawn (£2.25 million) but he was not to draw any more until the Bank had fulfilled its commitment to Morgan.

Bonar Law Threatens to Resign

Cunliffe had blundered. He had given orders to a Treasury official, the representative of government. He had not consulted the Chancellor, nor had he spoken to anyone in the Treasury. Bonar Law was so angry he told Lloyd George that either Cunliffe must go or he would. Clearly Law could not go, and Lloyd George got on well with Cunliffe. Law then suggested that both men should work together, but that the government should always have the final say when there was a difference of opinion. It amounted to an admission that Cunliffe was extraordinarily powerful. When Lloyd George put the proposal to Cunliffe, inviting him to sign a memorandum confirming the arrangement, Cunliffe said he could not sign it without consulting his Directors. Lloyd George then hinted that the government might take over the Bank.

The Bank Holds Out

The Bank's Committee of Treasury, the most important committee in the Bank, backed up Cunliffe, saying that it would be 'impossible for the Bank thus to renounce its functions'. That in itself was an astonishing statement, tantamount to claiming that its functions were superior to those of the Treasury. Lloyd George retaliated by warning that if the Bank did not sign the document the government would take control of the Bank. But the Directors were obdurate. They believed that Cunliffe's handling of the Ottawa affair was the only course he could have taken in view of Morgan's sudden demand for money. Their reply did not go down well with Lloyd George. Cunliffe took a holiday and the opportunity to write to the Chancellor, under a covering letter to Lloyd George, a letter that showed apparent signs of humility but not of contrition. He told Law that the Bank would not fail to confer with him over matters such as the National Credit or the Bank's gold holdings. But at the same time he indicated to the Bank's Committee of Treasury that changes in Bank Rate were not the Chancellor's business; they were the prerogative of Threadneedle Street.

If Cunliffe had continued as Governor there is little doubt that relations between the Bank, the Chancellor and Lloyd George would have gone from bad to worse, probably culminating in a State takeover of the Bank. As it was, the Committee of Treasury a few months later decided to recommend Brien Cokayne for Governor in the coming spring elections, with Montagu Norman as his deputy. The embarrassment of Cunliffe had effectively been removed.

Montagu Norman; the Bank is Nationalized; More Governors

What was not so easily disposed of was the legacy Cunliffe left behind. His relationship with the government may have fallen into disrepair during his final term, but he bequeathed to the Directors and the nation an institution as solid as rock and indispensable to City and financial life. A committee was set up under Lord Revelstoke and recommended that future Governors should not be in the position of exercising autocratic control; in future, Governors would be obliged to tell the Committee of Treasury what the Bank was doing. Cunliffe's example had struck home. Among its other recommendations were that the Committee of Treasury should be smaller – nine members in all, including past Governors – and that it should be elected by secret ballot. Lord Revelstoke's wise men concluded that they were not in favour of the Bank being controlled by the State.

The Greatest Governor

The post-war years at the Bank were dominated by Montagu Norman, who became Governor in 1920 and held the job for no fewer than twenty-four years. Norman had been educated at Eton and Leipzig, joined Martins Bank and later worked for his grandfather's bank, Brown, Shipley. He fought in the South African war, won the DSO and was invalided home. He became a Director of the Bank in 1907 and eight years later gave up his other banking interests to devote his services full time to the Bank.

Norman is generally regarded as the Bank's greatest Governor. Threadneedle Street was substantially reorganized under his direction: he laid down the principle that Governors should have no other business interests, that their deputies should be full time and that people from outside the Bank should be represented on the Court of Directors. He also established the principle of salaried executive directors, who are now among the most important people in the Bank.

Norman realized that there had to be some kind of co-ordinated monetary policy within the Empire. That involved the establishment of central banks, which could consult with each other about policy. Between 1920 and 1934 five central banks came into being – India, South Africa, Australia, Canada and New Zealand. The Bank not only co-operated actively in setting them up, but provided

three Bank of England men for the central banks of South
Africa, New Zealand and Canada.

Lender of Last Resort

Norman had always accepted the notion that the Bank
should be the 'lender of last resort' – a concept over which
his predecessors differed. It meant that the Bank should be
willing to lend to the banking system at all times. While
other central banks have always lent to their commercial
banks, the Bank of England does not. Its lending function is
normally restricted to the discount houses, which frequently
call on the Bank's discount office for cash to balance their
books. The Bank lends to them on its own terms, which
means that it can influence interest rates and the money
supply.

The 'New' Gold Standard

It had always been Norman's intention that Britain's gold
exports should no longer be prohibited. Winston Churchill,
Chancellor in Stanley Baldwin's Cabinet, announced the
return to gold in his Budget speech of April 1925. The most
important point about the restoration (apart from the
unusual fact that notes were no longer to be convertible into
gold coin at the Bank, although the Bank was obliged to sell
gold bars of not less than 400 troy ounces in exchange for
legal tender) was that anyone who wanted to sell pounds for
foreign currency knew exactly how much currency he was
going to get in exchange – provided he was buying currency
that was linked to a gold standard of its own. In effect, this
was a gold-exchange standard and it lasted until 1931 when
the United Kingdom came off gold altogether.

The Bank Stops Competing with Commercial
Banks

Maintaining the 'new' gold standard was one of the Bank's
preoccupations. It was during this period, though, that Norman was detaching the Bank from its commercial activities
– it was still competing with the joint-stock banks – so that

it could properly become a central bank. It was Norman's view that central banks did not compete with commercial banks for business and to that end he closed down the discount side of all the Bank's branches and sold off the West End branch in London to the Royal Bank of Scotland.

The Wall Street Crash

Norman, however, was not involved solely in the Bank's reorganization. The prelude to the Wall Street crash of 1929 was marked by heavy speculation when investment funds left the UK for America and gold left the Bank for France. Bank Rate was increased to stem the outward flow of funds, but the City and the banks could not maintain any kind of stability as short-term money shot around foreign markets looking for a bolt hole.

When the crash came, its reverberations were felt in Europe with the force of an earthquake. First, the Credit Anstalt in Vienna – a Rothschild bank – stopped payment. Then the Reichsbank, the German central bank, lost a large part of its reserves. American, British and French credits and backing from the Bank of International Settlements could do nothing to stop the rot. The German economy collapsed. In July 1931 the Bank of England began to lose gold at the rate of £2.5 million a day. Bank Rate was increased without having any effect. Credits were arranged with France and America, but the gold drain continued. It looked as if the credits would run out within weeks. Taxation was raised and government expenditure – mainly on social security – was cut, but not without bitter divisions in the Labour cabinet. A National Government was formed under Ramsay MacDonald. Chancellor Snowden's economic housekeeping produced more credits from France and America and for a time it looked as if the crisis was over.

Invergordon Mutiny

But a few weeks after the National Government was formed there came the Invergordon 'mutiny'. The government's measures to cut the pay of all public-service workers,

including the armed forces, had triggered off a protest by the
sailors. It was not in itself particularly serious, but it upset
foreign sentiment. There was another run on gold – £30
million in three days. Britain's credits were close to being
spent. Bank Rate was raised to 6 per cent and the Gold
Standard Act of 1925 was suspended, in effect abandoned.
The UK's reserves were simply not large enough to with-
stand any sustained selling in volume.

A few months after the UK went off gold in September
1931 steps were taken to ensure that there were not any
violent fluctuations in sterling as a result of the measure.
The government set up the Exchange Equalization Account,
which was run, and still is, by the Bank. Its objective was to
iron out sudden shifts in the value of the pound caused by
speculators or large movements of capital out of sterling
looking for a safer place. But such an account could not hope
to work if it did not have funds. It started life with assets of
£17 million, with borrowing powers for a further £150 million. This was later increased to £200 million in 1933 and
doubled in 1937.

Fixed Rates of Exchange

Sterling at this time had a fixed rate of exchange against the
dollar, which it does not have now. Once sterling showed
signs of falling from this rate, the Bank used the account to
sell dollars and buy sterling, bringing the two currencies
into their former relationship. It depended, of course, on the
'theology' of the fixed exchange rate. That theology was
largely abandoned in the early 1970s in favour of a 'managed' float, which depended on the government's view of
what value sterling should be. That was influenced by factors such as the balance of payments and the competitiveness of British goods in export markets. But no policy is
ever perfect. In the first Reagan Administration, the US
Federal Reserve (a law unto itself, unlike the Bank of England) opted for high interest rates to reduce inflation and
fund record budget deficits. Consequently the dollar soared
against sterling and it was still doing so early in the second

Reagan Administration. The Bank used the Exchange Equalization Account only marginally, then preferred to let interest rates take the strain, stabilizing sterling at a lower rate. The use of the account tends to be a short-term palliative only, wasteful of reserves. It is also vitiated by the problem of secrecy. Once speculators know the Bank is 'in the market', selling dollars and buying sterling, they can organize their affairs to make the maximum profit.

Exchange Control

However, with the advent of World War II, exchange *control* became a necessity and it was administered by the Bank. Its purpose was to conserve foreign exchange needed to finance imports during the war. British residents were prohibited from moving capital out of the country – it had to be available, if required, for the prosecution of the war or for the maintenance of essential civilian supplies and services. The same regulations applied to banks and industry. Apart from this essential control (it was abolished only in October 1979, one of the first acts of Mrs Thatcher's new Conservative Government), Montagu Norman argued for, and got, a remarkably cheap war. Government funding programmes in earlier wars – particularly World War I – had been expensive operations. Norman wanted a 3-per-cent war, but the Treasury did not believe it was possible. The first War Loan – for £300 million at 3 per cent – was accompanied by a statement that simply said that subsequent loans would not have a higher coupon. That, accompanied by an unvarying Bank Rate of 2 per cent, left the public with little choice. Later loans came on to the market at 2½ and 3 per cent and the government's funding programme was achieved at relatively low cost.

Norman Goes

Bad health forced Norman to retire in 1944. Lord O'Brien, Governor of the Bank from 1966 until 1973, was Norman's last private secretary and an unstinting admirer. He remembers him not just as an exacting taskmaster but as 'the most magnetic personality I have ever met. He dominated everyone around him. He had effortless superiority and great personal magnetism. Whenever he went abroad or on holiday the Bank just sank back on its heels.'

The Bank is Nationalized

Lord Catto succeeded Norman as Governor and two years later found himself dealing with Clement Attlee's Labour Government, which had decided to nationalize the Bank. Surprisingly, the debate was not a furious one but muted by a sense of inevitability. Nationalization was not a new notion. All the central banks, apart from the Bank of England and the German Reichsbank (a fact that did not go unnoticed), had been taken under State control. The Tories had tried to take over the Bank as far back as the reign of Queen Anne but had failed. Lloyd George had threatened it because of the Cunliffe row, but had never carried it through.

The paranoia of the Labour side centred not on the Bank's ambiguous relationship with government but on what it took to be the Bank's control of the country's economic policies, particularly during the inter-war years. The return to the gold standard in 1925, assumed to be a Bank decision, was blamed for deepening the depression. The Bank was a sinister conspiracy against the national interest. It was a racket and a monopoly, supported by the State. In fact, the Bank had nothing to do with the return to gold, it was not even represented on the committee that made the recommendation. The Wall Street crash, which led to the depression of the 1930s, was not of its making either.

Lord Catto, the Bank's Governor, was not alarmed by the nationalization proposal. The Chancellor of the Exchequer, Hugh Dalton, had made it plain that apart from compensating the Proprietors of the Bank (it was still a quoted Stock Market security) very little would be changed. Although the Directors of the Bank would now be appointed by the government, the administration of Threadneedle Street and its day-to-day running would be solely the concern of the Bank; there would be no outside interference. Just as important, the Bank's relations with the Treasury would not change either. The Act was passed on 14 February 1946.

Cromer, a Patrician Governor

Catto was succeeded as Governor of the Bank by Cameron Cobbold and then, in 1961, by the Earl of Cromer, one of those Establishment figures who had a daunting gift for taking pretty well what he wanted as a right. Cromer was a Baring, a scion of the great merchant bank, a connection that gave him an entrée not merely to every banking parlour in the country but to international institutions, industry, diplomacy (Ambassador to Washington) and to the Court (Page of Honour to George V and Queen Mary at their Coronation). It was the kind of career that ambitious men lust after but rarely attain. He came out of World War II as a lieutenant-colonel at the age of 27 and then Barings groomed him for stardom. The bank sent him to America for a three-year stint where he worked, in succession, with J. P. Morgan, the bankers, Kidder Peabody, Morgan Stanley and the Chemical Bank. At the age of 30 he returned from the States and became Managing Director of Baring Brothers for thirteen years, during which he sandwiched in two years in Washington as Economic Minister and UK Director of the International Monetary Fund, the World Bank and the International Finance Corporation. When he was 43, he was appointed Governor of the Bank by Harold Macmillan.

Cromer and Wilson

Cromer was a patrician and, according to Denis Healey, later Labour Chancellor, *dégagé* to the point of insolence. Harold Wilson and Cromer, apparently, did nothing but have rows. It is not surprising that the two men did not get on. Socially, and in every other way, they were poles apart. Yet in spite of being a Macmillan appointment, Cromer was very much in the central tradition of Bank Governors – a banker appointed from outside Threadneedle Street, a man who had a firm grasp of international banking and its problems. Lord O'Brien (Wandsworth School and a lifetime Bank of England man) takes the view that outsiders – particularly merchant bankers – make the best Governors: 'They have a far wider experience of international banking. The problems they run up against in merchant banking, which are often very complex, give them an exceptionally good background for running the Bank.'

The man who followed O'Brien, Gordon Richardson (Nottingham High School, a Cambridge law degree) had all those qualifications. But Richardson did not come to banking until he was 40, after he had ceased to practise at the Bar. Two years later he was a Director of J. Henry Schroder, the merchant bank, and four years after that became Chairman of Schroder Wagg. He had been a member of the Bank's Court for six years before he was appointed Governor.

Competition and Credit Control; the Secondary Banking Crisis

Ironically, just as he had settled into the Governor's chair, Richardson found himself in the middle of a major banking crisis very largely of O'Brien's making. The policy at the core of 'the worst financial crisis since the 1930s' was a discussion document issued by the Bank in May 1971 called Competition and Credit Control. The background to it is tortuous and complex, but it can be crudely simplified by some black and white brush strokes, which inevitably exclude the political and financial tints that fill in the picture of how and why there are changes in policy.

Until the late 1960s, the Bank had managed the financial markets by discreet pressure – the kind of pressure that was understood and acknowledged by City institutions. Like the Bank, they believed that what went on in the City was not the concern of government and, more particularly, the Treasury. There was nothing new in that: indeed, Treasury officials rarely, if ever, met City people in the course of official business. It was tacitly assumed by the Treasury that it was the Bank's role to act as a filter for City opinion and to represent it to government if the Bank thought it necessary. And the Bank did nothing to disabuse the Treasury. In other words, the City was the Bank's jealously guarded preserve. When he was Labour Chancellor, Denis Healey recalls that the Bank did not really approve when he held lunches for City people, but it reluctantly came to the conclusion that that was his style. Healey, however, was not even at the Treasury when Competition and Credit Control came along; Anthony Barber was, the man who was later to be blamed for the 'Barber boom', although it was Edward Heath and not Barber who went for 'growth'.

Requests

In return for acting as guardian and representative of City interests, the Bank had always made it clear that there should be a *quid pro quo*. It was not, of course, put in those terms. But there was a clear understanding that when the Bank 'requested' the banking community to do something – such as restrict the level of its lending – then the request would be complied with. From this understanding between Threadneedle Street and the City there stemmed the received wisdom – made clear to the Treasury – that the Bank and City together knew what was best for financial markets because they alone had the expertise and practical good sense. There was a close and obvious relationship.

The second point in favour of the argument was that the Treasury could not hope to understand the complexity of financial markets; that was best left to the experts. Moreover, the Bank's influence on financial markets was not in any way statutory; it was not in a position in law to tell City institutions what to do. And both the institutions and the Bank preferred it like that. Once something became law, then outsiders such as politicians would be tempted to interfere.

The system of 'requests' by the Bank on the whole worked well during World War II and through the fifties. During that period the Bank had to deal with only a small body of

people, the clearing banks. But the 1960s were to prove
much more problematic. Post-war London was reviving as
an international financial centre; foreign banks were setting up subsidiaries and branches, and the finance houses,
the exponents of hire purchase and personal loans, had
grabbed 90 per cent of all instalment-credit business. Very
quickly, the Bank found itself making 'requests' not merely
to a handful of important banks like the Big Five (Barclays,
Lloyds, Midland, National Provincial and Westminster) but
to more than 200 institutions, many of whom were lurking
on the fringe of the established banking system and taking
business from those who were obeying the Bank's 'requests'
by restricting their lending. The 'good boys', who had followed the Bank's guidance not just on how much they
should lend but to whom, were losing out. If there was to be
any fairness in the marketplace, therefore, the guidance and
administrative controls exercised by the Bank should apply
to everyone. That was easier said than done. The capacity of
the financial system to innovate and avoid, to sophisticate
its market operations to obfuscate policy, has always been
capacious.

Determining Credit by Price

Competition and Credit Control set out to abolish these
anomalies by replacing them with a system of credit that
would be determined by its price or cost – or, as O'Brien put
it, 'to permit the price mechanism to function efficiently in
the allocation of credit, and to free the banks from rigidities
and restraints which have for too long inhibited them'. It
would be idle to pretend that the Governor had not been
influenced by a number of reports published before the
Bank's discussion paper. Lord Crowther's *Committee on
Consumer Credit* a few months earlier argued that all
restrictions on hire-purchase credit should be abolished;
they were, seven months later. But well before Crowther,
the Prices and Incomes Board observed in 1967 that restrictive practices among banks was bad for the allocation of
resources, not just in banking but in credit allocation as a

whole. O'Brien said the report had been taken seriously by the Bank.

The Money Supply

In the first two years of the scheme – beginning in September 1971 – something occurred that would have made a Thatcher Government blanch with horror. The annual rate of increase in the money supply, as measured by M3, rose by no less than 26 per cent. A monetarist government would have taken immediate action by raising interest rates. But, curiously, no one took much notice. In the early 1970s there was much scepticism, not to say confusion, about the validity or meaning of money-supply measurements. Indeed, as late as the Spring of 1973, the Deputy Governor of the Bank, Jasper Hollom, said that changes in banking behaviour (through Competition and Credit Control) made M3 (the broad measure of money supply) an unreliable indicator. He could see that the changes had caused disortions but he could not account for them. He hoped, however, that they would be transitional. Hollom was not the only one to reflect doubts about the accuracy of the measurements. Government Ministers were doing so as well, but for rather different reasons: the Heath Government had embarked on a policy of economic expansion; if it were to curb the money supply it would have to do so by raising interest rates; if it did that, it would inhibit economic growth. It was convenient, then, to assume that the figures were unreliable and they were supported by the government's Chief Economic Adviser who as early as June 1970 had delivered a paper saying that all economic indicators were unreliable. But as Michael Moran points out in his book *The Politics of Banking*, while the government was emphasizing the unreliability of the figures, it had no hesitation in responding very quickly to disquieting figures about unemployment and output.

Wage Demands

What would have been obvious to any present-day commentator or economist was that the increase in M3 was caused by an excessive increase in the money supply caused by Competition and Credit Control. Recognition of that fact, however, was not politically convenient. The government believed that it had identified the cause of inflation, but it had nothing to do with the expansion of credit. The main cause, so the argument ran, was the rise in costs – particularly labour costs caused by excessive wage demands. Get those down – or at least decrease the rate at which they rose – and inflation would look after itself.

Interest Rates

When interest rates rose sharply in July 1973 – mainly to protect sterling – logic would have dictated that bank base rates would rise too. But the banks did not increase base rates to match the levels in the money market. There were two main reasons for this contradiction in the working of market forces. If base rates were to rise, they would knock on to the mortgage rates charged by the building societies. The relationship between the two, as most people know by now, is indissoluble and hinges on the fact that societies have to compete with banks for deposits. A rise would have been politically sensitive and the Heath Government had gone to great pains to avoid this earlier on when it forbade banks to offer more than 9½ per cent on deposits of less than £10,000. Bank profits were also large. Any increase in the rate of borrowing to customers would have laid them open to the charge of profiteering.

Companies Cash In

This led to an added confusion in the market: there was now a disparity between base rates and the rates in the whole-sale money market, which were higher. At this point, the treasurers of large industrial companies saw an opportunity to make a lot of money. They borrowed from their banks at base rate or just above and lent that money to the wholesale market where the rates were higher. The banks themselves were borrowing from the money market – frequently the same money they had just lent to companies. As Moran

points out, this 'round-tripping' of money did two things: it
distorted M3 even further to an annual rate of 36 per cent
without actually adding to the volume of credit, and, faced with
these alarming measurements, the authorities were panicked
into abandoning some of the principles embodied in Competition and Credit Control. They raised Minimum Lending Rate,
set levels for bank borrowing in the money market, and rein-
troduced controls on hire purchase. But what they could not do
was interfere with competition in the money market itself: too
many large institutions were doing far too well. The new
measures, however, had a beneficial effect on the money supply
in the sense that M3 grew at only half the rate in 1974 that it
did in the previous year.

But the damage had been done. The huge expansion in credit
created by Competition and Credit Control had already been
harnessed to the one commodity enjoying a spectacular boom –
property. It had been unintentionally boosted by Harold Wilson's administration almost ten years earlier. Understandably,
it had wanted bank lending to be channelled into manufacturing industry, the wealth and job-creating sector, and not into
property speculation. Property controls seemed to be the
answer. At the end of 1964, the government imposed a ban on
further office development in London and also restricted
development in the South-East. Office and commercial accommodation consequently soared to an enormous premium, fuelled by the demand for space from foreign banks and institutions
which had set up shop in London. Demand simply outstripped
supply. Between 1965 and 1970 office rents in the City's banking sector rose by 400 per cent. And although the clearing
banks had been instructed not to lend for property development, there was no shortage of fringe banks to fill the gap. In
the two years after the introduction of Competition and Credit
Control bank lending to the property sector was eight times
what it was to manufacturing industry.

The Fringe Banks

It meant the fringe banks were heavily committed to the
property companies and were often involved in schemes them-

selves. They were also borrowing short in the wholesale money markets and lending long – so there was a gap between their long-term loans to the companies and what they were borrowing. They tried to cover this by renewing existing deposits or, if they could not do that, they created new liabilities. But when interest rates rose by government decree at the end of 1973 the secondary banks found themselves in difficulties. Competition for money intensified. Borrowing short and lending long at fixed rates of interest meant that many banks were facing losses on their lending. London and County Securities, of which Jeremy Thorpe was a director, collapsed – a combination of dishonesty and mismanagement. It did not take long for the rumours to gather momentum, namely that the fringe banking sector was in trouble, that it was finding it difficult to raise new deposits. Consequently, existing depositors took their money out of the fringe banks and put it into the trusted favourites like the clearing banks. It was the beginning of the end.

The Property Market Crashes

The collapse was hastened by two things. At the end of 1973 property values finally peaked, the steam having gone out of the market. The financial roller-coaster on which companies borrowed and bought, sold at a profit, then borrowed and bought again, sold at a profit and so on, had come to a full stop. In many cases, their liabilities were bound to exceed their assets. If that was not enough, the Heath Government compounded the agony by imposing a freeze on office rents at the end of 1973. The rot set in early in 1974 as prices began to fall. By the end of the year property values had halved. Worse still, the share prices of property companies (in which secondary banks had so much money at stake) were quite simply butchered. No one could repay interest or capital. The banks were locked in. If they tried to realize the security they had – property shares and physical property that they had as collateral against their loans – they would be realizing assets that had declined steeply in value and would decline even further if they sold.

The 'Lifeboat'

In December 1973 the Bank of England under Richardson set about trying to pick up the pieces against the background of a miners' strike, an impending 3-day week and a stock market that had been drained by gloom and pessimism. The Bank could not allow confidence to fall any further, otherwise the whole banking system would be threatened. It set up a Control Committee to supervise the rescues – an operation that was later called 'the lifeboat'. The Committee was chaired by the Deputy Governor, Jasper Hollom, and each clearing bank had a member on it. The clearers were co-opted for one good reason – the Bank had the power to do so. It did not have the power, on the other hand, to co-opt the pension funds, which lay outside its jurisdiction. The clearers also had vast resources, although initially the members of the Committee did not envisage that any money would have to be spent at all – quite the contrary, in fact. They believed at that stage that the banking system was fundamentally sound; it had simply been shaken by lack of confidence. They even thought the rescue would be profitable for the participants.

This rosy view was quickly confounded by events. The Committee's original intention was to 'recycle' those deposits taken from the secondary banks and deposited with the clearers. These would be recycled back to the fringe banks, thus relieving the secondary-banking system of its main problem. Three months later, the lifeboat had committed £400 million to recycling, but that was far from being the end of their commitment. Nine months later, at the end of 1974, they were in for nearly £1,200 million and decided to call a halt, complaining that they had now put up 40 per cent of all their reserves and assets. The Bank had no alternative but to pitch in £85 million of its own money, in addition to the 10 per cent it had already contributed to the Committee's resources. According to Moran,

> The Control Committee itself helped twenty-six institutions, of which eight were eventually put into liquidation or into the hands of a receiver. The amounts used to provide support outside the Control Committee cannot be accurately calculated; the best-informed journalist to follow the affair puts the total used in the whole rescue at about £3,000 million.

Slater and Matthews

When the clearers called a halt, the Bank had to go it alone but no one knows at what cost. Slater Walker was its most important rescue, probably involving the Bank in about £110 million. Inside the lifeboat itself there were a number of household names familiar to anyone who was involved in those days with hire purchase: United Dominions Trust, the largest of the finance houses, and First National Finance Corporation – both of which cost the lifeboat millions of pounds. FNFC was the creation of Pat Matthews, who was the darling of the industry. He is no longer heard of. Jim Slater came out of the crash without a penny and was saved by a million-pound loan from his friends. It has all been paid back. Slater now writes children's books and runs a property company. He is comfortably in the millionaire class again and does not look likely to leave it.

Shareholders Are Dumped

While all the depositors involved in the secondary-banking crisis got their money back, the shareholders did not. The Bank treated them as second-class citizens, the first-class citizens being the big depositors from industry and elsewhere. But shareholders are an important source of funds for companies. It is one thing to argue that if a large company goes into liquidation then shareholders must take their place in the creditors' queue. It is quite another to argue that the same, crude rule applies when a whole industry gets into trouble – as the property market did. The secondary banks fuelled the property boom, indeed were its main propellant, and like it or not were part of the banking system. The two were tied together; it was not a freak or fortuitous occurrence. In that sense – because of its particularity – the Bank should have paid some attention to shareholders. By not doing so, it did nothing to help investor confidence.

Nor was the Bank itself blameless in the secondary-banking crash. When the crisis was actually rolling, it gave 'authorized' status to Edward Bates, a fringe bank, which in the event it had to bail out. Bates was authorized by the Bank to deal in foreign exchange. This was not merely extraordinary; it showed that the Bank was singularly ill-equipped during this period for its supervisory function. It was trying to supervise more than 300 financial institutions with a staff of fifteen people, a task that would have taxed the wisdom of Solomon.

'Banks' that were not Banks

But there was an added complication to a system which the Bank was quite happy to assent to. In the bad days of secondary banking there were many financial institutions that were able to give themselves the label of 'bank' – thereby creating the impression that they conducted their affairs prudently, when that was the last thing they were doing. In the end, 'bank' means only one thing: an institution where prudent men conduct affairs prudently. How is it, then, that a fringe banking community could grow up appearing to be banks but without any supervision from the Bank of England? The law of the time was extraordinarily lax: all a fringe bank needed was a certificate from the Board of Trade, which looked for only 'a minimum level of banking characteristics'. Supervision did not enter into it. Since these authorizations came from Whitehall and not Threadneedle Street, the Bank apparently felt no responsibility for supervision. In effect, then, the fringe was certified but unsupervised. As Whitehall supervision was non-existent, it was only a short step to chaos and mismanagement.

Muddle

If we assume that the Bank was thoroughly conversant with what was happening in the property and money markets, or at least had a grasp of it, why didn't it seek to do something about it? Because the fringe was the creature of the Board of Trade and not the Bank? Because the banks Threadneedle Street recognized as in its domain – the clearers and the merchant banks and, to some extent, the discount houses – were *the* banking system and anything else was, literally, on the fringe and not of much account?

In the first place, the fringe was not entirely the creature of the Board of Trade although the Board issued the certificates. Before it did that, however, the Department invariably consulted the Bank's Discount Office. The Bank said a certificate was issued only when an applicant was 'soundly based and operating fairly'. How it could be sure of that with a staff of only fifteen, who theoretically had to check the information and monitor the applicant's subsequent operation, was not merely questionable but impossible. Consequently, many applicants were slipping through the net, and staying beyond it, because any examination of their suitability was, to say the least, cursory. If the Bank was satisfied with the quality of the people it was vetting, it was singularly ill-equipped subsequently to forestall the crisis.

Confusing the Elite with the Fringe

The explanation for its sanguineness must be historical, a received notion that bankers of all kinds are *per se* sound people. Before the emergence of the fringe the City knew its bankers intimately. They came from a long line of City families, established backgrounds and school and university contacts. Few of them ever stepped out of line because there was no need to. Everyone knew the rules and there was no incentive to break them. However, the fringe was not composed of Hambros, or Warburgs, Beavans, Tukes and Cattos; it consisted very largely of people the City had never heard of or, if they had, knew only slightly. Does one treat, for example, John Stonehouse, the former disgraced MP and boss of the British Bangladesh Trust, in the same way that one would treat a Hambro? Of course not. Yet Stonehouse slipped through the net, as did many others. It was sheer *naïveté* on the part of the authorities to imagine they were dealing with people who, either by background or by custom, would understand the City's unwritten rules and play the game the City's way. Many of them did not know the rules or, if they did, they broke them and were quite happy to walk away from the shambles with a great deal of money in their pockets. For a society that is built on the caste system, particularly a financial caste system, this aspect of the affair is the hardest of all to understand, especially when the City has been assiduous in keeping out of its ranks, indeed its environs if at all possible, people like Tiny Rowland and Robert Maxwell who, however distasteful to the Establishment, have been around for years and are likely to be so for some time yet.

Change

Lord O'Brien still believes that Competition and Credit Control could have worked: 'It just came into effect in the worst possible conditions.' He also thinks that the edict to the clearers not to go into hire purchase and loans (outside the corporate sector, that is) pushed a huge volume of business straight into the hands of the fringe, which, unlike the clearers, was not capable of handling it prudentially. Two things are quite clear, though. By rationing credit through price and not controls, the scene was set for a rapid expansion of 'banking' institutions outside the traditional banking sector. The fly in the ointment was the property market, where freak conditions had ironically been created by the Wilson Government and were later exacerbated by the Heath Administration through freezes on office rents. One brought growth, the other – combined with the peaking out of the market – hastened decline. That was O'Brien's misfortune.

What the crisis did, however, was to shake up the traditional relationship the Bank of England had with the banking community. Informal contacts, based on a shared view of prudentiality, were to go. However much the City wanted to cling to its world of private politics, free from Whitehall interference, it is inconceivable that the system could have continued for very long. The number of foreign banks and subsidiaries alone demanded a change in the structure. It would have been irrational and dangerous to have a two-tier banking system composed of the traditional core of clearers, merchant banks and discount houses on the one hand and on the other a large rump of unregulated banks that were not part – either by custom or practice – of the old Lombard Street.

The Banking Act

What emerged, after several years of discussion, was the 1979 Banking Act, which obliged the Bank to regulate the banking system. What it did do was to make a clear distinction between licensed deposit takers and banks proper. In February 1984 there were 290 recognized banks (banks proper) and 308 licensed deposit-taking institutions. The Act itself was far from perfect. The secondary-banking crisis showed there was considerable mismanagement and sometimes fraud among those operating on the fringe. The flaw in the Act related to deposit-taking institutions and particularly partnerships. Here, the Bank used what it called the 'four eyes' criterion. It is worth quoting:

> These provisions are designed to ensure that at least two minds are applied both to the formulation and implementation of the policy of the institution. The Bank would not regard it as sufficient for the second person to make some, albeit significant, decisions relating only to a few specific aspects of the business. Both must demonstrate the qualities and application to influence strategy, day-to-day policy and their implementation, and both must actually do so in practice. Both persons' judgements must be engaged in order

that major errors leading to difficulties as a whole are less likely to occur. Both persons must have sufficient experience and knowledge of the business and the necessary personal qualities to detect and resist any imprudence, dishonesty or other irregularities by the other person.

It is a statement of aims, rather like house rules in boarding schools. In any partnership one partner is likely to dominate the business more than the other; it is a fact of life. It is also a fact that many partners are likely to devote themselves to certain aspects of the business rather than others because that is where their interests and expertise lie. My own recollection of an association with a licensed deposit taker in the mid-sixties – it called itself a merchant bank – was that the board of directors was dominated entirely by one man. He took the decisions and virtually ran the bank. The directors were happy to take the money. The institution came to grief. There were provisions in the Act to deal with such an occurrence, but no legislation can ever provide for concealment or deceit, especially where the profit motive overrides all other considerations.

The Johnson Matthey Scandal

It was ironic, therefore, that while the Act was supposed to deal primarily with irregularities in the licensed deposit-taking sector (the assumption being that banks proper always behaved themselves) it should be blown to smithereens by a proper bank acting – as the Chancellor of the Exchequer, Nigel Lawson, put it – 'with an appalling and bizarre record of incompetence'. Johnson Matthey was a long-established gold house that had branched out into commercial banking through Johnson Matthey Bankers and it had thus asssumed the mantle of a bank proper. The Bank of England felt obliged to rescue it when it got into deep trouble, although the obligation is arguable: if JMB had been allowed to collapse it would not have brought down the banking system; it would have caused tremors, certainly, but dealing with that kind of problem is precisely the Bank of England's job. (It does not, it is worth noting, express its concern about the commercial banks' huge exposure to sovereign loans in overseas countries, at least not in public.)

There was also a number of other factors at work that argued against a Bank of England rescue. The first was JMB's incompetence in the loan market – £248 million lost, mostly because of its rapidly growing loans to two Asian businessmen who were known to be dubious credit risks. This was banking *naïveté* at its worst, an example of commercial banking failing hopelessly to do its business on commercial terms – a secure return on its loan book. These loans amounted to substantially more than JMB's total capital, although JMB's reports showed them to be equivalent to no more than 72 per cent of capital. This was a case of gross underreporting. (Later JMB was to become a case for the City of London Fraud Squad.) The affair, then, was not a matter of bad luck or due to circumstances outside JMB's control, two factors that could have argued for a rescue.

Blunders

Yet in November 1984 the Bank of England capitalized a £100 million deposit it made with JMB to give it working capital. Why? The Bank never seeks to give explanations if it can avoid doing so, but it's clear that it was embarrassed by its own failure of supervision. How did the Bank explain the astonishing fact that the quarterly return from JMB that was due in mid-April 1984 was not received until June and that it did nothing to chivvy JMB to provide the return by the due date? Why was it that the Bank – when it professed it was concerned by the developing crisis – did not arrange a meeting with JMB until August? If anything, both these discreditable lapses were due to a total failure of its supervisory role.

The Chancellor is Left in the Dark

But the Bank, apparently, had a skin of rhinoceros hide. Way back in November 1984 it made the deposit of £100 million with JMB, by which time it was generally known throughout Parliament and the City that something was badly amiss. The Chancellor was obliged to make a statement to Parliament in December of that year without knowing that the Bank had made the deposit a month earlier. The Bank, in other words, had not bothered to inform him. Understandably, the Chancellor had every right to be furious; predictably, the Opposition asked whether he could any longer have confidence in the Governor, Robin Leigh-Pemberton. A clear invitation, not accepted, to sack him. The Bank's behaviour was not merely high-handed, it was outrageous. Yet there is no reason to suppose that Leigh-Pemberton had suddenly assumed the autocratic mantle of Cunliffe – he had neither the temperament nor the skills. Moreover, he was in Moscow when the loan was made – no doubt one of the reasons why the muddle had occurred. If anyone had bothered to tell Leigh-Pemberton about the deposit, he had not thought the information important enough to pass on to the Chancellor.

A White Paper

Nigel Lawson ordered an immediate inquiry into the Bank's supervisory role and a year later produced a White Paper on banking supervision, the forerunner of a new Banking Bill. One of its main recommendations, which was not entirely complimentary to the Bank, was that a Board of Banking Supervision should be set up to help the Governor with his supervisory duties. Members of the Board would be appointed by the Governor with the agreement of the Chancellor. They would include the Governor, the Deputy Governor and the executive director of the Bank responsible for banking supervision and they would be permanent ex-officio members. But the Board would be beefed up by five outside members. They would be senior bankers, either recently retired or having no executive responsibilities in the private sector, and members with legal and accountancy qualifications. They would serve for a fixed term and would be remunerated by the Bank. In addition, the Board would be

obliged to include in the Bank's annual report to the
Chancellor a section giving an account of its work over the
previous year and expressing its views on current issues
within the field of banking supervision.

New Rules

That dealt with the supervisory set-up. On the question of
bank lending, which led to the collapse of Johnson Matthey
Bankers, the government decided that any bank would have
to notify the authorities if its exposure to a single customer
rose above 10 per cent of its capital base. Exposures in
excess of 25 per cent of capital base would require prior
notification to the supervisors. Any serious breaches of these
rules could lead to revocation of a bank's authorization to
accept deposits.

No Discrimination Between Banks

The two-tier system of banking – that is, the distinction
between recognized banks and licensed deposit takers
created by the 1979 Banking Act – would be abolished. But
it would continue to be a requirement for authorization that
at least two individuals effectively directed the business of
an authorized institution. There was one other aspect of the
government's legislation that caused accountants to worry
about their confidential relationship with their customers.
The government made it quite plain that auditors of banks'
accounts should report to the Bank of England any fraud or
wrongdoing by their clients. It said that a regular dialogue
should take place between the Bank and a bank's auditors
and that the Bank should have new powers to obtain
information. In the JMB affair, the bank's auditors were
Arthur Young, who appeared to believe that JMB was sound
until very late in the day. The Bank of England and Johnson
Matthey plc, JMB's parent company, decided to sue the firm.
If that case goes against Arthur Young, it will have
enormous repercussions throughout the accountancy industry. Auditing – a very rewarding activity – will become a
minefield, fees will almost certainly rise and the cost of

professional indemnity for incompetence or negligence will not only become more expensive; it will become harder to obtain. JMB will have rocked more than one boat.

JMB – the Good Bits Are Sold

Litigation apart, the Bank of England went some way towards clearing off the JMB debt when it sold, in April 1986, the good bits of Johnson Matthey to Westpac (what was the Bank of New South Wales) for £17.5 million. Westpac already had a bullion subsidiary and by buying the bank and its bullion-dealing business it joined the exclusive band of five bullion houses which arrange the London daily gold-price fixing. (The others are Rothschild, Samuel Montagu, Sharps Pixley and Mocatta & Goldsmid.) But the bad loans made by JMB remained with the Bank of England, as did the legal actions.

Influence and Invisibility

Bank supervision is, of course, a delicate business because a whiff of scandal can trigger off a panic that has reverberations in every City market. Once the tip of an iceberg has been sighted the City presumes immediately that what lies beneath the surface is of unimaginable proportions. It is one of many reasons why men of power within the Bank have long espoused anonymity, discretion and a closet culture that has made them faceless and nameless to all but a few hundred City people with whom the Bank has regular contacts. The Bank prefers suggestion to direction; when the Bank proposes, the City disposes.

'Mrs Thatcher's Poodle'

The authority and image of the Bank of England are vested in the Governor. When he speaks in public – whether on interest rates, City regulation or financial services – he is expressing the views of the Bank, handed down to him by an impressive array of advisers and directors. Some strong Governors – like Gordon Richardson, Leigh-Pemberton's predecessor – were independent enough to express their own views in forceful terms to the Treasury or in public. Mrs Thatcher reputedly never got on with Richardson. He had views of his own – no bad thing but not easily forgivable by a Prime Minister who believes in consent but not consensus. Leigh-Pemberton, a clearer and not a merchant banker, was appointed, according to her critics, by Mrs Thatcher as her poodle at the Bank. Certainly, the new Governor indicated on his appointment that he was in total accord with the government's policies. Professional critics thought it was a disaster: he was a clearing banker, not a central banker, a man with no experience of the wider issues. He had one thing in common, however, with many of his predecessors – he was an Etonian and a squire. And he had the abiding virtue of being keen on cricket. But he is said to be a man who's willing to learn. The Governorship of the Bank of England seems a curious post for on-the-job learning, suggesting that a pliant Governor under a Thatcher Administration is more important than a man who is well versed in international banking.

The Man They Preferred

Barring any candidate from the merchant-banking community, the man people preferred for the job was Christopher ('Kit') McMahon, the very able Australian who has been Deputy Governor since 1980. McMahon had intellectual distinction, something Leigh-Pemberton is not noted for, by virtue of his academic posts, notably at Oxford where he was Fellow and Tutor in Economics at Magdalen. But well before he came to the Bank he was thoroughly versed in the habits and thinking of government: four years as Economic Assistant at the Treasury, followed by three as Economic Adviser to the British Embassy in Washington. McMahon entered the Bank as Adviser in 1964 and became Adviser to the Governors two years later. In 1970 he became an Executive Director, a job he held for ten years before being appointed Deputy Governor. He was a thoroughly rounded central banker whom Leigh-Pemberton was lucky

to have as his Deputy. McMahon eventually left Threadneedle Street in the spring of 1986 to become Chairman of
the Midland Bank.

City Reorganization

Both the Governor and the Deputy Governor have been
fairly well exposed to the media and to a far wider circle in
the City than was formerly the case. The one act by the
government that has given the Bank substantially more
exposure than before was the decision to keep the Stock
Exchange out of the Restrictive Practices Court. Leigh-
Pemberton devoted many of his early speeches to City reorganization, but the bulk of the work on reorganization has
been done by David Walker, the tall, personable and intel-
ligent Executive Director in charge of Finance and Industry.
Walker is too clever by half for some tastes. Immensely
articulate, he has a wide grasp of City markets and he has
been the driving force behind the new, larger financial
groupings in the City. Walker was quick to realize that the
abolition of minimum commissions and single capacity was
only a step on the steep road to creating sizeable institutions
capable of competing with the giant investment houses of
Wall Street and Tokyo. He has spent most of the last four
years cajoling brokers, bankers and jobbers into performing
acts of union, persuading them that the marriage bed –
however uncomfortable initially – was a better place from
which to fight international competition than the creaking
hammocks of individualism. If it had not been for Walker's
energy and talent for intellectual persuasion it's unlikely
that the City's reorganization would have gone as far as it
has done.

Walker has a Treasury background – he was Assistant
Secretary when Healey was Chancellor. Healey regarded
him as extremely able. Another Executive Director,
Anthony Loehnis (Eton and New College, Oxford) came to
the Bank by way of the Foreign Office and the merchant
bankers, J. Henry Schroder Wagg (Lord Richardson's old
firm). Eddie George (Dulwich College and Cambridge), who

runs the Policy and Markets Division – a complex
embracing home finance, the money markets, monetary
policy and gilt-edged – joined the Bank when he was
twenty-four and has had various secondments to the Bank of
International Settlements and the IMF. Rodney Galpin, the
Executive Director in charge of Operations and Services,
entered the Bank from Cambridge. The four Executive
Directors are, of course, members of the Court of Directors.
They are mostly under fifty and paid between £50,000 and
£60,000 a year.

The Court, as one might expect, is composed of worthy
men who are not likely to run off with anyone's money. The
non-executive Directors include two merchant bankers – the
Hon. Sir John Baring of Barings and David Scholey of
Warburg. There is also a smattering of industrialists –
people like Sir Hector Laing of United Biscuits and Sir
Adrian Cadbury of Cadbury Schweppes. There is a single
trade unionist, Gavin Laird, General Secretary of the
Amalgamated Union of Engineering Workers.

Some of the non-executive Directors sit on the Committee
of Treasury, the most important committee in the Bank, and
are supposed to lend their years of experience in the form of
distilled wisdom to the Governor. They do not make policy,
but they do play a role in the administration of it – mainly
in the other committees.

The Governor, his Deputy and the four Executive Directors are all paid more than any senior Civil Servant.
Leigh-Pemberton gets around £80,000 and George Blunden,
the present Deputy Governor, about £65,000. There is a
good argument for increasing the pay substantially. For one
thing, the work of the Bank has become increasingly
complex in recent years and much more demanding. Staff
numbers (in total about 5,750, including those at the Bank's
printing works) fell in 1984 by 100 and could hardly be
called Parkinsonian in their trend: Walker's department
has only 50 people, George's 340 and Banking Supervision
just 90 (to be increased). The difficulty arises at the top,
where there is a demand for trained Bank people with

considerable experience. They cannot be obtained from outside – by transfers from the Treasury, for example, simply because the required expertise does not lie in government departments. The Bank, apart from the Advisers, has to breed its own people. The work of the Executive Directors is quite as onerous as that of the chief general managers of the clearing banks, who are paid anything up to three times more than the Bank's executives.

Nor does the Bank lose money. It was the fashion – and still largely is – that the chairman and directors of nationalized industries should take salaries 'prudential' enough not to upset the trade unions or politicians. The Bank is not in that position. It has always made a profit, both before and after nationalization. Its long history may have been patchy – inevitable when one considers the turmoils of three centuries – but its authority in the City is indisputable and it has shown itself to be an innovator, often in the face of Establishment reluctance. Yet the old ambiguity still remains. It has persisted ever since 1694, raising doubts among politicians about its true role. Is it a creature of the State, or does it stand apart – independent, aloof, rarely explaining and never apologizing? Outside its crucial market functions, the Bank of England is, if anything, the leader of that curious amalgam of institutions called the City and its preferences lie there rather than in Whitehall. It is, after all, an immensely powerful parish, which even the most radical politicians are reluctant to take on.

THE CLEARING BANKS

The British clearing banks are among the biggest in the world and have generally had profits to match. Unlike merchant banks, they deal extensively with the public; keep the accounts of industrial and commercial companies, and are heavily engaged in foreign lending. They are very active in the money and interbank markets (banks lending to each other) and, to a lesser extent, they finance the needs of industry – although it is a bone of contention that they do not do nearly enough of it.

Getting to the Top

Their image is staid, prudential and essentially unexciting. They have none of the verve and colour of merchant banking; they lack the entrepreneurial flourish of stockbroking, and they are so deeply conservative as to raise serious doubts about their ability to modernize their role in a rapidly changing financial world. Enterprise is easily stifled in these monolithic institutions and brilliance is not at a premium. It took Geoffrey Taylor thirty-nine years to become a director and Group Chief Executive of the Midland Bank. NatWest's Group Chief Executive, Philip Wilkinson,

took forty years to attain his present post. Even Sir Timothy
Bevan, Executive Chairman of Barclays, with a long family
tradition in the bank behind him, took thirty-one years to
become the top man. The wheels of promotion grind exceed-
ingly slow and the story is repeated time and again. It is
small wonder that the ambitious middle classes can find
better things to do.

Security and Perks

For clearing-bank employees, however, security can often be
an agreeable compensation for tedium, and a surrogate for
quick promotion. The branch manager plays golf with his
clients; supports local activities and probably belongs to the
Rotary Club. He is well paid (in the City of London anything
from £30,000 to £40,000). He will get a cheap mortgage at
an interest rate of 5 per cent or less; a personal loan at the
same kind of rate; a non-contributory pension scheme; non-
contributory life assurance up to three to four times his
salary; private medical facilities (in most cases extended
free to his family); subsidized lunches, and interest-free
loans for his season ticket. In addition, he is likely to be fired
only if he causes a scandal or gives away the bank's money –
as one manager did in 1984 to a woman he was besotted
with. It is a formidable package of benefits. Responsibility,
but not too much of it, and respectability have their own
rewards.

Clearing-bank staff would not get pay and perks of this
kind were it not for the intense competition among banks to
get competent and experienced people. With 450 banks, the
bulk of them foreign and mostly in the City, tussling for
good personnel, some of the financial packages are even
better. Most foreign banks also place a much bigger
emphasis on ambition. The British clearing banks pay lip
service to ambition, but regard patience as a virtue.

The Clearers

Everyone who has a cheque book knows that cheques have
to be cleared. They are debited from one account and

credited to another. The term 'clearing bank' simply means any bank that is a member of the Bankers' Clearing House in Post Office Court, Lombard Street. It was formerly run by the Committee of London Clearing Bankers. There were ten members: the Bank of England, the 'Big Four' clearing banks (Barclays, National Westminster, Midland and Lloyds), the National Giro, the Trustee Savings Bank, the Co-op Bank, Coutts and Williams & Glyn's (the two latter belong, respectively, to NatWest and the Royal Bank of Scotland). All that was changed in December 1985 with the formation of the Committee of London and Scottish Bankers, a trade association dealing with regulatory, legislative and fiscal matters. At the same time a new body called APACS (Association for Payment Clearing Services) was set up to oversee and manage all the payment and money transmission systems. There are fourteen settlement members – the ten banks mentioned above, with some important additions: the Bank of Scotland, the giant American Citibank, Standard Chartered, the Clydesdale and the Royal Bank of Scotland (in place of its subsidiary, Williams & Glyn's). All the clearers keep their accounts with the Bank of England and the daily settlements between banks are debited or credited to these accounts. The Bank itself plays no part in the administration of the Clearing House. Membership signifies that the banks can clear each other's cheques through a number of clearing systems at an astonishing annual cost of £2 billion. Clearing systems grew up because the majority of cheques drawn on a branch bank have to be paid into accounts at other branches or banks. If a cheque is paid in at a different branch from the one where the payer's account is held, it has to be passed back to the home branch to check the signature and ensure that there are sufficient funds in the account to meet the payment. The payment is then approved and recorded. Banks in the same vicinity can clear cheques locally, but most cheques pass through the UK clearing system. Nor is it just cheques that have to be cleared: there are also clearing systems for automated electronic fund transfers.

How Clerks Started the System

Naturally enough, it has not always been like this. The clearing system of the early eighteenth century was ramshackle and cumbersome. Humble clerks from the City and West End banks tramped the street, calling on one bank after another to collect payment for cheques drawn on these branches. Among themselves they decided to rationalize the business. They met daily for lunch and beer at the Five Bells chop house in Dove Court, Lombard Street, where they simply compiled a list of each bank's claims on the others and settled the difference in notes and cash. It may have been rough and ready, but it proved so sensible and satisfactory that the bankers, who were alarmed by the amount of physical cash involved in the clearing, rented a room in the Five Bells where the clerks could exchange their drafts. This happened around 1770 and the logic of this basic clearing system soon caught on. Membership of it was eagerly sought. If a bank did not have a seat in it, it had to use the services of a bank that had. That holds true today. The result was that many banks amalgamated so that they could become members.

The General Clearing System

These days the majority of cheques, by volume and not value, passes through the General Clearing system – a process that generally takes three days. Once cheques have been paid into a branch bank, they are sorted into bank order, batched with control totals and sent to the banks' clearing departments in London, each of which employs hundreds of people. That takes a day. Each clearing department processes and adds together their cheques separately and the sorted cheques are then exchanged with those from the other clearing banks at the Bankers' Clearing House. That is another day. Once the cheques have been exchanged and the net balance to be transferred from one bank to another is agreed, the exchanged cheques are sorted at the receiving banks' clearing department and returned to the branches on which they are drawn. This is the third and final day. And it's at this stage that the bank either 'bounces' those cheques drawn on accounts that do not contain enough money to meet the payments, or it debits the accounts in the normal way. Bounced cheques are returned to the payee and the bank washes its hands of the affair, leaving it up to the drawer and the payee to settle matters between themselves. A post-dated cheque is usually a sign that the person who has written it had not got sufficient funds to pay immediately, but reckons that he will have by the time the cheque is presented for payment. The General Clearing system is now almost fully automated.

Town Clearing

However, it is not the most sophisticated of the clearing systems, nor the largest in money terms. The palm for sheer monetary value goes to the Town Clearing system, which grew out of the original London-based clearing system for the settlement of interbank money market dealings and stock transfers. It now handles the City's big money transactions – cheques of £10,000 or over, which have been drawn on, and paid into, offices and branches within the City of London. The number of cheques by volume is small (about 21,000 cheques a day) as against General Clearing's 12 million. On the other hand, Town Clearing's daily value runs at £36 billion, compared with General Clearing's £2.8 billion. The latter figure is so small because 70 per cent of the cheques passed through the General Clearing system are for £50 or less.

CHAPS

Town Clearing is also much quicker. The City's geographical limits mean that Town Clearing can operate same-day clearing, using a fleet of highly trained messengers. Cheques must be delivered to the Clearing House by 3.50 pm each day, giving the branches in the system until 4.45 pm to examine the cheques and return any that they cannot pay to the Clearing House. The net balance to be transferred between banks is then settled. In February 1984 the clearing system was given an electronic face-lift through CHAPS (the Clearing Houses Automated Payments System), which handles 9,000 payments a day (minimum cheque value of £10,000) totalling £10 billion, and which gives same-day settlement. CHAPS does its talking through a series of computers in each major bank, which are linked together by the British Telecom Packet Switching Service. Each bank has a gateway connected into its own payments system through which customers gain access to the settlement process. But it is a crediting system, not a debiting one: banks instruct accounts to be credited rather than debited. And once an instruction has been issued, it cannot be cancelled. It means that banks must be quite sure of their customers' standing. The funds in the system are also guaranteed by the clearing banks, unlike the parallel system in the US – CHIPS (Clearing House Interbank Payment System) – where banks have to wait for final settlement at the end of each day to know whether funds are genuinely available. What Town Clearing guarantees is same-day value: even if, for one reason or another, payment is delayed, the account is still credited on the same day.

Technically, CHAPS has had very few problems. Not everyone was equally elated by its introduction. There is the rigid deadline for payments, for example. Under the old system, a brief phone call and a quick scoot round the City on a bicycle would usually allow a late payment to be slipped in after closing time. The non-clearing banks grumbled that the clearers were gaining a competitive advantage by allowing themselves extra time to settle in the late afternoon. It had some effect. In 1984 the clearers agreed to stop the practice.

Computers

There are also snags at the technical level, which have nothing to do with the system itself. Each clearer has tended to invest in a different computer package. Barclays and NatWest opted for Olivetti equipment, Midland for ICL and Lloyds for NCR. This was interpreted by the non-clearers as a deliberate ploy on the part of the clearers to hook their customers permanently to one clearing bank. If that was the idea, it didn't work. The non-clearers opted for most of the systems, so that they interfaced with more than one main clearer. It proved to be terribly expensive, but it was an investment based on the suspicion that if a non-clearer used just one clearing bank it would expose the whole of its business to the clearer. The clearing banks tend to regard this as a ludicrous allegation. But the expense has meant a virtual boycott of the system by most of the merchant and foreign banks in the City, with some large and notable exceptions like Citibank and Bank of America.

Credit Clearing

Two other clearing systems are worth mentioning. The first is Credit Clearing, which is similar to General Clearing but almost entirely manual. It is part of the bank giro system for transferring money between branches of banks. These are bank giro credits and standing orders (sums transferred regularly on a given day from one account to another). Each day the credit-transfer documents are sorted at the branches, then sent to the bank's clearing department. Each bank's credit transfers are collected together and exchanged at the Clearing House, with the net balance to be transferred settled on the following day.

BACS

The other system is BACS – the Bankers' Automated Clearing System Ltd – a company formed by the clearers to reduce the amount of time spent on processing money transactions and the inevitable paperwork involved. It owns the computer centre that is used to transfer funds electronically between customers' accounts. This has proved to be very useful for non-bank customers, such as corporations, who have a high volume of regular payments like salaries and pensions. BACS can provide an interface with the customer's own computer system, which then gives BACS its payment instructions. BACS forwards the relevant information to the banks and their computers automatically process the transmission from the customer's account.

Clearing at Point of Sale

There is one more system, experimental and still in its infancy, which could well transform banking, retailing and the role of the credit-card companies. It suffers from an appalling acronym – EFTPOS, or Electronic Funds Transfer at Point of Sale. The key phrase here is 'point of sale' – in other words, a shop, store or garage. Having made his purchases, a customer will hand over a card (effectively any type of bank, cash, credit or in-store charge card) to the sales assistant. This is run through a machine that will give access to the customer's bank account without revealing any of its details. The assistant types in the value of the purchases and the account will give a positive or negative reading. If the account says there are sufficient funds to make the payment, the customer types in his PIN (Personal Identification Number) and the money is automatically transferred from his account to the shop's account.

The system has enormous advantages: it is very good for cash flow; it cuts down on bad debts; it reduces the shop owner's time spent at his local bank paying in large amounts of cash; it reduces the cost of banking, and it cuts down on credit-card administration. But the snags are also numerous: it is very expensive to put in (the cost of the system would have to be shared by banks and their customers); it could not be anything like totally effective (that is, cashless) because a large swathe of the population (25 per cent) is 'unbanked' – it is paid in cash and it shops in cash. But it is intellectually appealing. It is a clearing system in itself and in an ideal world it comes closest to being cashless.

Cheque Truncation

In the next two years, money transmission and clearing is likely to be speeded up by a system known as 'cheque truncation'. This means that a cheque paid into a local branch by a customer would never leave that branch, as it does today. It would be read electronically and the credit and debit made by computer. There are one or two difficulties attached to the system, not least of which is verifying the signature on the cheque – which at the moment is done by the drawer's bank. Another problem is that many customers want their banks to keep the cheques they have paid as a form of permanent record. Cheque truncation would not allow that because the drawer's cheques would be at different banks around the country. Despite those inhibitions, the Clearing House believes that 60 per cent of customers would agree to the system initially and would be quickly followed by the rest.

Opening Up the Club

In 1983, the UK clearing system handled about 13 million payment items a day in England and Wales. (Scotland and Northern Ireland have their own clearing systems.) But non-clearing banks have always been obliged to clear their payments by using one or more of the Clearing House members as their agents. In other words, the clearers were operating a cosy club, a monopoly that stifled competition. In late 1983, the National Consumer Council said that the government should take action if the clearing system was not opened up. In that year, Citibank caused a stir by asking to become a member of the clearing system, and it was followed by Standard Chartered. Then, in March 1984, the Committee of London Clearing Banks, a very powerful club and lobby, initiated a full-scale inquiry into 'the various elements of the clearing system, taking into account recent developments in technology'. Denis Child, Deputy Group Chief Executive of NatWest, headed the review and reported back at the end of that year.

The Child Report recommended that the clearing system should be thrown open to all 'appropriately regulated institutions' that wanted to join, subject to certain provisions. It acknowledged the rapid changes in the financial-services field and the emergence of building societies as major competitors to banks. The Child proposals were remarkably liberal, bearing in mind that Child was a clearing banker, a breed steeped in tradition and wary of innovation and outside competition. The clearing system itself would be comprised of three companies: one covering the general clearing and the credit clearing; another dealing with CHAPS and the town clearing; and a third to look after BACS.

More Clearers

Cost alone might prove a deterrent to a long list of applications. But the report did recommend that Citibank and Standard Chartered should be admitted to the charmed circle. Apart from the big building societies, which would want to join anyway, the only non-clearer with the volume to qualify for General Clearing membership would be the Yorkshire Bank. But there will be new members and that can only lead to a more aggressive and competitive approach to the provision of clearing services.

Intermediaries

While rapid money transmission is important to the life blood of the banking system, it is money itself that is central to its function and profits. Essentially, the clearing banks are financial intermediaries: they channel cash from those who have a surplus to those who need it. The surplus belongs to customers who hold money at their banks in the shape of deposits and current accounts. This is then lent on to borrowers who will want it for a variety of purposes – anything from buying a car to building a new factory. The deposits take two forms: term deposits, when the customer agrees to keep his money with the bank for a certain length of time in return for interest paid by the bank; and demand and short-term deposits, which give the depositor the right to withdraw his money after giving appropriate notice. These, in turn, fall roughly into two generic types: wholesale deposits, which are large sums obtained from corporate sources through the money market; and retail deposits, which are smaller amounts obtained over the counter from the bank's customers.

The Decline of Current Accounts

Current accounts have traditionally proved a major source of funds for the clearing banks. But these have come under pressure from the building societies and National Savings. When bank customers see more attractive rates of return elsewhere, they draw down their current-account balances to the minimum they need for daily cash requirements and transfer the surplus to the Halifax or the Nationwide, or whatever savings institution will give them a higher return. Competition of this kind has led to a sharp depletion in bank current accounts. A decade ago, for example, current accounts represented half of the banks' total sterling deposits. Since then, they have declined by almost 50 per cent. In 1984, the Midland Bank reported that in the previous year the growth in personal accounts had been 'minimal'. The truth is that customers have been using building societies like banks, and the societies have done all they can to behave like banks. New legislation will help them further along that road.

In the high-street battle for personal savings, the figures speak for themselves. The building societies have dramatically overtaken the banks as market leaders. They hold 47 per cent of the liquid assets in the personal sector, compared with only a third in 1970. In the same period the banks' share has dropped from 43 per cent to about 36 per cent. And it looks as if that trend is going to continue. The building societies' share of new personal deposits has climbed steeply from 45 to 65 per cent in roughly three years, leaving the banks sliding downhill from 35 to only 10 per cent over the same period. National Savings has also increased its market share, mainly at the expense of the banks. But the 28th Issue of National Savings Certificates also hit the societies particularly hard.

Current Accounts without Interest

Of course, current accounts do not usually bear interest and the banks have been sharply criticized for not paying it. They are getting the use of the money for nothing. The banks have always contested that proposition. They argue that the cost of servicing current-account holders is equivalent to paying interest of about 10 per cent on all outstanding credit balances – even after recovering some of that cost through bank charges. So, with the decline in current accounts coupled with falls in interest rates, they have been tempted to increase bank charges to personal and corporate customers. In 1983, for instance, the amount earned by banks in charges rose by 25 per cent. But there is a limit to how long that can go on as customers become more canny. Bank charges are a sore point. A *Which* report noted that 22 per cent of bank customers were 'positively dissatisfied' with the service for which they were charged and many others with the way bank charges were calculated. There was also a lack of information. Fuelled by resentment, many customers voted with their feet and transferred to banks offering free banking. And it has paid off. In 1984, for example, Yorkshire Bank reported a 171 per cent increase in new current accounts in the three years since it started free banking.

The Banks Fight Back

After watching their decline in popularity and deposits with nothing less than lethargy, the banks decided to hit back. Back in 1982, Barclays started to reopen some of its branches on a Saturday morning, and two years later NatWest followed suit – citing building-society competition as the main reason. (Societies are open on Saturdays.) The Midland also returned to the Saturday banking habit. Early in 1985 it reopened 50 branches with the intention of extending that to 150 in 1986 – at a cost of around £3.5 million. In February 1984 the Midland followed the lead of the Co-op Bank and introduced a high-interest cheque account. The effect of that was dramatic. In just over six months, it brought in £725 million from 68,000 new accounts and helped to stabilize the bank's deposit base. Faced by retaliatory competition from societies like the Abbey National and the Alliance, Barclays joined the other two clearers in offering a similar facility.

But the Midland resolutely tried to keep ahead of the other three clearers, and abreast of some of the innovators, when it joined William & Glyn's, the Co-op, the Yorkshire Bank and the National Girobank by offering customers free banking if they were in credit. The Midland wanted to gain 100,000 new customers, marketing itself to the top socio-economic groupings who were the most vocal, so the Bank's research found, when it came to complaining about bank charges, and whom it assumed would be more vulnerable to persuasion and a better deal. In fact, in 1984 the Midland gave the impression it was the only major clearer that really had the bit between its teeth. Anxious about losing ground to the other savings institutions in deposits, it launched in September its 'Saver Plus' account, with higher interest rates than those for normal deposits (the rate depended on deposit size), together with facilities for automatic teller machine withdrawals from the account. The bank also aimed itself at the children's market, based on the received notion of many banks that if they get someone young enough they have got them for life. The Midland has turned out to be the most innovative of the lot, with a very successful children's account, which at the end of 1984 was paying 2 per cent above its normal 7-day deposit account.

Costs of Competition

But no one competes in the savings area without spending money hand over fist. By offering free banking, for instance, the Midland sacrificed £2 million it would have received in revenue from bank charges. It also spent a lot on advertising in an effort to attract 100,000 new customers to replace that lost revenue. The instinct of many banks is to let someone else make the running first and if it comes through as a plus on the balance sheet then it is worth considering.

Lending for Mortgages

Early in the eighties, the banks decided to lend money in the mortgage market – a logical enough step if they were to show that they could compete with building societies. Mortgage advances at the end of 1981 stood at just over £3 billion, then rose in the following year by 110 per cent to just over £7 billion. In 1983, there was a 36.5 per cent jump to just under £10 billion. The figures do not compare, of course, with the mortgage advances of the societies, which at the end of 1983 stood at £67.5 billion. But there is little doubt that the banks have made inroads into the societies' traditional market and could do more if they did not have commitments elsewhere. They have tended to undercut the societies on interest rates – an important marketing factor – but the mortgage field is not as profitable as lending to industry or providing personal loans for customers. There is no reason to suppose that they will ever be locked in head-to-head competition with the societies.

The Use of Deposits

Once banks have acquired their deposits, how do they put them to work? In the first place, they have to maintain sufficient liquidity to meet their day-to-day operational needs, as well as satisfy the requirements of the supervisory authorities. These liquid assets consist of money at call and at short notice with other banks and the discount houses, Treasury and commercial bills, and certificates of deposit (CDs). Clearing banks also hold portfolios of dealing assets (gilts and short-dated financial instruments), which can be realized very quickly. Besides maintaining adequate liquidity, the banks have to use their funds to buy, maintain and operate their branches – about 13,000 of them in England, Scotland and Wales. Then there are the computer networks to pay for. They also invest in, or lend to, their subsidiary and associated companies. But the bulk of their assets is available for lending.

Overdrafts and Business Lending

The form of lending best known to most of us is the overdraft. These loans are often secured on assets already owned by the borrower. The ordinary domestic customer, who is well known to his bank as a reliable and prudential citizen, will not have to meet this requirement for small sums. But if we take a small business, whose proprietor may want to borrow £20,000 or £30,000, the bank will certainly ask for security. In some cases, the security will be put up in the form of shares owned by the borrower, but if he has sunk every penny he has in the business then the security will often take the form of a second mortgage on his house. The morality of deals like this is arguable. Banks will say that they have to protect their shareholders' interests, that they are being prudential. On the other hand, if the worst comes to the worst and the borrower loses the roof over his head and anything else that he may have pledged, the bank may have pushed a customer into bankruptcy through no fault of his own and who may have been a valuable asset to the bank in the longer term. Customers are extraordinarily loyal to banks who treat them well. There have been many examples of successful businessmen who have never moved their accounts from their original branches and indeed often keep their companies' accounts with their first bank.

The difficulty is that bank managers are not so stereo-typed as people imagine. Some are excessively cautious, others less so. The younger, modern manager knows more about business than his counterpart of twenty years ago. He has a better understanding of the problems small businesses face and can often give sound advice or put a businessman in touch with someone who can help. Most of the banks have departments that specialize in these areas. The volume of lending to small businesses is now very large. Early in 1984, NatWest estimated that it had committed well over £4 billion to financing small businesses. Most of that was still in the form of overdrafts and loans, but its Business Loan Development Scheme accounted for about a quarter of the total. Under the scheme, amounts up to £250,000 can be borrowed for up to twenty years on a fixed-interest basis. In 1983, more than 37,000 small businesses used the facility to borrow £500 million. But the initiative has not been entirely the banks'. They have been able to expand in the small-business field partly because of the government's Loans Guarantee Scheme, which underwrites the greater part of the risk. At the beginning of 1984, Barclays reckoned that as much as 85 per cent of its non-personal lending was to small businesses – a commitment amounting to about £6 billion. It is a pattern that is repeated in all the major clearers.

Going by the Book

They also lend to much larger, established companies – a profitable form of financing, generally speaking, because the security is better, the loans are larger and the returns are lucrative. That is not to say that the clearing banks haven't had numbers of public companies in what they call their 'intensive care units', a medical euphemism that does not disguise the anxiety the clearers have felt during the recession for their less robust industrial patients. Some of them, like Laker and Stone-Platt, died in a blaze of publicity. The Midland called the receiver into Stone-Platt Industries, having taken the company's pulse more than once and found the patient was not responding to treatment. The chairman was Leslie Pincott, a senior executive from the oil industry, who had been recruited to revive the company. Pincott was angered by the Midland's high-handed action. He acknowledged that banks have every right to protect their security, but equally he thought they had a duty to protect the rights of suppliers, employees and shareholders. He received a bland reply from the under-taker, the Midland's Chairman, Sir Donald Barron, who said it was unjustifiable to jeopardize the Midland share-holders' funds by propping up a business that was failing.

Merchant Banks

During the early eighties the clearers were constantly under fire for not doing enough to help industry. The criticisms were rejected, of course, but at least corporate banking divisions have been set up to meet the needs of their major clients. More lending authority has also been delegated down the line. Barclays has set up its own merchant bank; so has NatWest. Both are making substantial contributions to the needs of medium-sized companies, which are sometimes neglected by the traditional merchant bankers. NatWest's County Bank, particularly, has been very active in corporate finance.

However, no one could accuse the clearers of inertia when it comes to international lending or overseas expansion. Some have developed their international business by establishing worldwide branch networks or by joining international consortium banks. Others have acquired established banks overseas. Until recently, this expansion looked as if it was going to be a path strewn with roses but in the last four years it has turned out to be a bed of nails. International trading profits have consequently been hit. The Midland, for example, made losses of £65 million and £21 million in the last half of 1983 and the first half of 1984.

Overseas Lending

The problem has been the Third World debt crisis, the huge amounts of money lent to the less-developed countries. Lloyds and the Midland are the two most heavily exposed banks. In 1984, each bank had half its capital lent to problem overseas debtors. Barclays' and NatWest's exposure was about half that level. It is not unique to Britain. In 1983, the exposure of the nine largest US banks to Argentina, Brazil and Mexico alone exceeded their capital, while their total exposure to all debtor countries was 250 per cent of their capital base. In that context, the British banks look comparatively healthy. But that is beside the point. What a British clearer cannot afford is to have a foreign debtor either default on its loan or fail to reschedule its debt. It would make a very large hole in a bank's balance sheet, alarm depositors and shake the banking system. Therefore, prudentiality dictates that they should make some provision for these debts should they turn sour. But, until 1983, none of the UK clearing banks had made any provision for sovereign loans to Latin America. In that year, and in 1984,

NatWest and Barclays made provisions of about 5 per cent of total loans to potential problem debtors. The Midland could not make any because of low profit levels and Lloyds made some provision, but probably less than 5 per cent. It can be only an estimate, but it looks as if total provisions made by the clearing banks in those two years were in the region of £1 billion. And that was bound to be reflected in reduced profits.

Midland and Crocker

The Midland's problems were compounded by its investment in the Crocker National Bank of California, the twelfth largest bank in the United States. The Midland took a majority stake in Crocker in 1980 for £576 million – the largest banking deal in American history. Three years later Crocker was steering a perilous course between the Scylla of non-performing loans to the Californian real-estate market and the Charybdis of equally dodgy loans to the wine industry. If one was a monster, the other was a whirlpool that sucked the bank into a loss of $10 million before tax because of a special $107 million charge for bad loans. One US bank analyst commented tartly: 'Crocker has been disastrously run. The only smart thing they did was to stick Midland with the stock at $90 a share.' What was clear was that the Midland had given Crocker an extraordinarily free rein to do what it wanted and did not really know what was going on. What the bank had done, in fact, was to agree to give Crocker's management 'maximum operational autonomy' – a fact that the American banking community found astonishing.

In January 1984 the Midland revoked that extraordinary agreement and appointed new top executives. Two months later the bank turned in a loss of $121 million after a further provision of $148 million for loan losses. In July 1984, the Midland announced its intention of buying the remaining 43 per cent of Crocker for $207 million. It believed that Crocker's outlook was improving. Three months after that Crocker sold its San Francisco building to raise $358 million and the Midland raised its buy-out offer to $275 million. In January 1985 that offer was promptly reduced by about $50 million when Crocker reported a loss for the whole of 1984 of $324 million, among the largest ever recorded by an American bank.

The Midland promptly advanced funds of $400 million to Crocker, but in the process reduced its own ratio of 'free capital', a key measure of a bank's strength. It announced that it would try to rebuild it, possibly with an issue of convertible loan stock. The bank also said that the Crocker losses would have a 'severe impact' on its 1984 results, but it pledged that it would hold its dividend to shareholders. The Crocker affair was by far the worst of the problems to hit any British clearer in the overseas market. In February 1986 Midland reached an agreement with Wells Fargo Bank to buy the good parts of Crocker for £750 million, but Midland was still left with difficult Crocker loans overseas.

More Competition

As we have seen, the competition in the domestic sector from building societies has eroded banking deposits. Then, in April 1985, the banks were obliged by the Chancellor to pay interest on deposits net of tax and not gross, thus bringing them into line with the building societies. That has put pressure on them to offer higher rates to match the societies' net yields. And while most foreign banks in the UK use London only as a base for their international operations, a few – such as the giant Citibank – are getting into the domestic banking market as well. There is also increasing competition in corporate finance.

There have been other aggravations, too, which have made the banks' balance sheets somewhat thinner than they used to be. Corporation-tax changes have helped to undermine their leasing business. The 1984 Budget told them that they would have to meet their deferred tax liabilities, for which they had made little provision. That has not merely weakened balance sheets; in one case at least it effectively wiped out a whole year's profits. Changes like these, together with competition from other institutions, have obliged some banks to raise new capital in the market.

The banks have not welcomed the government's attempts to make financial services more competitive. They have always thought of themselves as the first port of call for loans and deposits and have a highly developed self-esteem, which is beginning to look distinctly out-dated. Given the fact that they do not respond quickly to change, and show little inclination to do so, it is likely that these leviathans will have to stir themselves vigorously if they are still to be regarded as indispensable to our financial way of life.

THE MERCHANT BANKS

Merchant banks are easy targets. Labour politicians think of them as people who wear striped shirts, go to the best tailors and wear hand-made shoes. They have all been to the top public schools, have large houses in the country, hunt, shoot and fish and must be members of White's. If they are not already well born, they will join the upper classes by picking off the daughters of Dukes or Earls, thereby ensuring continuity for themselves and their children in the right social strata. Add to that the habit of making mounds of money and you have the Labour prototype of a merchant banker – élitist, clever and inevitably rich; enviable people who have plenty to be envious of. And totally British, a class that could just as well practise its mystical business in the depths of the shires as in the City of London.

Not All That British

Right in parts, badly wrong in others. First, the Britishness. The grandest of the merchant banks are foreign in origin. Hambros is Danish. Morgan Grenfell, American – founded by George Peabody. Warburgs is German. Lazards was founded by three French brothers. There are now three

Lazard houses – in London, Paris and New York. Rothschild was German-Jewish originally until Meyer Rothschild sent four of his five sons to colonize the financial capitals of Europe – Paris, Vienna, Naples and London. Kleinwort, Benson is German. Schroders is also German. Baring Brothers is arguably German as well – the grandfather of Sir Francis, the founder, was a Lutheran pastor in Bremen. The Honourable Sir John Baring, the present Chairman, stoutly maintains that it is British but there is little doubt that the bank would not be in existence were it not for its German antecedents.

Baring, Warburg, Kleinwort and Morgan

This did not happen because foreigners deliberately set out to take over bits of the City. They arrived in Britain for different reasons. Sir Francis Baring's father started a cloth-manufacturing business in Devon. But Francis was sent to study commerce in the London firm of Boehm. His natural genius for business made him a fortune, certainly the largest in that period, as merchant and banker. Siegmund Warburg, a star among merchant bankers, came to London from Germany in the mid-thirties convinced there was going to be a war. He stayed in Britain, but did not found the bank until 1946. The first Kleinwort, Alexander, went to Cuba from Hamburg in 1854. There he set up in competition with his employers, dealing in sugar and commodities. Sixteen years later he arrived in London. George Peabody, an American and the founder of Morgan Grenfell, set up a banking business in London in 1838 and was later joined in partnership by John Junius Morgan, the father of the great American banker, J. Pierpont Morgan. Grenfell, an Englishman, came into the partnership a little later. Peabody settled in Britain permanently only because his American firm had business connections with London. It is safe to assume that for whatever reason these bankers set up in London it was not because the City was a commercial backwater. It was the most important financial centre in the world. There was money to be made.

The Dynasties

There also exists a notion that merchant banks are family
affairs, controlled by dynasties of bankers who go on lining
their pockets from generation to generation. But that is far
from being the case. True, there were three Hambros on the
board of Hambros Bank, including the Chairman, and they
controlled the bank until recently through the family trust.
There are four Barings on the board of Baring Brothers and
the family has a strong grip on the firm through the Baring
Foundation, which is the holding company. There are three
Rothschilds in the Rothschild bank – Evelyn, Leopold and
Lord Rothschild. There were four until Jacob had a row with
Evelyn and set up on his own. But the family have kept
financial control of the bank. There is one Schroder, Bruno,
on the board of Schroders and the family has a large shareholding through various family trusts. These are the only
dynasties. There are no Warburgs or Lazards. There are no
Morgans or Grenfells. The last surviving banking Kleinwort, Sir Kenneth, lives in France for tax reasons and takes
no active part in the bank.

Together with Hill Samuel, totally British, these eight
banks form the élite of merchant banking. They are members of the Accepting Houses Committee, a club of sixteen
banks, which at one time enjoyed a special relationship with
the Bank of England. Nowadays its exclusivity depends on
keeping other banks out of the club.

There have not been any spectacular marriages among
the chairmen or any notable injections of wealth from outside sources. The Rothschilds have always been rich in their
own right and the Barings, Schroders and Hambros have
sufficient to keep them going because of their rich predecessors. They all make sure they pay themselves well, but not so
well as to cause raised eyebrows; no one at the time of
writing gets more than £200,000 (Ian Fraser of Lazards) and
most of the chairmen who are non-family have shareholdings in their banks. The days when Sir Cyril Kleinwort, a
former Chairman of Kleinworts, could say of a client worth
half a million 'the man's a pauper' are over. Eton does not

predominate (Sir John Baring, Lord Catto of Morgan Grenfell, Rupert Hambro). Harrow has one representative, Evelyn Rothschild. The rest of the chairmen went to middle-of-the-road schools like Ampleforth, Bedford, Wellington and Highgate.

Mystique

Yet merchant banking retains its mystique. Very few people outside the City know what it does. It is certainly not the same as clearing banking. Even a former Chairman of Lazards, Ian Fraser, had no idea what it was when he left Reuters in the 1950s for a new career in merchant banking: 'I'd never heard of it until my boss at Reuters, Christopher Chancellor, suggested it might not be a bad idea. He just gave me some introductions and I found myself a job.' Fraser's route to the top at Reuters had been blocked by a more senior man, who was next in line for promotion. So Fraser went to Warburgs, then headed up Lazards. Most people would regard it as an enviable substitute for Fleet Street.

The Bill of Exchange

All merchant banks, except the new ones, had their roots in merchanting of one kind or another. But whatever the business, it always involved credit and finance. Credit was the crucial factor. A merchant took delivery of goods and made delivery of goods. Payment came later and until it was made the merchant was either receiving credit from his suppliers or giving it to his customers. But the merchant, whether receiving payment or making it, had to be certain when and where the payment was to be made. This is where the bill of exchange came in. The seller wrote to the buyer telling him that he owed so much money on a certain date in respect of the goods he had supplied. The buyer either paid against the bill or, if it was to be paid in the future, he 'accepted' the bill, thereby showing his willingness to pay. Gerald Thompson of Kleinwort, Benson has said,

> The bill of exchange constitutes the most lucid and comprehensive instrument that man has ever devised. It expresses the nature and amount of the transaction which

is to be financed and identifies the parties concerned, and the agreed period of credit. Nothing could make it simpler for the burden of finance to be assumed by a third party. The sale of a bill to a third party enables the seller of the goods to receive cash, leaving the buyer with the full period of the credit allowed to him. The financial burden is lifted from the merchant and can be carried by the spare cash of others who have no part in the original transaction.

That third-party transaction was conducted by the London discount houses in the money market. The discount houses had their roots in merchanting as well, but there were other large and prosperous merchants who took to accepting bills of exchange – very often on behalf of merchants who were less well known to the international trading community. It was these large merchants who became merchant bankers, but their business was credit and not finance. It is worth looking in more detail at the business of accepting bills and how it works in relation to the provision of credit. Let us say that Company A is a Japanese steel exporter and it gets an inquiry from a German car manufacturer, Company B. Company A will not want to accept an order until it is quite sure it will be paid. Moreover, it does not want to lock up, say, £50 million worth of capital represented by the steel for the period it takes to get the shipment to Germany. That would run into weeks. Company B, on the other hand, does not want to pay until it takes delivery. There are two parties – one, which wants the money now, and the other, which wants to pay later. But they agree that the deal should be in sterling and should be payable in London.

The German company tells its local bank to ask the merchant bankers, Company C, to open a credit in favour of the Japanese firm. The merchant bank, which has good Far-East connections, knows that Company A is reputable and that Company B is a top German firm. The bank undertakes to accept bills drawn upon it by the Japanese in respect of their shipment to Germany, while the German company undertakes to provide the sterling to the bank so that it can meet the bill when it becomes payable – that will generally be 'ninety days after sight', plus three 'days of grace'. That period will comfortably accommodate the length of time it takes for the steel to reach Germany.

Once the steel is ready for shipment, the Japanese company will draw a bill for £50 million on the merchant bank in London and it will attach to it all the relevant shipping and insurance documents to show that the steel is actually on board. As soon as the merchant bank is satisfied that the documents are in order and that the steel is of the prescribed quality, it will 'accept' the bill. It is now almost the equivalent of cash, but not quite. The Japanese company still wants the cash, but the acceptance by the bank means that it can now be discounted through the London discount market. A London discount house will buy the bill at face value, less a very small percentage. The Japanese company gets its cash well ahead of the 90-day period.

This, in a simplified form, is how the bill of exchange is used. Behind it, of course, there is a network of overseas agents, shippers and insurers. But we have seen that the merchant bank has not provided any finance at all. It has provided credit – and done it for a very modest commission. The standing of its name in the market is vital; so, too, is its knowledge of the people it's dealing with. But once that bill has been accepted by the bank it is a guarantee that it's as good as cash. And it is precisely for that reason that the bill can be discounted in the money market.

Monarchies and Governments

The 'bill on London' was an important staple of the early merchant banks – indeed it was virtually synonymous with financing international trade and in that the merchant banks played a crucial role. That was on the commercial level. But it was their foreign connections, too, that helped to lubricate their balance sheets. These connections were not at a mundane level; they were with monarchies and governments. In 1820, the first of the Hambro bankers,

Joseph, became court banker to King Frederick VI of Denmark. It was to Hambros, then, that Denmark eventually turned after it had defeated the Prussian invasion of Schleswig-Holstein, at that time part of the Danish kingdom. The war was expensive and money had to be raised. Rothschilds and Barings turned down the bond issue, but Denmark played on the Hambros' dislike of the Rothschilds (they were too arrogant) and Carl Joachim, Joseph's son, managed a successful issue for £800,000.

Nevertheless, it was a near thing for Hambro, who by nature tended to be conservative – 'experience and knowledge, commonsense and calm', his father used to say, and Carl Joachim was no different. Yet with the Danish loan he was closer to playing roulette than being a banker. It was a gamble, but he got away with it and made a fortune on the issue. He was rewarded with a Danish barony, which the head of the Hambro family still bears today. Hambro bought Milton Abbey for a quarter of a million pounds and put his crest – modified by the Royal College of Arms – over the fireplace in Hambros Bank. As a London merchant banker, he had arrived. In fact, the Hambros showed they were notably successful at ingratiating themselves with Scandinavian royalty. Bernadotte, who later became Charles XIV of Sweden, made the Hambro family court bankers to Sweden and Norway.

Rothschild's Domination

Curiously, it was the ascendancy of the Rothschilds over much of Europe's sovereign finance that led to Hambro taking on the Sardinian loan for £4 million in 1851. Italy had been known as 'Rothschild's country' since the Napoleonic Wars – Baron James in Paris and Baron Carl in Naples had the country's provinces neatly tied up for many years with various loans, and their hegemony looked impregnable. Their dominance was altogether too much for Barings when they were offered the chance of undertaking the loan. Sardinia's Minister of Finance, Camillo de Cavour, remarked contemptuously: 'These gentlemen are reluctant

to enter into a struggle with the House of Rothschild.'
Cavour wanted to break the Rothschilds' Italian monopoly
and hoped in the process to raise money more cheaply.
Carl Joachim Hambro decided to take it on, more out of
pique with the Rothschilds, who had always been
patronizing and condescending towards his father, than
from any idea of making a fortune. He had resentment
working for him, but precious little else. He knew
Denmark like the back of his hand, but the kingdom of
Sardinia – which then comprised Piedmont, Savoy and the
island itself – was unknown country. Moreover, the
Sardinian loan was fives times larger than the Danish
one.

Hambro Goes for Broke

There was some initial bickering over the opening price of
the bonds. Cavour wanted 90, Hambro 85. The Hambro
price was prudential, the Cavour price speculative. For a 5
per cent loan at that time the market rate was about 85.
Hambro had no intention of subscribing anything himself,
but it was made clear to him that he should – it would
show his confidence in the issue. He then did something
extraordinary. He subscribed £400,000, or 10 per cent of
the loan. It was the whole of his fortune. If the loan failed
he would lose everything – the bank, his prestige, his
credit. A price of 85 was eventually agreed, pitched rather
higher than any of the Rothschild loans, a fact that would
raise the hackles of James Rothschild in Paris. It was
called the Anglo-Sardinian Loan and it was offered in
London in May 1851. By August it was limping badly –
only £2.2 million of the £4 million had been subscribed at
the agreed price of 85. The Rochschilds had taken a hand
in the affair. James Rothschild was advising customers
not to buy until the price had fallen substantially. He was
telling Cavour in no uncertain terms that in Hambro he
had backed the wrong man. By September it was
rumoured in London that the price of unsold Anglo-
Sardinians was going to be dropped to avoid a disaster.

Carl Joachim had become manic about the Rothschilds, but Cavour encouraged him not to drop the price.

The Gamble Works

At this point Hambro was becoming desperate. He found a British speculator, Lewis Haslewood, who was a gambler to his fingertips; he subscribed £400,000 at just under 85. Haslewood's brother was despatched to Turin to investigate the Piedmontese railways on which the whole loan had been predicated – under Hambro's scheme buyers of the bonds would be able to convert into railroad shares. Edward Haslewood came back with the news that the railroads were so secure that widows and orphans could safely invest in them. The market was unimpressed. The price fell to 79½ and even Cavour was talking about selling them at the best price Hambro could get. Hambro took the suggestion manfully, but at this point his luck turned. Cavour became Minister of State. His popularity in England was gaining ground because of his unremitting campaign to unify Italy. Lord Russell, the Foreign Secretary, launched the slogan 'Italy for the Italians' and suddenly the bonds began to recover. Early in 1852 they had risen to 90 and Carl Joachim made a substantial profit on his £400,000.

The Barings

Hambros is simply illustrative of the role merchant banks played in international finance. Rothschilds was always the biggest. In the hundred years from the Napoleonic Wars to the beginning of World War II the bank brought out eighteen government loans to the tune of £1.6 billion. But well before Nathan Meyer Rothschild set up N. M. Rothschild in 1804, it was the Barings who were the great bankers of Europe. Even in 1903, by which time the Rothschilds were a prodigious force, a German diplomat told the German Foreign Office in Berlin: 'Anybody who wants to place a loan in London on a grand scale must apply to the Barings.'

The Banks' Spread of Business

Foreign government loans on a grand scale are still quite common. The nineteenth-century Rothschilds, Hambros and Barings were always competing for that kind of business, but today the merchant banks could not hope to make a living from it. Over the years they have developed into multi-faceted businesses, which require a wide range of skills. They still deal in bills of exchange, of course, but to that have to be added the operations of foreign exchange, corporate finance, banking, fund management, life assurance and investment services. It is an extensive spread of business, but each house tends to lay a different stress on what it does. Some do not touch life assurance, for example. Some have very few outside investments; others make a point of it. But all of them put a strong emphasis on corporate finance.

Takeovers – ICI and Courtaulds

The mechant banks' involvement with the corporate sector of industry hit the limelight only in the sixties when takeover bids became the fashion. One of the most spectacular was in January 1962, when ICI suddenly made a bid for the textiles giant, Courtaulds. Takeover bids bring out both the worst and the best in people. Inert managements, sleepily content with their balance sheets for years, suddenly become galvanized at the prospect of losing their jobs. Predators lick their lips as they contemplate underused or undervalued assets or the masses of cash lying in the bank. Each side brings in its merchant bank; the battle lines are drawn; the language becomes less diplomatic; circulars fly out to shareholders; profit forecasts are revised, and the professionals on the sidelines watch with amusement as antagonist and protagonist give their versions of events to investors. These can be funny, pompous or hurtful: when directors are fighting for their companies they assume all sorts of postures. It is up to the merchant banks advising them to do the best they can, frequently with unpromising material.

Barings Shun The Limelight

Courtaulds called in their merchant bankers, Barings. Barings is immensely conservative. It is not a bar-room brawler, like some other banks who do not mind using their knuckles when the chips are down. Barings' first reaction was shock. ICI had made the announcement in the papers. This indicated it was sure of victory. ICI, moreover, was an industrial giant, a blue chip that could not be brushed aside. Barings had no choice but to say that the price was not high enough. ICI bid again. Barings still said it was not enough. Balance sheets were pored over – Courtaulds assets looked undervalued. The company told shareholders that it would double its profits in two years.

Enter Frank Kearton

Barings is not comprised of people who enjoy the vulgarity of publicity, but if Courtaulds was not to be swallowed by ICI then the company would have to fight. The City itself was split by the takeover bid. There were those who thought it time that Courtaulds, almost as conservative as Barings, was shaken up. Others saw the bid in personality terms and backed the textile company because they did not like ICI's Chairman, Sir Paul Chambers, a dry tax man with little public appeal. Barings advised Courtaulds to change its corporate image as quickly as possible. The company had to convince its shareholders that the bid was not in their interests. That meant showing them that future profits were good, that it had an expansion programme and that ICI had a poor research record. This was done through an advertising campaign, bolstered very largely by the best weapon Barings had – Frank Kearton, Courtaulds' Deputy Chairman. Kearton was a brilliant chemist and a former ICI man who later collected a Barony for services to industry. He was a fighter, the only man on the Courtaulds' Board who did not mind taking the gloves off in public. Kearton talked freely to the press, massaged the Courtaulds image and attacked ICI day after day.

105

In 1984 Kearton told me,

> We came to the conclusion that what ICI was really
> after was our 50 per cent shareholding in British Nylon
> Spinners and that once they got that they would close
> the rest of Courtaulds down. That wasn't good enough.
> Barings were very supportive, very helpful, but they
> were the most reticent bank of the day. The aggression
> had to come from us.

In the event, ICI only got 37 per cent of Courtaulds' shares
and the company doubled its profits in two years, as it had
forecast to shareholders. Later on, Kearton did a deal with
ICI:

> We sold them our share of British Nylon Spinners,
> which was worth about £128 million, in consideration
> for giving up their 37 per cent in us. By 1970, nylon was
> beginning to do badly and since then it has lost hun-
> dreds of millions.

Playing With Figures

When Kearton became Chairman and started buying companies on behalf of Courtaulds he had an opportunity to see
how merchant banks behaved.

> I saw how unscrupulous they were in dealing with the
> figures of the companies we were taking over. They
> bore very little relation to the facts.

Later, when Kearton became Chairman of the Industrial
Reorganisation Corporation, he organized some very large
takeovers and mergers for nothing:

> I became very unpopular with the merchant banks,
> who were not getting the business and in consequence
> were losing out on fees.

Ironically, Kearton was to become Chairman of the merchant bank, Hill Samuel.

The takeover battles of 1985 and 1986, however, were to
dwarf anything that had been seen in the sixties or
seventies. While the numbers were huge and ran into
billions of pounds, they were no larger in real terms than

the bids of ten or fifteen years ago. But two, in particular, caught the headlines week after week. They were Hanson Trust's bid for the food, drinks and tobacco giant, Imperial Group, with Sir Hector Laing's United Biscuits acting as a 'white knight' for Imperial. (The white knight lost.) And another three-cornered battle between Guinness and the Argyll Group who were fighting for the ailing body of the Distillers Company. Distillers wanted Guinness to win so much that it even entered into an agreement with Guinness to pay all the costs of the bid (advertising, merchant bank fees and underwriting), which amounted to about £30 million. Guinness won.

Personalities and a Resignation

The total value of the two bids was £5.7 billion. The figures, of course, were enormous but it was not that which made the battles come to life. It was their animosity. When boards of directors were fighting for their personal prestige, their jobs, their comfortable salaries and their perks, the urge to survive led to personal enmities between the opposing parties that were frequently aired in public. Advertising was the medium for their expression and something like £15 million was spent in telling shareholders just how bad and unsuited the other side was for the stewardship of their companies. The bidders, with the exception of Lord Hanson, were equally hostile. Hanson, who had advertised barely at all, eventually felt obliged to issue writs against Imperial alleging 'injurious falsehood' in their advertising and Argyll received writs from Guinness. It was the first time in takeover battles that such naked aggression had been seen in public. The senior director in Imperial, Michael Pickard, who had masterminded Imperial's defence against Hanson, resigned as soon as Hanson had won. Disturbed by the nature of the advertising throughout the two campaigns, the Takeover Panel decided to tighten up on what could or could not be said. It acted from hindsight: throughout the bids all the parties had been obliged to submit their advertising copy to the Panel for vetting. It should have acted then and not later.

Morgan's Aggression

One of the City's most powerful merchant banks, Morgan Grenfell, played a prominent and controversial part in both bids. Acting for United Biscuits, Morgan bought £360 million worth of shares in Imperial (with an agreement that it would be indemnified by UB if it lost on the deal), and acting for Guinness it acquired £180 million worth of shares in Distillers. Together, the purchases amounted to three times Morgan Grenfell's last (disclosed) net worth of £170 million.

That prompted some new rule-making on the part of the Bank of England – namely that Morgan Grenfell, or any other merchant bank, would not in the future be allowed to buy shares in another company to a value of more than 25 per cent of the bank's capital base. Morgan was unrepentant. But those deals – together with an extraordinarily high competitive profile – have given Morgan the reputation of the most aggressive bank in the City.

Takeovers, of course, are an integral part of corporate finance. Although they are frequently glamorized they nevertheless help to keep merchant banks in the City eye, especially when they are on the winning side. In other words, they can be good for business and often help to attract new corporate customers. Lord Catto, the Chairman of Morgan Grenfell Holdings and former Chairman of the bank, illustrates the point precisely:

> Our general image in the late sixties and early seventies was a stuffy one. We've always been called blue-blooded, largely because there were lots of Lords on the board. We didn't look after our corporate customers very well, expecting them to come and see us when they had problems, rather than the other way round.

Morgan's Morale Grows

Catto believes the turning point came in 1972 when Morgan Grenfell did something very aggressive and, by City standards, unheard of. The bank intervened in a takeover bid in which it was not representing any of the parties. P. & O. were bidding for Bovis, a client of Warburgs.

> What P. & O. were actually doing was bidding for one man, Frank Sanderson, the property expert who was on the Bovis board. They weren't really bidding for the company. We thought that was wrong. So we rang all the big institutional shareholders, got a group of them together and after a great proxy battle we won.

Catto, son of a former Bank of England Governor, says that morale in the bank grew after that:

> We now have much the biggest list of any of the merchant banks as far as British corporate clients are concerned.

Those clients include Lloyds Bank, Guinness, Arthur Bell and Costain. It's this side of the business that accounts for two-thirds of Morgan Grenfell's profits, fee income earned from advising companies on raising money, restructuring, takeovers and mergers.

Fees

When merchant banks advise clients in takeover situations they make their money by charging fees. This is a murky area because there is no set scale. The amount of work involved in takeovers varies a good deal – some are comparatively simple, others detailed and complex. However, when a merchant bank is asked by a company it has never met to mount a takeover, or more probably to mount a defence, it will either propose a fee or the company will ask for an indication of costs. Foreign companies generally ask for a contract, particularly if they're in the British market for the first time. In the case of a takeover, a merchant bank will probably split the operation into parcels: a study and recommendations as to technique; a valuation of the company to be taken over; and a recommendation about the price the bank thinks the company can get away with (obviously, the cheaper the better). If a bank is suddenly asked to mount a defence, it will have to do a certain amount of preliminary work before it can decide what kind of defence it can make. A fee will be agreed for that. It will cover expenses and a small profit.

Takeovers, of course, do not always run the full distance. The bidder might pull out for a variety of reasons – he may realize he cannot afford it. But if it is decided to 'go public' on a takeover, the company and the bank will agree a failure fee – relatively small, and which will just cover costs. The next stage will be a success fee, charged as a percentage of the value of the deal. When BTR succeeded in its bid for Thomas Tilling, the bank representing BTR (Morgan Grenfell) probably got rather more than £1 million, while Warburgs, who looked after Tilling, probably got rather less than a million; in other words, the difference between the two fees was probably in the region of £500,000. Sometimes the failure fee can be quite large, simply because the defending bank managed to screw a higher price out of the aggressors than might otherwise have been expected.

The Money in Mergers and Takeovers

A glance at the 1983 league table, showing which banks did best in mergers and takeovers, shows the amount of money involved. It is not what the banks charged; it is the amount of share capital involved. The figures are impressive. Morgan Grenfell did 39 takeover and merger deals with a total value of £2.737 billion, almost double the business that Warburgs did in the same year. (In 1982 Warburgs headed the table with £1.188 billion, but Morgan Grenfell was only a few million behind.) In the same two years, Hill Samuel was always in the first four, with Lazards coming fourth from nowhere in 1983.

Income from takeovers and mergers is not something that is entirely in the control of the banks. If a bank happens to have clients who are hyperactive in a particular year – either because they are bidding for someone else or they are the target of a takeover bid – then the bank is likely to do

particularly well from fee income. Nor is it the amount of
deals that matters; it is much more the quality and size.
While Morgans did the largest number of deals, the average
was only £70 million. Lazards managed only 25 per cent of
Morgans' numbers, but averaged £166 million for each
takeover or merger. The rough and ready rule is that the
bigger the takeover or merger, the higher the fees. Uncontested takeovers, of course, involve the banks in much less
work, although it's quite likely that a merchant bank will
advise its client that the price is not good enough. That, of
course, will affect the fee it charges, particularly if it wins
its case.

Getting the Business

A list of inert or inactive clients does not always mean that
merchant banks will wait for something to turn up. Very
often they will spot a situation that will generate good
business. A bank may see that a certain company can be
bought dirt cheap and would suit another company particularly well. In this case it will make the proposal and
expect to get the business, even if the company it is selling
the idea to already has its own bank. It may occasionally
have to share the business with the other bank, but that is
part of the game. Nor are merchant banks necessarily pass-
ive when they see a company that is not one of their clients
being attacked. 'It might well be a defence situation which
we think we're particularly good at,' says Ian Fraser of
Lazards. 'In which case we will be round to their offices first
thing to see if we can get the business.'

The 'Star' System

But merchant banks are also prone to the effects of the 'star'
system. All banks who are active in the takeover and merger field have one or two directors who acquire a name for
their skills in defence or attack. They are quoted in the
financial press; the banking community talks about them
and in a very short time they become the flavour of the year.
The problem is that the flavour can linger indefinitely, so

111

that clients demand their services and no one else's. They have become the established gurus of the takeover trade. Clients who are offered alternatives think they are getting second best. Michael Hawkes, Chairman of Kleinworts, recalls that in the major battle between Thomas Tilling and BTR, Tilling asked for Lord Rockley, who was not available: 'We should probably have sent a helicopter for him, but we didn't. Tilling abandoned us and went over to Warburgs.'

Kleinwort and British Telecom

Hawkes regards the personality cult as a bore: 'We're trying to play it down. There are plenty of young people in Kleinworts who've got the ability to handle takeovers. It's just a question of educating people out of the star system.' However, it has not materially affected Kleinworts' capacity for getting first-class business. In 1982, it pulled off a major coup when it was appointed as adviser to the government on the sale of 51 per cent of British Telecom, a share amounting to £4 billion and quite the biggest of the government's 'privatizations'. Warburgs acted for the company. 'We made comfortably the best presentation,' says Hawkes – a reference to the now mandatory fashion among brokers, bankers and advertising men for displaying their wares and skills to potential clients. While it is difficult to estimate Kleinworts' fee from the sale, it was probably close to £4 million and involved some of the most complex work ever in a major flotation. In February 1984, for example, Kleinworts together with Hoare Govett, the lead broker to the issue, visited no fewer than 120 City institutions on what was nothing less than a major campaign to persuade them to buy heavily into BT. Their job was to prepare the ground and ensure that a sufficient number of institutions would give the sale their backing.

Flotations

Kleinworts has generally been among the first six merchant bankers in the flotations league. Schroders took first place in 1982 and 1983 and Kleinworts, Morgan Grenfell, Lazards

and Warburgs were all in the first half dozen. The money
involved was not so spectacular as it was for takeovers and
mergers. Schroders' flotations came to £1.589 billion in
1983, a good £600,000 ahead of Kleinworts. Significantly,
Hambros made no showing in the first ten in either year.
The rankings for rights issues (new shares offered to existing shareholders on preferential terms) showed Morgan
Grenfell either first or second, with the emergence of Hill
Samuel and N. M. Rothschild as front runners. Rothschilds'
performance in the three areas of flotations, rights and
takeovers was distinctly patchy for a bank that has a 'mystical' reputation.

Outside corporate finance most merchant banks practise
the traditional range of activities: domestic banking – the
provision of advice, loans and overdrafts to corporate, local-
authority and other public-sector borrowers, often involving
a high degree of creativity in developing new financial
instruments to fund medium- and long-term debt; capital
markets – the playground of the Eurobond (now a huge
market) as well as the sterling 'Bulldog'; international work
– export and project finance, loans to the developing world,
finance for energy schemes; investment advice and management, both in Britain and overseas, for innumerable clients,
among them the pension funds, foreign governments and
private clients; and, of course, foreign exchange and the
management of Eurocurrency and sterling deposits. They
also underwrite share issues and loans.

Profits

The diversity of their business, and its complexity, suggests
that their profits should be correspondingly large. But they
do not begin to match those earned by the large British
industrial companies. Of the eight top banks, for instance,
profits range from the £6 million mark to £19 million (Hill
Samuel), with Barings' last reported profits as low as £1.25
million. Their 'inner reserves', however, which do not have
to be disclosed and never are, are assumed to be large.
Hambros, for example, had no trouble in finding £10.5

million from its reserves to write off a bad shipping loan. Profits are disclosed only after transfers to reserves have been made.

The disparity in profits between one merchant bank and another can probably be explained by the differences in style of the people who run them. Ian Fraser of Lazards, a relaxed and patrician Scot, says, 'We're a boutique, not a general store.' It is an indication that Lazards are prepared to go so far and no further in spreading their interests. Fraser has been careful to keep the bank out of the fashionable stampede by other bankers to merge themselves with stockbrokers and jobbers: 'It's a question of risk management. It isn't easy to manage one major risk. If you're managing six big risks simultaneously, you're quite likely to get into trouble.'

Fraser, who was the highest paid of the merchant bankers, until he retired, exercises the same caution when talking about the amount of money owing to the bank by foreign governments. In 1983, by which time the sovereign debt problem had assumed alarming proportions for the banking community, he told shareholders:

> The board takes the view that debts owing or guaranteed by foreign governments deserve the same treatment as commercial debts once these governments have demonstrated that they cannot keep up with the originally agreed schedule of service payments. Accordingly, it is our policy to make substantial specific provisions against the amounts which are owing to us in this category and the profits are thereby reduced.

Some Lazard Clients

On the takeover front, however, Lazards had a very active year. They appeared for BAT Industries against the German company, Allianz, which wanted to take over Eagle Star Insurance. It was a battle keenly watched by the City since it was nothing less than the biggest takeover seen in Europe at that time, worth £960 million. It was a major contest for

Lazards since Allianz had a head start, already owning 29 per cent of Eagle Star. BAT and Lazards eventually won. Lazards also represented the American millionaire, Alfred Taubman, when he fought for, and eventually got control of, the Sothebys auction house. During the same period Lazards launched three regional exempt unit trusts, which were formed to specialize in local unlisted investments – very much in line with the bank's increasing penetration into the field of venture capital for smaller and unlisted companies.

Sir John Nott, Mrs Thatcher's former Defence Secretary, is now Chairman of Lazards. He spent six years with Warburgs as General Manager before he went into full-time politics. He was one of fourteen managing directors and worked as a director of Lazards' international and corporate-finance divisions. Viscount Blakenham, the Chairman of S. Pearson & Son, the industrial and financial conglomerate that owns the *Financial Times*, is also a managing director – reflecting the fact that Pearsons virtually owns Lazards. The shareholdings of the directors are expressed in Pearson ordinary shares and one of the managing directors, M. W. Burrell, at the end of 1983 held rather more than a million, worth at that time about £5 million.

Rupert Hambro

Lazards has never bustled for the limelight. In contrast, the house of Hambro at 41 Bishopsgate fizzes with activity, people and ideas. The fulcrum of much of this energy is the new, young Chairman, Rupert Hambro, who exudes enthusiasm and charm in roughly equal proportions. He is an empire-builder by nature but immensely conscious of the bank's image:

> We had a survey done which showed that we were the best-known name after the Prudential and Legal & General. There was a 35 per cent recognition factor.

Taking over the High Street

The question is what do you do with such information? Rupert Hambro is sure he knows:

If you look at the future, there's the whole area of retirement. There's redundancy. There's a huge group of people
aged between 18 and 50. They all need motor insurance,
life assurance and a whole range of financial services. The
obvious place to sell all those is in the high street. We're
planning to set up 250 money shops on the Marks &
Spencer principle.

He then started talking about buying a building society.

Not All Gilt-edged Business

Hambros have done some curious business in their time. They
had an interest in honey: 'A whole consignment exploded.'
Kippers: 'A shipment went bad.' A hairdryer: they lost £50,000.
They now have an interest in cellular radio. Their most outstanding investment was the £1 million they put into Mark
Weinberg's Hambro Life in 1971. They sold that in 1984 for
£123 million – as much a tribute to Weinberg's extraordinary
entrepreneurial flair as to their own foresight. Their least
spectacular investment was a £70 million loss they accrued
over the years by lending to Hilmar Reksten, a Norwegian ship
owner, who was a friend of the family. Reksten was a personal
and financial embarrassment. The Norwegian was charged for
failing to declare the profit on a tanker sale. Hambros, by
implication, became tarnished by the Reksten image until a
commission eventually cleared them of condoning his activities. One suspects that Carl Joachim Hambro would not have
got himself into the same fix – at least not to the tune of £70
million. The whole unfortunate affair is something the bank
has taken very much to heart. It was one occasion when their
valuable Scandinavian connections let them down.

The business of the bank is masterminded from the Front
Room where the senior directors, including the Chairman, sit
at substantial antique desks listening to each other talking on
the phone. The idea is that everyone should know what the
others are doing. 'Everything is run from the Front Room,'
Hambro says.

Ideas start here, then get given to the executive directors
and so on down the line. On the other hand, anyone in the

bank can come to us with an idea, provided it's on one
side of a piece of paper.

Hambro enjoyed the fruits of nepotism from an early age.
He was a director by the time he was 26 and running a
division when he was 30. He's conscious of his luck:

> They gave me all the breaks when I was young, so I
> don't see why our young people shouldn't get them as
> well.

The bank's board is the most youthful in the City, with an
average age of 43. There are directors in their twenties,
some of whom are getting £45,000 a year, added to which
there are bonuses and stock options. But they are not big
payers; indeed they are well below the rest of the market.
Hambro got £83,000 in 1984, but if he is to attract the talent
the bank needs, he will probably have to pay senior people a
good deal more. He pulled off a major coup in 1984 when he
poached John Padovan, the Chairman of County Bank.
Padovan played a major role at County Bank, a subsidiary
of National Westminster, in building the corporate-client
list and Hambro wanted him for precisely that job. Hambros' client list is small for a bank of its size. Recently, it has
been concentrating on small companies and those on the
Unlisted Securities Market in an effort to get close to
rapidly growing firms who could emerge as major clients in
the future.

Savoir-Faire

Hambro makes no secret of his preference for people from
public school: 'They've got more *savoir-faire*, more self-
confidence and they panic less.' But curiously, for a man who
exudes self-confidence and ebullience and who has an
appetite for expansion, he has not yet followed his competitors into that major, if high-risk, area of growth – the
financial conglomerate, the merger of merchant banks with
stockbrokers and jobbers, which has been seen by the Bank
of England as the City's answer to the growing dominance of

Wall Street and Tokyo over the provision of financial services. The Hambro family, as it turned out, was never to go down the big-bang route. It was in mid-1985 when I talked to the expansionist Rupert. Almost a year later the Hambro dynasty split up, marking the end of an era for a household name.

No Tantrums

It was a split between two cousins, Charles and Jocelyn, Rupert's father. Jocelyn, together with Rupert and his two brothers, left the bank to set up a corporate finance business of their own in Threadneedle Street. Charles, on the other hand, remained as Chairman of the Hambros holding company. It was all very amicable, so they said, and there were no temper tantrums. But, of course, not even the Hambros could set up on their own without some capital behind them. This was done by opening up the Hambro Trust, through which the Hambro family owned the group. The trust had 13.5 per cent of the shares but almost 50 per cent of the voting rights. That gave them virtual immunity from a takeover.

Money for a New Business

The deal was that Hambros would buy all the issued equity capital of the trust. This would give the Jocelyn side of the Hambros about 3 per cent of Hambros stock after the changes, worth about £13 million, some or all of which they would sell to put towards their new venture. If it was the end of an era for the family – Carl Joachim would not have been pleased – it was the beginning of a new one for the group. The protection of the trust had been removed, to be replaced by a normal shareholding and voting structure. That made it easier for the group to go to market for new capital, but also much easier for predators to gobble it up.

An Uncertain Future

The difficulty it had, both before and after the deal, remained: proving that it could stand on its own two feet. There were plenty of sceptics about who doubted that the group really knew where it was going – probably reinforced by Rupert's dreams – and there was a real fear that the best of the group's management might well depart. The group never whole-heartedly embraced the retail customer apart from its purchase of Bairstow Eves, the estate agents. Its commercial banking operations were allowed to shrink and its corporate finance ambitions did not come to much. But the name was worth a lot – particularly to someone prepared to use it to sell every type of retail financial product.

Hambros was the only major merchant bank that did not embrace the big bang. The pacemaker here has been Mercury Securities, the holding company of S. G. Warburg. Warburgs are widely respected by their fellow merchant banks – and not simply because there are a lot of former Warburg men to be found at other banks. They are very good at what they do, largely because their style was formulated by one man, the founder Siegmund Warburg, and it has been rigidly maintained. 'Siegmund', said a merchant banker when the great man was alive, 'is the mixture of Jewish dynamism and German thoroughness – an unbeatable combination in modern merchant banking.' He was also a paradox – he thought a working knowledge of Latin and Greek was a better preparation for merchant banking than economics and management techniques. Reticence is part of the style. 'Siggy was intensely reluctant for his New Trading Company to be called S. G. Warburg,' says David Scholey, Mercury's Chairman, a large man who prefers invisibility to the headlines.

Warburg's German thoroughness lives through his successors. The bank believes in textual precision. Bad words are 'sloppy' (particularly written material) and 'complacent'. The buzz words are 'thorough' and 'creative'. The staff practise internal courtesy, which means they can be critical of one another without leaving blood all over the floor. The morning mail is summarized and circulated to all directors before they meet at 9.15. The bank has two sittings for lunch – one at 12.30, the other at 1.30 – and it's hard to get a drink. Scholey's office is cramped for a man who earns

£168,000 a year. The company's annual report and accounts are a drab, spartan affair. It is undoubtedly the most ascetic bank in the City. And although Warburgs abhor the personality cult, Thomas Tilling insisted that Scholey headed the defence team against BTR and Morgan Grenfell. It is not always possible to practise what you preach.

Mercury

While it is not the biggest of the merchant banks, Warburgs took the plunge into expansion with verve and nerve. Under their Mercury umbrella, they drew into the fold two stockbrokers – Mullens and Rowe & Pitman – and one of the biggest jobbers, Akroyds. It was a complex deal, involving £125 million in shares and various types of convertible paper, and it was certainly the largest. It will probably turn out to be the most significant as well. The new holding company contains major players in corporate finance, broking and market making, and it has a strong international flavour through Warburgs' Euromarket activity.

Some Marriages

No other merchant bank has formed such a strong conglomerate at the time of writing. During the same period of consolidation and acquisition Kleinworts got together with the brokers Grieveson Grant; Hill Samuel bought 29.9 per cent of brokers Wood Mackenzie; merchant bankers Samuel Montagu did the same with brokers W. Greenwell; Barings bought a majority holding in Henderson Crosthwaite (Far East); County Bank took a small share in Fielding Newson-Smith, the brokers; N. M. Rothschild bought 29.9 per cent of Smith Brothers, the jobbers, for £6.5 million. Morgan Grenfell took 29.9 per cent of the jobbers Pinchin Denny. And the list of mergers and acquisitions does not end there.

The brokers and jobbers have on the whole done quite well from mergers. Some partners became millionaires when they received shares in the new conglomerates. But it is doubtful whether the merchant bankers have profited equally. It is they who have done the courting and the paying and they decided to do it at a time when brokers' and jobbers' profits were at an historic high – thus putting a much larger valuation on these firms than might otherwise have been the case. However, they did not have much choice. Once the wagon started to roll – with the Bank of England's shoulder firmly behind it – they had no option but to jump on it. There was a danger they might be left out in the cold if they hung back, or might be left to buy firms without much clout in the marketplace. The new groupings were very largely acts of faith. The logic behind them was that the banks had the capital and the brokers and jobbers the retail distribution and market-making skills. Whether that will make them strong enough to fend off the big predators from Wall Street, like Goldman Sachs or Salomons, is quite another matter. But one thing is certain: the game is now being played in quite another ball park and there will be plenty of injuries and shouts of 'foul'.

THE MONEY MARKET

THE DOMESTIC MONEY MARKET

The Bank of England's Role

The Bank of England is rather like a spider sitting at the centre of a web of money. That may not sound elegant but the money market has no clear, settled geometry and it is always changing as its exponents devise new financial instruments. On the other hand, it has a powerful and watchful centre, the Bank, which can manipulate the strands at any time it wishes. The strands spread out through the banking system, composed of the discount houses and the commercial banks, to international trade, industry, commerce and the domestic consumer, providing them with liquidity. The Bank can tighten the strands by using its power in the money market to raise interest rates. This makes money more expensive and reduces the amount of credit in the system. Or it can loosen the strands by lowering rates, consequently expanding credit and giving the consumer – whether a company or an individual – easier access to money for investment in plant, machinery, or a house or car.

The Use of Interest Rates

This is broadly how monetary policy works. A government
bent on economic expansion will use low interest rates to
encourage investment, but in doing so it incurs the risk of
rising inflation and decreasing competitiveness. A government wanting to curb inflation, on the other hand, will use
higher interest rates to reduce the liquidity or credit in the
system, thereby incurring the opposite risk of lower investment and higher unemployment.

Bank Rate

Until fourteen years ago the Bank used the mechanism of
Bank Rate to increase or reduce interest rates. The Government Broker walked into the Stock Exchange, generally on
a Thursday (unless there was a crisis, when any day of the
working week would do), to announce any change in the
Rate. It was the rate at which the Bank lent to the banking
system. From it there stemmed a multiplicity of rates: the
rate at which the discount houses dealt with the banks; the
rate at which the banks dealt with each other (the interbank
rate); and the rates at which banks lent to their customers –
dependent also on the standing of the customer and the
length and type of loan. There was, of course, another tier of
rates – those charged by the building societies for mortgages
and those fixed by the finance houses for hire purchase and
personal loans. The latter bore no relation to the rates
charged in the banking system, were scandalously high and
depended largely on the *naïveté* of individuals whose concern about what they were paying was in inverse proportion
to their desperation for cars and fridges. This part of the
borrowing and lending market has not changed much nor,
regrettably, have the rates at which finance houses lend.

Bank Rate Effects

Changes in Bank Rate had two effects: the first on the level
of short-term interest rates in the money market; the second
on the movement of international capital. If Bank Rate was
higher in London than in other international centres then

126

investment capital from abroad would be attracted to the City – simply because it would earn more. If Bank Rate was lower, then there would be the opposite effect. But the Rate sometimes fell into conflict with itself. A low level of economic activity, for example, often required a low Bank Rate to stimulate business investment, but if Britain was running a deficit on its balance of payments at the same time – and consequently sterling was under pressure – a higher Bank Rate would be required. This conflict of interest between the desire to generate economic expansion on the one hand and defend the pound on the other often led governments to shore up sterling by the wasteful expedient of spending large amounts of reserves defending the pound until so much had been spent, or borrowed, that devaluation was the only answer.

Minimum Lending Rate

Bank Rate was also the rate at which the Bank of England lent to the discount houses as lender of last resort and it was supposed to be 'penal'. However, there were other rates outside those the Bank charged, which were often higher – those fixed by the clearing banks and finance houses, for example, for deposits and loans. Consequently, Bank Rate came to mean less and less and with its abolition in October 1972 there also disappeared an inhibiting psychological factor – that movements in Bank Rate were often interpreted, both domestically and abroad, as indications of shifts in economic policy, whereas they were often technical. It was replaced by Minimum Lending Rate, which was set by the Bank according to an automatic formula. But MLR, too, was suspended, in August 1981. The clearing banks' base rates are now a much more important guide to what is happening in the interest-rate market and they also indicate to potential borrowers the base from which they will have to work if they want to borrow money.

The Discount Market

The money market deals in short-term loans and securities, anything from a day to three years, and in the narrowest sense comprises those institutions – the discount houses, commercial and merchant banks – who deal in Treasury bills, bills of exchange, other financial instruments and money 'at call' (money deposited for a very short term, even a day). For convenience it can be called the discount market. The market handles between £8 billion and £12 billion each week, so it is not a minnow in financial terms. Over the course of a year an amount equivalent to the Gross National Product flows through the market more than fifteen times. Its size alone, therefore, shows it has an important function, but what exactly is it?

What the Market Does

In the first place, it provides a home for the short-term liquid funds of commercial and other banks who may need the money quickly to settle liabilities but want those funds to earn interest while they are lying idle. The institutions that want this liquidity are the London clearing banks, the accepting houses (merchant banks that 'accept' bills of exchange), the overseas and foreign banks and the Scottish banks. There are around 450 potential lenders to the discount market, of which some 300 are active. It's from them that the market gets its finance.

The Discount Houses

Between the banks, who provide the finance, and the Bank of England, which is the market's pinnacle, there stand the discount houses – a small, élitist group of companies, no more than nine in number, who form the London Discount Market Association. The members are the only people – apart from the Government Broker – who wear silk top hats when they go about their official business (no one seems to know why) and according to Michael Lisle-Williams in his doctoral thesis, *Continuities in the English Financial Elite,*

1850–1980, three-quarters of the directors of the discount houses are Etonians. That is not surprising. The houses have a long history and many of their founders must have sent their sons to Eton, as did their successors. The continuity carries through to their jobs. The discount brokers are a very small group of people, no more than 600, and they rarely change their firms or jobs. At one time most of them had their offices in Lombard Street, now only one has – Gerrard & National. The big houses have luncheon rooms that are better appointed than the stockbrokers'; their offices are much more comfortable, and their dealing rooms are considerably more civilized. On the other hand, they are paid a good deal less than successful stockbrokers who have never paid much attention to creature comforts – outside, that is, their dining rooms.

Laid Back

Their profiles are also much lower than those of many people in the City. By comparison with brokers, merchant bankers or the clearing bankers they belong to that part of the submerged City iceberg that outsiders never see. They do not court publicity like stockbrokers, who use economic analysis and research as part of their public relations, and they do not use advertising, like the commercial banks, to promote their image. The merchant banks are quite happy, when good news comes their way, to take some of the credit. But the discount houses have never been 'up front' in any sense.

This is understandable because they have never had products capable of catching the public imagination. There is nothing glamorous or eye-catching about the discount houses' origins, which were in the mundane but profitable business of discounting bills in the early nineteenth century. They were not public companies then, as they are now, but were humble brokers in pieces of commercial paper, which simply said that Person or Company A would, on a given date, pay Person or Company B a certain sum of money. Because the banking system did not have its present sophistication (that is, a branch system that could handle these transactions quickly and simply), there was often a substantial time lag before Person or Company B got paid. What the bill brokers shrewdly identified was that when Company B wanted to turn its bill into cash quickly (for example, to pay wages or other debts), they had a market on their hands. They simply plugged the gap by offering to buy the bill from Company B at its face value, less a percentage discount for paying the company straightaway. The broker later presented the bill at a bank and received the full amount, his profit being what he had charged Company B for transacting the bill immediately.

The Quality of 'Paper' and Customers

Superficially, it looked like easy money. But the bill broker had to be sure about the 'quality' of the paper he was dealing with, in the same way that shops or stores try to be sure that customers' cheques won't bounce. A bill broker, therefore, was not merely using his own capital to pay other companies for a premium, he was also underwriting one company's debt, which was payable to another company. The discount he charged was a mix of two items: his own profit and the chance that when the bill was presented for payment it might not get paid. So knowing the quality of the customers and the worth of their paper was an essential part of the business. That is still true today, but the Bank of England, as we shall see, is very fastidious about the quality of the bills it accepts.

Later on, the brokers began to buy bills for their own account with money borrowed from the banks and deposited the bills with the banks as security. In 1829, the Bank allowed leading bill brokers to discount approved bills at Threadneedle Street and this gave the discount market a helpful push. By the mid-nineteenth century London banks were lending money at call (short-term money that could be called back quickly from the market) to the leading brokers and this was secured on first-class bills that could be discounted at the Bank of England. In the period up to World

War I the discount market found itself short of domestic bills because the commercial banks had extended their branch systems and were able to offer local customers loans and overdrafts. Fortunately for the brokers there was a compensating factor. This was the growth in international trade financed by foreign bills of exchange, which were accepted by the City's merchant banks. The discount brokers bought these bills from the accepting houses and sold them (at a profit, of course) to the commercial banks, which generally held them as part of their liquid assets because they could be turned into cash very quickly.

Banks versus Discount Houses

When international trade came to a virtual stop during the war the market was left without a product to deal in. But wars, as we've seen earlier, always lead to an increase in government expenditure and this was partly financed by the issue of Treasury bills, which the houses discounted through the market. The post-war period, of course, led to a revival of international trade and a consequent up-turn in foreign bills of exchange. But it was an interval that lasted no more than twelve years. It was followed by the great Depression of the thirties during which economic activity went into steep decline. This was a period of considerable pressure for the discount houses. The demand for money had fallen off and the banks had large surpluses on which they were anxious to get some return, however small. They began to compete for Treasury bills at the weekly tender at the Bank, shaving the discount rate to a point where the discount houses' business became unprofitable. It might be thought that when the heat in the kitchen becomes too hot the cooks, the discount houses, would get out. But the City does not work like that. An accommodation was reached whereby the banks agreed not to tender for bills themselves but to buy from the market after the bills had run for at least seven days. This left the discount houses with a clear field, but their profit margins were still tiny. When margins are small, volume becomes all-important; the larger the volume, the higher the gross profit.

The difficulty was that the houses were in competition with each other for Treasury bills and this depressed margins as well. So a second accommodation was reached. They agreed not to compete against each other at the weekly tender, but to make syndicated bids for bills. This meant that they were all bidding at the same price. The amount of bills each house got at the tender was allocated according to each house's capital resources. The market also agreed that they would take up all the bills on offer, irrespective of the amount. Effectively that meant the Treasury was guaranteed a market for all its short-term borrowing.

Years without Profit

But the measures were only a palliative: discount rates and margins still remained low and when World War II came along the market did not get a boost with better rates. Since 1930, therefore, the discount houses had made virtually no profit. They were likely to continue like that if their sole source of revenue during the war years was confined to Treasury bills. They had, however, a useful alternative and one that received the support of the authorities. The houses had been buyers of government bonds in a small way since the 1920s and became much bigger buyers when Treasury bills ceased to make a profit. During World War II they increased substantially their holdings of low-coupon short-dated government stock and this helped the government to sell debt to pay for the war. It would not have been possible, however, if the clearing banks hadn't recognized government bonds as security for the loans they made to the discount houses.

Public Companies

For six years after the war the houses continued to be active dealers in government bonds as they were still the main source of revenue. (Treasury bills remained at a low ebb.) Government debt during this period rose by about £8 billion and the main source of its borrowing was the bond market.

To help the government's funding operations, the authorities encouraged the discount houses to raise new capital. Many of them became public companies and the resources of the market grew from £22 million to £34 million, giving the houses a substantially larger capital base.

But from 1951 to 1960 there was an awkward shift in the market. It was true that a flexible monetary policy meant the houses could at last make profits from dealing in Treasury bills, even though there was an element of risk involved. The dificulty arose because interest rates fluctuated over very short periods and the houses could find themselves borrowing at one rate from the banks, having discounted bills at another rate. If the rates the banks charged the houses for loans suddenly shifted upwards the houses found themselves with a discount rate perilously close to the rate at which they were borrowing. Their margins, in other words, were being eroded. Consequently, the houses dealt only at rates that gave them a buffer against sudden shifts in the borrowing rate. This stabilized when there was a return to an interest-rate policy by the authorities and the gap between the borrowing and discount rates actually widened. That was bound to prove attractive to institutions outside the discount market and they promptly started to compete for bills on offer. Outside holdings of Treasury bills rose by very nearly 1,000 per cent in the years to 1960.

How the Discount Market is Used

We have seen, then, that the discount market provides two important functions: it is a home for the banks' surplus funds, which in turn lubricate the market, and it provides the government with funding for its short-term debt, which of course is managed by the Bank of England. However, it has a third function: it is used by the Bank of England to influence interest rates. It is a rule of money that when there is plenty of it about interest rates fall; when it is scarce the rates rise. Being at the centre of the banking system, the Bank of England can create either a shortage or

a plentiful supply – depending, of course, on the requirements of monetary policy.

Discount Rates

At this stage, it is worth looking at the role of the Treasury
bill, which the government uses for short-term borrowing.
When discount houses buy these bills from the Bank they do
so at the prevailing rate in the market. If the rate is 13 per
cent they will buy £1 million of 91-day bills for £967,589.04.
That goes to the Treasury. The balance of £32,410.96 is
pocketed by the houses. They will either hang on to the bills
until maturity, getting the full £1 million back from the
Bank at the end of 91 days or they will sell them on to the
banks at a slightly higher rate of discount than they bought
them – as little, say, as a thirty-second of 1 per cent or a
sixty-fourth. It is not much, but it is still money. The banks
can hold on to them until maturity, selling them back to the
Bank of England at the end of 91 days or, if they are short of
cash, they can sell them back to the discount houses before
maturity. The latter puts the houses in the position of
having to hold the bills until they can be fully paid at the
end of 91 days or finding another market for them. So the
flow of bills is two way – from the Bank to the discount
houses to the banks and then back again to the Bank,
though not necessarily by the same route.

The Bank of England's Refusal

Therefore the key to the whole process is the Bank of England. It is in a dominant position to influence interest rates
as a whole. Let us say, for example, the Bank thinks interest
rates should rise because sterling is under pressure. The
Bank has an obligation to buy back Treasury bills from the
market once they have reached maturity. That is the theory.
But the Bank can refuse to buy them. The effect of the
Bank's refusal is to make the discount houses short of cash –
cash they need to repay the money they've borrowed from
the banking system to finance their money-market operations. This in turn forces the houses to borrow from the

Bank of England in its role as lender of last resort. And this is where the squeeze comes. The Bank will then lend to the houses at a 'penal' rate – a rate, that is, above base rate and pitched at a level where the Bank thinks base rate should be. The net effect of this pressure is to push up rates all round. The market response is so quick that it's a very short time indeed before the man in the street learns that his bank's base rate has risen and his cost of borrowing is going to be that much more expensive.

The Bank of England's Acceptance

Suppose, on the other hand, the Bank wants rates to fall. It no longer refuses to buy bills; it may well overbuy – thus creating easy conditions in the money market. So by using its power to turn the tap on and off at will it can control the direction of interest rates. By indulging in a buying spree the Bank is pumping money into the market, increasing its liquidity and therefore reducing the cost of credit. By refusing to buy, on the other hand, the Bank forces up rates – the market becomes short of liquidity, credit is not so easy to obtain and the cost of borrowing rises.

Both these examples assume that the Bank has chosen one of these options. More often that not, it does neither. When monetary conditions are stable – and there is no need for rates to rise or fall – the Bank's main concern is to smooth out monetary flows in the system so that there are no hiccups, no immediate shortages or surpluses of money, which could affect interest rates unnecessarily. Obviously there are periods in the government's financial calendar when the State is short of ready cash – for example, when there's a lag in tax revenues. These have to be met from the money market and the Bank's job is to see that these demands are met without any sudden distortions.

Other Bills and Bonds

Up till now we have assumed the Bank handles these arrangements entirely through the instrument of Treasury bills. But they are much less important now than they used to be. The Bank also deals in 'eligible' paper (bills it approves of, whose security is unquestionable), which includes corporation bills, eligible bank bills and occasionally local-authority bonds. They are all known as 'short-term' instruments, which is what one would expect of a short-term market. Treasury bills are more than a hundred years old and are issued in denominations ranging from £5,000 to £1 million. The £5,000 bill is red print on a grey background, the £1 million bill black print on a white background and is much more reminiscent of the old black-and-white fiver before it was replaced by a note that was tawdry by comparison. Anyone can buy them but they must do so through a bank. They are generally issued for 91 days but they represent immediate liquidity in the sense that they can be sold to the discount market and the cash realized immediately. In fact, they are not a bad investment. If we look at Treasury bill rates for mid-July in 1984 we see they were yielding the investor around 11 per cent, less commission. A sum of £5,000 invested in the money market at a fixed rate for three months would have yielded 10½ per cent.

The Corporation Bill

Another instrument, the corporation bill, is a local-authority bill and it is drawn on a local authority. Rates tend to be slightly higher than Treasury bills, but they normally run to 91 days like their government counterparts. They're accepted by the Bank of England and are essentially bearer bills – that is, payable to the person who presents them. They usually come in rather larger denominations than the Treasury's at the bottom end – for example, £25,000 and £50,000 – but smaller at the top end (around £100,000), although they sometimes rise to £1 million.

Eligible Bank Bills

Then there are eligible bank bills. One might think that anything that came from a bank is eligible, but the Bank of England does not think so. There are some 120 banks, ranging from Barclays and the Bank of America to Hambros and the Mitsubishi Bank of Japan, whose bills are rediscountable at the Bank of England. But as one discount house points out, even an eligible bank can produce an ineligible bill if the underlying clausing is not correct.

Even experts in this complex market tend to glaze over when they are asked to explain its technicalities. They have been at it so long that it has become second nature. But its functions are perfectly clear and so is the broad role of the participants. The Bank is at the top, holding the reins. Beneath the Bank there are its agents, the discount houses, who alone can borrow from the Bank in the last resort but borrow primarily from the commercial banks whose surplus funds are made available to the houses at market rates of interest. This money is 'at call' – in other words, the banks can get it back at any time if they need to meet their liabilities quickly. If that happens, then the discount houses can go to other banks for loans, or alternatively to the Bank itself. Like so many other things in the City it's a case of borrowing, lending and borrowing again.

Parallel and Secondary Markets

Just to add to the complexity, there are also what are called parallel or secondary markets to the discount market. These deal in other short-term financial instruments that cannot be discounted at the Bank of England but can be discounted between institutions such as the discount houses, commercial and merchant banks and so on. They include sterling certificates of deposit, Eurodollar certificates of deposit (CDs to the trade), foreign currency bills of exchange, variable-rate Treasury and corporation stock, local-authority bonds and stocks, short-dated gilts (up to five years) and even building-society certificates of deposit – a recent invention of the London discount market. At time goes on – and the financial markets show their customary ingenuity and innovation – other 'negotiable' instruments will appear, each of them endorsed for flexibility, liquidity or tax efficiency. Some, perhaps, may even carry a financial health warning.

FOREIGN EXCHANGE

No one who goes into their bank and asks for dollars or francs for their holidays can do so without the foreign-exchange market. It could well be that demand for those currencies at that particular time is so large that the bank doesn't have enough dollars or francs to take care of their customers' needs. They can quickly be satisfied, of course, by the simple expedient of buying them from elsewhere. It could well be that the bank has those currencies 'in stock', as it were, but at some point – perhaps even hours or minutes before – they were held by another bank or banks in totally different parts of the world.

The World's Largest Market

Currencies, except in those markets where they're controlled, like Russia, are extraordinarily mobile. They change hands or banks in seconds and they move in very large quantities. The foreign-exchange market is unique in two respects: first, it's the largest market in the world, with a daily volume of around $200 billion; the second is that there's no physical marketplace where currencies are exchanged – like the Stock Exchange for shares or the Baltic

Exchange for shipping contracts. A South Korean who wants dollars doesn't slip into his nearest foreign exchange; he instructs his local bank and the bank will make the arrangement for him. A corporation or a bank acts in exactly the same way. A bank, for instance, may need $100 million it hasn't got, in which case it will instruct its foreign-exchange department to buy that amount in the market in exchange, say, for sterling. The dollars could come from anywhere. Barclays might find itself buying from the Midland in London or Chase Manhattan in New York or a merchant bank. Of the $200 billion traded daily, probably 90 per cent is accounted for by the banks dealing with each other or with central banks, the interbank market. The remaining 10 per cent represents the needs of governments, companies with overseas trade interests and international investment money.

The market is the world and there are no opening or closing hours. Its common link is the telephone, backed up by visual display units, calculators and computers. The manpower is provided by foreign-exchange dealers whose work has little affinity with any other area of banking. Their working lives are totally committed to dealing across the world's exchanges. They live in nothing short of bedlam, a telephone at each ear, shouting rates, accepting prices, making markets. It's a young man's business and it needs a quick mind.

The Main Dealers

Not all of London's 450 banks are active in the foreign-exchange market. Perhaps fifty of them are market makers. They are prepared to quote a two-way price, a buying rate and a selling rate, and they are happy to do this even when they have no special interest in dealing – in other words, there may be no profit at all. As long as a customer wants a currency in which they specialize, and as long as the currency is dealt against the dollar, they will make a market in that currency. These main dealers are the British clearing banks, the major merchant banks and the London branches of overseas banks, such as Citicorp, Morgan Guaranty and the Deutsche Bank. The structure of the market is such that it's possible to find a bank at any time of the day or night that is willing to make a price in a currency. It's a 24-hour market simply because the world is conveniently divided into time zones: when London is trading at lunchtime, New York is just beginning; California takes over from New York and stops dealing just as Tokyo is starting to trade. Not that foreign-exchange dealers observe conventional office hours – several London banks kept their dealers up all night in June 1983 to buy and sell sterling as the General Election results started to come through. Banks are quite capable of dealing at all hours to protect their interests and those of their clients in very volatile markets. However, the volume of trading in the main financial centres is not shared equally. London and New York have the lion's share and anyone wanting to deal in large amounts would do so when both markets are open so that he could get a more competitive price.

The Benchmark Currency

The first rule of the 'Forex' market is that all currencies are quoted against the dollar. Only sterling is quoted as so many dollars to the pound; the other major currencies are quoted in reverse: so many Deutsche Marks to the dollar and so on. In fact, the DM against the dollar is the most widely traded currency – almost a third of total market turnover. It's for this reason that the DM is used as the benchmark for assessing the strength or weakness of the dollar. When a dealer talks about the dollar being strong, he generally means that the dollar is strong against the Mark. Sterling is the second most widely traded currency – around 23 per cent of turnover – and it's followed by the Canadian dollar, the Swiss franc and the Japanese yen; each has about 10 per cent of the market.

The Dangers of 'Taking a View'

When it comes to buying and selling currencies, the banks act very much in the same way as jobbers do in the stock market.

Each dealer keeps a book of the currency he is dealing in and he tries to 'square' his position at the end of the trading day – in other words, he has bought as much as he has sold and he is not 'long' (or has a surplus) of a particular currency. A dealer who goes home at night 'long' of $500,000 may go into the office in the morning to find that the market has turned against him and that he's made a nasty loss. Banks impose strict limits on the size of positions, but there are occasions when dealers will take a very big position (an abuse of privilege, as one dealer told me) in the hope of making substantial profits. That happened to the Fuji Bank of New York late in 1984. The Fuji's dealers took the view that the yen would rise against the dollar and bought billions of yen with the object of cashing in when they were proved right. They were proved hopelessly wrong. The yen went down and the bank was caught with a loss of £38 million. The chief dealer was sacked and others were forced to take pay cuts and lose their annual bonus.

Prudent dealers do not do that kind of thing. They will take positions, of course, but they are very short term – anything from five minutes to five hours. 'In this market,' says Geoffrey Munn, the Morgan Grenfell director who's in charge of the bank's foreign-exchange department,

> you don't go into the office saying to yourself that the dollar is going to rise and the Mark is going to fall and deal on that basis for the rest of the day. That's asking for trouble. If you're wrong, it will cost a lot of money. Flexibility must be the order of the day.

The Spot Market

Let us see how the market works in practice. The majority of currency deals are struck between banks, the interbank market, where one bank deals with another and probably many more during the course of a trading day. A typical deal in the 'spot' market (a currency for immediate delivery) would run along these lines: Barclays Bank calls the foreign-exchange room of the Midland and asks for a dollar–Mark quote. The Midland quotes 45–50. (Dealers always talk in shorthand. Expanded, the quote means 3.1145–3.1150 – the number of Marks to the dollar. The Midland is saying that it will buy (bid) dollars at 3.1145 and sell (offer) them at 3.1150.) The Barclays dealer might say '10 at 50', meaning he will buy $10 million from the Midland at 3.1150. In practice, that's all that needs to be done. The verbal order is enough to complete the deal and it is regarded as binding. A formal telex of confirmation will go out a little later.

The Barclays dealer has done his job. The Midland, however, has some way to go before it 'covers' its position. The Midland dealer is now 'short' of $10 million. Markets move very quickly, in a matter of minutes. He has two options. If he thinks the dollar will fall against the Mark in the next five or ten minutes, he might be prepared to leave his position uncovered. But he might not want to take that risk. So he goes straight back into the market and buys dollars. He will do that through another bank or through a broker – the broker acts as an intermediary between banks matching up buyers and sellers, but he is not allowed to deal on his own account or take positions in currencies. Unless the Midland dealer buys back his dollars at less than the 3.1150 he sold them for, he has lost on the deal. This is how profits and losses are made on foreign-exchange dealing. There are no commissions or dealing charges or concealed payments. If he buys back his dollars at 3.1147, he has made a profit. If he pays 3.1152, however, he has lost. When the sums are very large, the profits and losses are, of course, proportionately larger.

The Spread

In that particular deal we have seen a very small 'spread' on the buying and selling prices. These narrow spreads generally occur on sums between $2 million and $10 million. Smaller amounts will get wider spreads, while very large amounts will be priced by negotiation between buyer and seller. Banks tend to give each other narrow spreads and their customers wider spreads – although these days this type of business has become very competitive and the corporate customer wanting to deal in amounts over $500,000 will probably get prices no more than ten 'pips' wide. A pip is 0.0001.

The Squeeze

Let us suppose now that Ford UK wants to buy components from Germany worth £100 million and that the goods are payable in Marks for immediate delivery. This is, of course, a very big order. It is also where competition in the foreign-exchange market plays an important part. Ford will want to buy its Marks as cheaply as possible. It won't, therefore, ring up just one bank; it will probably contact half a dozen. The banks know immediately that there is a very large customer in the market for Marks. Each bank will almost certainly buy a hefty wodge of Marks straight away without knowing whether it has got the order or not. This has two effects: if Bank A gets the order, it has already got some Marks under its belt; if it doesn't get the order, it knows that the bank that lands the deal will be in the market for Marks and will be a buyer for the Marks it sold. Multiply that by five banks and you have a powerful squeeze on the bank that gets the order.

The Deal

Let us now examine the process by which a bank makes the deal for Ford, remembering that at the end of the day it wants to be 'square' on its position, neither short nor long of the currencies it is dealing in.

	BANK BUYS	BANK SELLS
1	**Sterling** from Ford	**Marks** to Ford
2	**Marks** from market	**Dollars** to market
3	**Dollars** from market	**Sterling** to market

Stage 1 is perfectly simple. The bank takes Ford's sterling in exchange for which it gives Ford spot (immediate) Marks. The bank is now short of Marks, so in stage 2 it has to buy

Marks from the market, in exchange for which it sells dollars. It is now short of dollars, so in stage 3 it buys dollars and sells sterling.

The deal has been done in dollar–Marks with sterling as the originating currency. The deal closes with the originating currency, Ford's £100 million. If we look at the BANK BUYS column, we can see that the currencies used exactly match the currencies used in the BANK SELLS column, although they appear in a different order. In other words, the bank has squared its position and has not left itself short or long in pounds, Marks or dollars. The bank has had to cover its one transaction with Ford (Marks–sterling) by two transactions in the market because the competitive quotations in the market are always for currencies against the US dollar. Settlement is two business days afer the deal is struck.

The Forward Market

So much for the spot market, which accounts for some 60 per cent of all foreign-exchange dealings. The balance is made up by the forward market where a customer may want a bank to buy a currency for it to be available in one, two or three months' time. Suppose that General Motors are purchasing components from Japan, worth $100 million, which have to be paid for in yen one month from now. GM tells the bank that it is a seller of dollars for yen one month forward. The two parties agree the price and the deal is done. The bank, in other words, has sold forward yen. To cover that trade it will firstly buy spot yen. But since it does not have to deliver the yen to GM for a month, it will go into the forward market.

One Month Yen–Dollar

This is where foreign exchange assumes the twists of a financial labyrinth. Banks will always quote a two-way price in forward currencies, but the figures will look very different. For example, we know by now that if a bank quotes spot yen against the dollar as 246.60–246.70 it is saying that it will buy dollars for yen at 246.60 and sell them at 246.70. In the forward market, though, it will quote on a totally different basis. For one-month yen–dollar it may say 55–50. This means that it will buy spot yen and sell one-month yen at a differential of 55 points (246.75 against 246.20) and at 50 points it will sell spot yen and buy one-month yen.

Let us pause for a moment because we want to know exactly what it is that the bank is saying. The differential of 55 points means that the bank will sell less one-month yen for a dollar – 246.20 as against the 246.75 it will buy spot yen for. The differential of 50 points means that the bank will sell spot yen for 246.70 and buy one-month yen at 246.20. In both cases, the one-month yen is more expensive than the spot yen, whether the spot is being bought or sold.

The reason for this is that the forward markets are based on the interest rates that the two currencies can earn. A figure of 55 points indicates that the differential between one-month yen on deposit and one-month dollars on deposit is $55 \times 12 \div 246$, which is 2.68 per cent per annum.

So how has the bank dealt? We can see its 'balance sheet':

SPOT	ONE MONTH
Bought **yen** from market	Sold **yen** to GM
Sold **dollars** to market	Bought **dollars** from GM

ONE-MONTH SWAP DEAL

Sold **yen** to market	Bought **yen** from market
Bought **dollars** from market	Sold **dollars** to market

The bank's position is now square. In fact, the same result could have been achieved by another process. After buying spot yen for US dollars, the bank could have replaced the swap deal by lending the yen for one month at 6⅜ per cent per annum and borrowing US dollars for one month at $9\frac{1}{16}$ per cent per annum, which is the 2.68 per cent differential we saw above. A bank will always try to find the cheapest way to cover its exposures, but in this particular example it preferred to deal in the forward swap market because it simplified the accounting. It can be seen that a swap is one settlement date against another for the same amount of the base currency, in this case US dollars.

The rates of spot 246.60–70 and one month forward 55–50 show that GM would be able to buy one-month yen against US dollars at 246.60 (the bank's selling price for spot yen) minus 55 points (the bank's selling price for one-month yen on the swap). One-month yen would therefore cost GM 246.05. The company will therefore pay more for one-month yen than it would for spot yen because it is retaining possession of the higher-yielding currency – US dollars – for one month. The difference in rates, however, has nothing to do with what the spot price is likely to be in one month's time – that is determined by the volatility of currencies and economic factors, not by a superhuman effort of forecasting.

Numeracy and Instant Decisions

Even in this cursory examination of a complex market, it is obvious that banks do not take young men and throw them in at the deep end straightaway. It is a business that needs a phlegmatic temperament, however hectic the pace of dealing. Geoffrey Munn says dealers have to be highly numerate and capable of taking and standing by an instant decision:

> If they stop to think about a situation, they won't make an instant decision and that is what foreign-exchange dealing is all about. They have to be flexible and have above-average common sense. It isn't a business for natural worriers, there's an awful lot to worry about without even looking.

At Morgan Grenfell, Munn eases his young men into dealing, starting them off with the smaller currencies until they've got a feel for the business. A year later, perhaps, they will graduate to 'Cable' (dealerese for the dollar–sterling spot, a throwback to the days when dealers would inquire the spot rate in New York via Western Union cable), or 'Swissies' (the Swiss franc) or 'Copey', the Danish kroner. By and large, it is not a business for Etonians.

EURODOLLARS
AND EURODOLLAR BONDS

Few financial instruments designed by the international financial community have enjoyed quite the success of Eurodollars and Eurodollar bonds. In the last twenty-five years these markets have expanded and flourished and the City, of course, has plunged its fingers deep into this pile of wandering currency and made it work profitably.

What They Are

Eurodollars are exactly the same as US dollars, with one crucial difference: they reside outside the United States in bank deposits and investments that cannot be controlled by the US authorities. Their natural domicile is Europe, where there are hosts of banks only too anxious to put them to work. Their arrival there was not by accident. The dollars that came into European hands had their origins, of course, in America: they had been used to pay for goods and services purchased from Europe. When America began to run balance-of-payments deficits during the sixties and seventies the flow of dollars into banks in Switzerland, London and Germany swelled into a torrent. But it was to assume enormous proportions as successive rises in the price of oil brought 'petrodollars' flooding into Europe from the immensely rich Middle East oil producers.

Political and Tax Advantages

The European holders of dollars could just as well have placed them in banks in the United States, but they chose not to. For one thing, European banks were not under the jurisdiction of the American government and monetary authorities; more important, perhaps, the imposition of an interest equalization tax by the American authorities, which ran from 1963 to 1974, meant that interest on deposits held in US banks was paid net of tax and not gross. They had no such problems with European banks. It is thought, but it cannot be proved, that the initiators of the Eurodollar market were the countries of the Soviet bloc who moved their dollar deposits from America to Europe because they were worried that their dollar balances in America could be frozen by the administration if the political situation merited that kind of economic warfare. Europe was safer and less sensitive politically.

The Swiss: Security and Anonymity

Typically, it was the Swiss banks that were the first to recognize the potential of the market. Switzerland, supremely, is the home of banking anonymity; accounts are known by numbers rather than their owners' names and the Swiss authorities sturdily resist attempts by the revenue departments of other countries to reveal the financial details of their customers. Substantial amounts of Eurodollars flowed into Switzerland in search of security and anonymity. The Swiss realized that here was an opportunity for a deposit market in Eurodollars on which interest could be paid. The habit quickly caught on. Now, all international banks in every financial centre handle Eurodollars, but because of its size London has become the focal point. The numbers are very large indeed. The gross size of the Eurodollar market between 1975 and 1982 soared from $377 billion to $1,620 billion.

And the bulk of this money was held on deposit in London banks.

Syndicated Loans

It must not be thought that that was where it stayed. The banking system exists to lend money at a profit. While it was paying interest on Eurodollar deposits to Arabs or whoever, it was lending out the same dollars to the banking system itself (the interbank market) and to countries overseas, in the form of syndicated dollar credits. Banks clubbed together into syndicates – the size of the loans was too large for a single bank to handle – which lent to governments, government agencies and government-sponsored corporations. These credits were medium term, anything from three to ten years, and were 'without strings' – in other words, the banks did not impose conditions on how these countries' economies were to be run. The profit came from charging fees to arrange the credits, together with interest rates, which were pitched above the rates they had to pay their deposit holders.

Defaults and Rescheduling

But there are snags to unfettered loans of this kind. Unlike the International Monetary Fund, which is in a position to make loans conditional on economic performance, the commercial banks have no such powers. The recent history of 'sovereign' lending (lending to countries, rather than specific corporations or agencies within those countries) has shown the agonizing reappraisals, the constant rescheduling of debt and the continuing fear of a major default that these loans have involved. Syndicated Eurodollar credits were no exception.

There is, however, another financial instrument which precludes many of these risks. It is the Eurodollar bond, which emerged in 1963 when the deterrent of the interest equalization tax in America made bond issues less appealing to investors. Until then, most bond issues had been raised in New York in domestic dollars. Foreign borrowers in the American market were disadvantaged; so were domestic borrowers. It did not take long for sharp-witted bankers to realize that they could all be accommodated by bonds raised in Eurodollars.

For the domestic borrowers – the big corporations, for example – it was a godsend. All they had to do was set up an offshore company, a company away from the United States mainland, and dip into the deep Eurodollar pool. One of the major attractions of raising money through Eurodollar bonds is the speed of the operation. Once the deal has been agreed with the lead managers for the loan, such as Morgan Stanley or Credit Suisse First Boston (the biggest player in the field), the bonds can be on the market at the right price in well under a week.

A Market for Big Names

The big users have been governments – the Scandinavian countries, particularly, and Australia and New Zealand – and, of course, the big American corporations. The World Bank and the European Investment Bank are also heavy borrowers. On the other hand, British companies are not prominent in the bond market, largely because the pre-requisite for successful issues depends on corporations being internationally known. It does not matter that Entwhistles of Huddersfield make the best sprockets in the world. If they do not have an international name they can forget any aspirations they may have to using the Eurobond market. For ICI or GEC, on the other hand, there is no identity problem.

Coca Cola for Preference

In the early days of these bond issues, the mid-sixties, the Swiss took roughly 40 per cent and tucked them away in those numbered accounts which represent thousands of investors from all over the world, the faceless rich seeking tax advantages under the cloak of secrecy. But they have curious preferences. One London Eurobond dealer told me that one of his clients, an extremely rich woman who deals through a Swiss bank, wanted to buy a dollar bond. He offered her two: one an Austrian bond, guaranteed by the Austrian government; the other, a Coca Cola bond, which had a lower yield than the Austrian and which was even lower than the yield on a US Treasury bond. She chose the Coca Cola bond. He was puzzled:

> She told me that she'd seen Austria disappear once in her lifetime and it might happen again. There is this feeling among a lot of people that they want their money in America, in American dollars and in major American corporations, because that's going to last forever. It's obviously emotional as much as logical.

Eurodollar bonds are issued at a par value of 100 per cent. Let us say that an American corporation wants to raise $100 million for five years on a coupon of 11½ per cent. They will be redeemed at 100 per cent five years from the date of issue. Few issues are for longer than ten years and dealings tend to be very active. Rather like gilt-edged stock, they can rise above par or fall below. In 1984 alone interest payments and redemptions amounted to $30 billion, much of which will have found its way back into the Eurodollar market, where it will have been recycled into further bond issues and syndicated loans.

Who Can Buy

In theory, any investor can buy Eurodollar bonds. There is just one snag: although the minimum denomination of most bonds is $1,000, the minimum practical amount in which it is financially viable to deal is $50,000. It's a market, therefore, for the better off, particularly those whose tax arrangements are unconventional. Otherwise, it's the large institutions who tend to be big buyers, along with central banks. Commissions are the same as the Stock Exchange's for smaller amounts, but drop quite sharply when large numbers are involved. The main advantage of Eurodollar bonds, as one dealer sees it, is that they are issued in bearer form. This means that they are payable to the person who presents them at a bank. No questions are asked. The bank tears off the coupon and hands over the cash. It is this anonymity that appeals to so many investors, who, for whatever reason, prefer to keep their financial and tax affairs to themselves.

THE COMMERCIAL
PAPER MARKET

On 29 April 1986 the government gave permission for a significant new financial market in sterling 'commercial paper'. It was a response to pressure from both the UK financial community and from large companies who were keen to copy the highly successful commercial paper market pioneered in the US.

Short-term Borrowing

Its most important function was to extend the range of financing options available to UK companies who were traditionally reliant on banks, the stock market and other financial instruments for raising money for expansion and acquisition. Companies wanting large amounts of cash would be able to issue unsecured promissory notes in minimum denominations of £500,000 which would have maturities ranging from seven days to one year.

Matching Borrowers and Lenders

Effectively, the new market means that large borrowers and investors like the institutions, and indeed companies with short-term cash surpluses available, will trade short-term money directly with each other in the form of unsecured paper. Thus it directly connects those needing money with those who have it available, bypassing the banking system and the usual securities exchanges. It is a cheap and flexible form of funding, very popular on Wall Street where the market has doubled since 1980 to $300 billion.

Up to now, top-grade British companies have had to go through all kinds of contortions to obtain money more cheaply than it can be had in the UK. They have found it cheaper to go through the rigours of the US rating system and swap the proceeds of dollar borrowing into sterling. Those who use the new market – and it is expected to become very large – will cut out banking intermediaries altogether and thus reduce the volume of bank lending.

When the new market was launched the main query was about the cost of commercial paper relative to other sources of finance, particularly the Treasury Bill market where rates had been artificially low for some time and could still undercut commercial paper rates. But it was thought that the Bank of England would not have agreed to the new market if it had clashed with its monetary operations.

Limitations on Access

By no means all companies will be allowed access to the market. They will have to have ordinary or preferred stock listed on the London Stock Exchange, have net assets of at least £50 million and will have to show that there has been no material change in their circumstances since their previous financial statements. These requirements will restrict borrowers to large, well-known UK companies – about 300 in all – plus several dozen foreign ones. There will be no need to issue prospectuses, which eliminates a boring and expensive hurdle, but it will take time to see whether the market will demand credit ratings for companies, as it does in the US.

The establishment of the commercial paper market meant that there had to be an amendment to the 1979 Banking Act to exempt the paper from the definition of a deposit, the main legal obstacle to the new financing facility. Companies borrowing through the market would in effect be deposit takers, an activity permitted only to licensed banks.

Companies will issue their paper through dealers acting either as agents or underwriters. Those acting as underwriters will have to be UK-licensed banks to ensure a degree of market supervision until the new regulatory framework for the Big Bang is fully established. The new paper has a number of attractions: it will be exempt from stamp duty, which will give it an advantage over the domestic securities market but put it on a par with the still-exempt Euromarkets; the return on the paper can be paid in full, without any withholding tax; and the cost of setting up a commercial paper programme will be a permitted business expense.

THE COMMODITIES MARKETS

THE STOCK EXCHANGE

The Stock Exchange, as its name implies, is simply a market where the stocks or shares of companies can be bought and sold. However, it would not have come into being without the existence of trading and manufacturing firms. The same can be said of the City's other markets and exchanges: the Baltic Exchange for shipping, the Metal Exchange for metals, the Corn Exchange for cereals, the foreign-exchange market for currencies. As commercial companies proliferated, specialist markets were set up to make the handling of cargoes, shares, finance and commodities both simpler and more centralized so that anyone involved in these activities knew which markets and specialists to use.

They are all service industries. Stockbrokers who deal in shares are not manufacturers; they do not take part in the management of companies whose shares they sell, although sometimes they are non-executive directors. A metal broker does not own or produce the metal he is dealing in; he is simply the intermediary between producer and buyer. Banks do not own the money they lend; it belongs to their customers. In the end, all these markets are dependent on the primary creators of wealth, whether they are engaged in mining minerals, farming, or producing cars and chemicals.

Today's supermarkets sell baked beans, canned in tins that have their origins in mining. Supermarket shares are quoted on the Stock Exchange – and that would never have been possible without the farmers who produced the beans or the miners who mined the tin. The beans and the tin have their separate markets and they are specialist markets served by experts who buy and sell on behalf of clients who want these metals and commodities.

Most of that is self-evident. What is not so obvious is that in the early days of Britain's economic history, when trading really began, there was no need for a stock market or exchange. A stock exchange has two main purposes: to raise money for companies through the sale of shares to give them the cash to finance their operations. This is often called the primary or new-issue market. It also provides a market for investors so that they have an opportunity of making a profit or earning an income, sometimes both, from the shares they buy and sell.

Self-financing Enterprise

Yet the earliest trading companies had no need for a stock exchange. Money was easy to come by, largely because there was not a demand for it in any great quantity. There were enough merchants and people of means who were prepared to finance a promising venture. In 1553, for example, a group of merchants led by Sebastian Cabot, the cosmographer and mapmaker, set up the first trading company in British history. Cabot was the life governor of the Merchants Adventurers whose objectives were redolent of romance and optimism: 'The discoverie of regions, dominions, islands and places unknown'. They did exactly that, but no one could claim that their initial success was anything but haphazard. The company's immediate purpose was to discover a north-east passage to China and the Indies. But two of the ships were lost in the Arctic pack ice.

The third accidentally discovered Russia. Richard Chancellor, the captain, made his way to Moscow where he pulled off a remarkable coup by securing from Ivan the Terrible a monopoly of trade with Russia and any other territories that could be opened up by the adventurers. The Russia, or Muscovy, Company had been born.

The expedition was financed privately by merchants who thought there was a profit to be made. Originally they bought shares in the company at £25 apiece – enough to raise the £6,000 to build the ships and pay the crew. As the company grew and trade flourished a number of calls were made on the same shareholders for more capital; the original £25 shares were raised to £200 and the company was capitalized at £48,000.

The East India Company

A number of other companies were formed around this time, but they were not all engaged in overseas trade. A couple of mining concerns came into being, one producing zinc ore in Somerset, and they were followed by a rash of ventures in James I's reign aimed at colonizing everything from Bermuda to Nova Scotia. City entrepreneurs realized that the success of the Russia Company could be profitably emulated. Quite the best known of the trading organizations founded during this period was the East India Company. The East India trade, of course, was risky and ships had to be large and well armed. Consequently the company needed more capital than most.

It was the habit in the sixteenth and the early part of the seventeenth century for shareholders to commit themselves to take up a certain amount of stock when a company was formed and to provide more money when it was needed. In 1568 the Earl of Leicester found that he did not have enough cash to meet the extra calls made on him by the Mineral and Battery Works, so he sold part of his original holding to pay for them. Clearly, there must have been transactions in shares at this time but there was no formal market and there were no specialists who dealt in shares as a recognized form of livelihood.

Royal Charters and Monopolies

There were a number of reasons for this. Most companies
were formed by a Royal Charter of Incorporation and these
Charters gave them a monopoly of the business they were
in. As there were no competitors, it was logical to limit the
number of original shareholders. It was like joining a club.
When more capital was needed the existing shareholders
provided it. There was, of course, a narrow 'market' in some
shares created by people who were anxious to buy into
companies. But they paid a fee for the privilege in addition
to paying for their shares. And naturally the shares always
had to be available; that meant there were existing shareholders who were willing to sell at the right price.

Early Entrepreneurs and the Need for a
Stock Market

In addition to trading and mining companies, which were
pretty much the staple of industrial society, the latter half of
the seventeenth century saw a mild burst of innovation.
Nicholas Barbon, author of two works on money and trade,
not only rebuilt much of London after the Great Fire but a
year later started the first fire-insurance company, 'the
insurance office at the back-side of the Royal Exchange'. A
contemporary wrote that Barbon was likely to 'gett vastly
by it'. Whether he did or not, it is quite clear that Barbon did
not have any scruples about money. He instructed the
executors of his will not to pay any of his debts after his
death. The insurance company continued to do business for
twenty years and then disappeared.

While Barbon was insuring London against fire, someone
else dreamed up the idea of illuminating the capital. 'The
Proprietors of the Convex Lights' formed a company in 1684
to light the streets of London with a new reflector designed
by Samuel Hutchinson. Two companies were formed to
make paper and silk in competition with France. By the
time of the Revolution of 1688 there were probably fifteen
companies, apart from newcomers like Barbon, that were

162

active in business – among them the East India Company, the Africa Company, the Mines Royal and the Mineral and Battery Works, the Hudson's Bay Company and several water supply enterprises.

Flotations Boom

This period of placid stability vanished almost overnight. It is axiomatic that wars change not only people but economies, prices and commercial activity. The war with France shortly after the 1688 Revolution saw a huge rise in prices and government borrowing. But the years between 1690 and 1695 also fuelled a boom in commercial activity and speculation. Company flotations mushroomed. In just seven years the number of companies in Britain rose from 15 to 140 with a total capital of £4.5 million. Many of them had surprisingly modern overtones: enterprises for exploiting new diving equipment to raise sunken treasure; a drainage pump and 'sucking worm' engine – the precursor of the fire engine; a host of companies filling the gap created by the war with France and the lack of imports – manufacturers of wallpaper, fine linen, plate glass and tapestries; and, of course, firms associated with the war effort itself, which were producing ordnance, gunpowder and 'hollow sword blades'.

The Royal Exchange and Coffee Houses

It was not surprising that all this commercial and entrepreneurial activity led to a demand for capital and the services of stockbrokers. There was no stock exchange as such. The Royal Exchange and the City's numerous coffee houses like Garroways and Jonathan's gave brokers an informal venue to go about their business. There they met clients who inquired about prices of shares and who gave them instructions to buy or sell. There is very little difference between the practice of the 1690s and the present day, except that brokers were not yet specialists. There was no rigid demarcation between jobbing and broking. Today's jobber holds the shares in which he deals and uses his own capital, while the broker acts as middle man between jobber and client, taking commission in the process. He is an agent. But no such distinction existed in the latter half of the seventeenth century.

'Low Wretches'

Jobbing, however, was a pejorative term denoting sharp practice and it did not go down well with the literati. Samuel Johnson dismissed a stock-jobber as a 'low wretch who makes money by buying and selling shares in the funds'. Daniel Defoe, author of *Robinson Crusoe* and *Moll Flanders* and a noted polemicist, identified the type in his description of Sir Josiah Child, 'that original of Stock-Jobbing', who was an MP, Mayor of Portsmouth and victualler to the Navy – a post in which no one but a fool could have failed to line his pockets. Child was shrewd, ruthless and well capitalized, a man who knew the value of talk in the marketplace and manipulated rumour and greed to his own advantage.

A 'Capital Cheat'

This, according to Defoe, was how Child went about his business:

> It would be endless to give an account of the Subtilties of that Capital Ch..t (*sic*) when he had a Design to Bite the whole Exchange. As he was the leading Hand to the Market, so he kept it in his Power to set the Price to all the Dealers. Every man's Eye when he came to the Market was upon the Brokers who acted for Sir Josiah: Does Sir Josiah Sell or Buy? If Sir Josiah had a Mind to buy, the first thing he did was to commission his Brokers to look sour, shake their Heads, suggest bad news from India and at the Bottom it followed, I have commission from Sir Josiah to sell out whatever I can, and perhaps they would actually sell Ten, perhaps, Twenty Thousand Pound; immediately the Exchange (for they were not then come to the Alley) was full of sellers; no Body would buy a Shilling, till perhaps the Stock would fall Six, Seven, Eight, Ten per Cent, sometimes more. Then the Cunning Jobber had another Sett of Men employed on purpose to buy but with Privacy

and Caution, all the Stock they could lay their Hands
on 'till by selling Ten Thousand Pound at Four or Five
per Cent Cost he would buy a Hundred Thousand
Pound Stock at Ten or Twelve per Cent under the Price.

Clearly, the stock market of Child's day was not formalized, just as professions and trades overlapped and inter-
mingled without any clear demarcation. That is not to say
the market was disorganized – it was already quite accustomed to put options and time bargains and modern brokers
would be familiar with its techniques. But they would not
enthuse about their forebears' mode of operations. Defoe
refers to Child's men working in the Exchange – the Royal
Exchange, which had nothing to recommend it except as a
place where people could trade. The 'Alley' was Exchange
Alley (now known as Change Alley), a narrow passage
where brokers hustled for business. In fact, for rather more
than 100 years brokers and jobbers were footloose, homeless
(except for their offices) and had no settled marketplace in
which to do their deals.

The Bank of England and Government Debt

In the last few years of the seventeenth century England
was up to its neck in debt, a perpetual condition that got
worse rather than better – indeed the foundation of the
Bank of England in 1694 was a direct response to the
government's and the public's demand for more credit, and
the new bank guaranteed to raise £1.2 million immediately
as a loan to the state; in return it would receive a 'perpetual
fund of interest' of £100,000 a year. Although it was a
substantial loan, the government needed every penny. The
reign of the Stuarts had been profligate – arrears of interest
and capital had fallen further and further behind. The
funeral of James I's wife, Anne of Denmark, had to be
postponed because there was no money to pay for it. Thirty-
six years later Cromwell had incurred a debt of £700,000,
which rose rapidly to £2.25 million. By the time the Dutch
fleet sailed unopposed up the Medway in 1667, the British

fleet was unable to put to sea. Hopelessly short of cash, it had no provisions, munitions or stores and Samuel Pepys was bemoaning the fate of the 'poor seamen who lie starving ... for lack of money'.

Tallies and the Tontine

The government tried a variety of loans to fund its war programmes: some through 'tallies' – a tally was a hazel stick into which notches were cut to show the amount of the loan and then split, the Exchequer keeping one half, the wretched creditor the other; others through such ingenious devices as the 'tontine' – a method concocted by the Italian banker, Lorenzo Tonti, whereby the last surviving lender scooped the pool; and life annuities and lotteries.

Capitalizing on Monopolies

Brokers had little to do with the National Debt as such, but some – along with merchants who had a speculative turn of mind – gambled on tallies, buying them at a discount on the vague assumption that they would be redeemed in full at some time in the future. But their main business was trading in the shares of companies. Some of these companies, whose names were nationally known, were themselves to become involved in the funding of the National Debt, though not on their own initiative. Four years after the foundation of the Bank of England, the government came up with an unorthodox method of funding its debt. It reasoned that if it was granting monopoly privileges to companies (the Bank of England, for example, was a monopoly), then the privileges should be paid for. When the East India Company was formed in 1698 with a monopoly of the East India trade, shareholders immediately loaned £2 million to the government at 8 per cent. Four years after that, when the new company merged with the old one to form the United East India, it not only shouldered the £2 million debt but in 1708 lent a further £1.2 million to the state interest free.

The South Sea Bubble

The government stretched this principle even further in
1711 with a new Act to solve the problem of unpaid interest
on £9 million of debt; in fact it had made no provision to pay
any interest at all. A new company, the South Sea, was
formed and the whole of the £9 million debt was bundled
into it, leaving the government with just 6 per cent to pay
the South Sea – £568,000 a year. Among the monopolies
granted to the South Sea was one for the South American
slave trade.

Blunt's Scheme

The State's reasoning was extraordinarily simplistic. The
Bank of England, so it argued, had done well out of the new
funding arrangements; so had the United East India. Logi-
cally, the South Sea would profit as well. From its inception,
the notion was preposterous. The impetus came from John
Blunt, the Secretary of the Sword Blades Bank (effectively
the South Sea's financial backer), who was a speculator of
Homeric proportions. Blunt and his cronies proposed to convert the whole of the government's debt – then amounting to
£31 million – into South Sea stock, an act of privatization
that dwarfs anything attempted by Mrs Thatcher's Government. If the whole of it was successfully converted, it would
save the government enormous sums in interest payments.

This was the first attraction of Blunt's scheme, but it did
not stop there. Depending on the amount converted, the
South Sea guaranteed the Exchequer a cash sum of between
£4 million and £7.5 million – a sweetener to moisten the lips
of any Chancellor hag-ridden by debt. No matter that the
company had nothing like that amount of cash available.
What Blunt was banking on was a stock-market manipulation based on South Sea stock soaring through the roof – a
magnet to speculators and, as it happened, an enormously
popular stock with anyone of any account in the country,
including royalty.

A Useful Surplus

Initially, Blunt was careful not to announce the terms of the conversion, which meant that if South Sea immediately went to a premium, holders of public debt would not get £100 of South Sea for every £100 of debt they held, but rather less. This is what Blunt engineered, thus creating a surplus of South Sea stock, which he could use as bonuses or sell for cash. In other words, the higher the shares rose the bigger the surplus became – the reverse of stock-market practice.

Blunt pushed the shares up and up, using the cash to buy more shares and inflate the price still further. Loans were made to existing shareholders, who, of course, bought more, pushing up the price still further. As conversion followed conversion, South Sea rose from £130 to more than £1,000. But then the company began to run out of luck. The country was in the grip of speculative fever and companies were mushrooming, many of them worthless, some fraudulent. Banks were making large loans to investors, companies were making more cash calls on shareholders, and the result was a shortage of money – money that might otherwise have found its way into South Sea stock and inflated it still further.

Blunt Brings Ruin

Parliament – members of which were by now heavily involved in South Sea speculation – thought it had found the answer when it passed the Bubble Act of 1720, which effectively outlawed the company's competition by banning firms without a Royal Charter and penalizing those that had Charters but were trading in unrelated businesses – an insurance company, for example, dealing in property. The stock market took no notice of these prohibitions until Blunt, realizing that the Act was not preventing speculattion, decided to prosecute a number of firms that were breaking the law. The effect on the market was electric: it crashed as unnerved investors saw the prospect of endless litigation and a collapse in company values. And the South

Sea crashed with the rest of the market, despite desperate attempts by Blunt to keep the shares afloat. The Sword Blades put a stop to any more credit and cut off the cash flow on which Blunt depended.

The game, quite simply, was up. Stock-jobbers took much of the blame. The Chancellor of the Exchequer, John Aislabie, and the directors of the South Sea were made to forfeit their estates. But the South Sea crash, curiously, was not terminal in its effects. Arrangements were made to see that most shareholders were not so badly off (that would not have happened had so many important people not been involved) and most of the transactions were on paper anyway. But the really sound companies survived the crash – among them the two insurance companies, the London and the Royal Exchange, the Hudson's Bay and the East India.

Parliamentary Control over Brokers

Some years before the South Sea scandal Parliament decided to 'regulate' the stock market on the grounds that speculation was bad for industry and the economy. Brokers, of course, bore the brunt of the new Act since it laid down that no one could be a broker without first being 'admitted, licensed, approved and allowed by the Lord Mayor and the Court of Aldermen'. It limited the number of brokers to 100 and they were obliged to enter into a bond of £500 each in the event of misconduct. For unlicensed brokers who plied their trade in the market the penalties included the indignity of spending an hour in the pillory on each of three days.

This Act of 1697 brought out the brokers' infinite capacity for contentiousness. In one respect the legislation was not specific enough: it did not prevent unlicensed brokers from dealing in the shares of unincorporated companies. But in the other – the limitation of licensed brokers to 100 in number – it aroused envy, anger and resentment among those who were excluded from the 'club'. They raised a petition to Parliament, arguing that they could not make a living under the new legislation. The licensed brokers responded by saying that they could not make a decent living as it was. The petition was thrown out and the Act continued until 1711, when it effectively lapsed.

In fact, business was not good. There was active trading in established companies, but no new company flotations were coming forward in any number. On top of that, the few new flotations that came on to the market were largely self-financing: most wealthy businessmen could start up an iron-works or a textile company out of their own pockets. The Bubble Act had not helped either by outlawing companies without a Royal Charter. Fortunately, the collapse of the South Sea, which had shattered the government's illusions about hiving off its debt to the private sector, led to a huge increase in government borrowing – not merely through the Bank of England and the East India but by debt issues to the public, which was by far the biggest subscriber.

Contracting

Brokers were active not only in the issue of government debt, but in subsequent dealings, too – the 'after' market. But by the middle of the eighteenth century they had also undertaken a new role, contracting for government debt. The system was attractive to the government since it involved the contractors in taking up the whole of an issue, not just part of it, thus providing the State with a guaranteed sum. It was done by competitive tender and brokers were frequently involved.

'The Great Oracle'

The best known of these was the son of a Portuguese Jew, Sampson Gideon, who was not only the 'great oracle of Jonathan's Coffee House' but was virtually financial adviser to the government. Gideon raised substantial loans on its behalf, consolidated the National Debt and managed to reduce the interest payable on it. In the latter half of the century contracting took such a strong hold that it became the rule rather than the exception. It was nothing less than

170

'underwriting' government issues, a guarantee to take up everything on offer. But, naturally enough, contractors were loath to underwrite the whole of a risk. They took a part of it themselves and farmed out the rest to interested clients, who in turn became underwriters.

The First Merchant of Europe

A glance at a late eighteenth-century issue for £20 million shows that the contractor, Boyd, Benfield & Co., underwrote more than £5 million, but in reality bought just under £2 million – the rest going to private clients. The lists of subscribers to these issues were generally headed by the Governor, Deputy Governor and Directors of the Bank of England, together with people like Abraham Goldsmid who were not only contractors in their own right but bill brokers and moneylenders as well. However, it was not all easy going. Goldsmid committed suicide when a £14 million issue he had arranged to contract with Sir Francis Baring went badly wrong. Baring died in the middle of the deal, leaving behind him the reputation of 'the first merchant in Europe'. In the course of an extraordinarily prosperous life he had amassed £7 million. Barings was originally a merchant firm, but had turned to finance and competed for government issues with bankers like Robarts, Curtis & Co. In fact, bankers tended to dominate contracting and brokers took second place.

The First Stock Exchange

The expansion of the National Debt led to a change in brokers' habits. The Bank of England was playing an increasing part in the management of the Debt, keeping the registers of stock people bought and recording transfers of stock between one shareholder and another. Some transfers were still being made at South Sea House. Brokers dealt in both places – particularly in the Rotunda of the Bank, where they made themselves thoroughly at home preparing transfer tickets without using Bank staff.

The Bank had less to complain about when the first Stock Exchange was formed in 1773, an accident initially characterized by a row when the more substantial brokers, after arranging with Jonathan's Coffee House for the exclusive use of the place, ejected a broker who later appealed to the courts and won his case. Piqued, the brokers moved to premises in Threadneedle Street, where there was another wrangle, followed in 1802 by a decision to have a new building, a new exchange and, most important of all, an elected membership. The Exchange was opened in Capel Court, where the foundation stone not only recorded the names of the Exchange's proprietors but noted that 'the public-funded debt had accumulated in five successive reigns to £552,730,924'. The Exchange had no doubt about the importance of the occasion: 'The inviolate faith of the British nation, and the principles of the constitution, sanction and ensure the property embarked in this undertaking.'

Stock Exchange Monopoly

Others were far from convinced. The Exchange marked the arrival of exclusivity and in 1810 the objectors presented two petitions: the first to the Exchange itself, which predictably was thrown out; the second to the House of Commons, demanding an open, public stock exchange where anyone could buy and sell 'Stocks, Funds and Securities'. The Parliamentary petition, apparently presented by those who had been expelled from the Exchange for misconduct, was defeated at the report stage. The Stock Exchange lobby, which until recently had always been an effective force, had worked remarkably well. William Hammond, one of Capel Court's proprietors, wrote to an MP who had opposed the petition in fulsome appreciation of his 'distinguished ability and zeal', noting that the Exchange's managers had no desire to create a monopoly, but wished to keep their doors 'open to honourable men and closed for ever to notorious cheats'.

Hammond's tone was morally uplifting, but he was wrong on both counts: the Stock Exchange was well on the way to becoming a monopoly and cheats, notorious or otherwise, were not to be kept out of the City, whether in the Stock Exchange or any other market. Thirty years after Hammond wrote that letter, a young clerk called J. Beaumont Smith pulled off one of the most spectacular of nineteenth-century frauds: he forged Exchequer bills and pledged them as security for loans from Stock Exchange brokers. Beaumont Smith continued the fraud for five years until he was caught, having run up £270,000 worth of counterfeit bills. His sentence was extraordinarily savage by comparison with today's leniency towards fraudsters: transportation for life.

The Problem of Regulation

Even at the time of the fraud, the City retained jurisdiction over brokers, but it was becoming harder to enforce. There were still unlicensed brokers working inside and outside the Exchange, but prosecutions did not do much to deter them. However, the new Exchange, promoted by Hammond and his friends, was beginning to show signs of becoming a coherent body. In 1812, ten years after its foundation, it produced its first rule book – one of many, which were to become increasingly complex. It set considerable store by better behaviour, with provisions for suspending members who were disorderly – brokers enjoyed setting fire to colleagues' papers while they were reading; hurled books down from the gallery on to the floor of the Exchange; let off fireworks on Guy Fawkes Night; and often sold non-existent stocks, such as Chinese Turnpike bonds and Sky and Deep Sea Junction, to new and naive members.

Competition

They were, however, competitive. Anyone who was first to receive news from across the Channel about the Napoleonic Wars stood to make a fortune. A number of firms kept up pigeon lofts for regular news flights between London and Paris, although birds were often lost and messages fell into the wrong hands. In the early 1850s, submarine cables were

173

laid across the Channel and the first telegraph line was installed in the exchange shortly afterwards. By 1872, the Exchange had embarked on the trial use of the teleprinter, which had been introduced by the Exchange Telegraph Company. Extel, as it was later known, was allowed to collect information about prices and transmit it to surrounding offices. But this led to trouble. The subscribers were not only banks and merchant banks but outside brokers. Members particularly objected to the latter because they had not been admitted to the Exchange and were, of course, in direct competition with Capel Court. Eventually, Extel was forced 'to decline any further applications from outside brokers and dealers and open stock exchanges where dealings in stocks and shares are carried on'.

The new technology did not convince all brokers of its value (unlike today's Stock Exchange which is technologically very advanced). Members were equally cautious about the use of the telephone – one firm kept the instrument in the partners' lavatory in the firm conviction that clerks would waste time and money on private calls. In America, on the other hand, brokers lived on the phone. An American visitor was puzzled by his British counterparts' working methods:

> A broker often finds on his desk in the morning 300 or 400 letters and telegrams: the care and attention required to handle an enormous lot of orders given in this deliberate manner is something with which the New York stockbrokers are quite unfamiliar.

Single Capacity

With the total repeal of the Brokers Relief Act in 1886, the Committee of the Stock Exchange took over from the City the responsibility for supervising the stock market. In 1908, it took the bull by the horns and decided to split the dual role of brokers and jobbers. The new rules laid down that all members had to declare whether they were jobbers or brokers and they could switch roles only with the consent of the Committee. It meant that a broker could no longer make prices in securities on his own account and that his sole function was to act as the agent for clients who wanted to buy and sell shares.

The Jobber and the Broker

The jobber's role was equally explicit: he alone could 'make a book' in shares, paying for them out of his own capital, and dealing only with a broker. This division of functions became known as 'single capacity'. A few years later, another Stock Exchange rule introduced a scale of minimum commissions that brokers could charge their clients. It meant simply that a broker could not charge his client less commission than the minimum laid down by the Stock Exchange. It was, of course, a restrictive practice – one that was to be dismantled more than seventy years later.

Apart from the general principles of practice embodied in those rules, brokers were left pretty much to themselves to decide the style of their firms. Between the First and Second World Wars the style was that of a gentlemen's club. No one had to work hard to make a decent living. There was no aggressive selling to investors: brokers did not phone their clients, their clients phoned them. Women were excluded from the club, except as secretaries. And the public schools dominated the community.

Self-interest: Economic, Social and Political

It was largely an amateur's business. Buying and selling for clients did not require much effort – a quick trip round the jobbers' pitches, that was all. Investment advice to clients mainly took the form of 'tips', a gut feeling that certain shares were good. Brokers who knew senior company executives well enough to get their information from the horse's mouth passed it on to their clients, provided they were important enough. But there was no informed analysis of share sectors or the economy. There was no original research and, most important of all, there was no pressure

175

for it. Markets change or update themselves only when there is a demand for it.

So the Stock Exchange remained a club, a very good and comfortable one, in which any young man with the right background could be assured of a decent and not very demanding living. He was also working in a market that in every sense was more of a community than most and a highly protected one at that. It has always had good political contacts, some of them a little bizarre: Lord Balogh, the distinguished economist and former economic adviser to Harold Wilson and virtually the world at one time, once told me that he'd made £50,000 as a broker's economist in the City in the eight years preceeding World War II (that was out of investments, close to a fortune in those days).

It has a sprinkling of MPs, the most active of whom is Sir Peter Tapsell, a partner in James Capel and, of course, a Tory. The Conservatives have never had much reason to question the existence of the Exchange, basing their support on the fundamental tenets of capitalism, the machinery of investment and an ill-defined belief that it provides a gateway for the 'small man' to become a shareholder. The Socialists, on the other hand, have always regarded Old Broad Street as a casino, the playground of rich gamblers who get richer and an economic anachronism in a society that should be able to order these things on a better and fairer basis. But they have never proposed an alternative. Furthermore, Mrs Thatcher's corner-shop economics have managed to give a boost to the notion of a 'share-owning democracy' through a number of privatizations: notably British Telecom, to which the employees of that vast organization were enthusiastic subscribers for shares. But, in the end, the Stock Exchange has always survived suggestions that it is a prime subject for government regulation by flourishing its rule book, an immensely complex and ever-changing bible of practice and conduct, which has proved an effective deterrent to political meddling. Within that framework the Stock Exchange has enjoyed a remarkably successful monopoly: self-regulating, self-electing and self-governing, a community based unashamedly on self-interest.

Clubs

At the social level, the sense of community has always persisted. Today, for example, the Exchange has twenty-six clubs and societies. There is a point-to-point club, a sailing association. There are clubs and associations for chess, bowling, darts, snooker, rugby and male-voice choirs. There are benevolent and provident funds. There is a branch of the British Legion and a Christian Association. Athletics, walking, cross-country running and skiing are all catered for. The range of hobbies and interests makes most public schools look impoverished.

The Exchange

But these are not really important in the sum of things, though they might be pleasant to have. The centrepiece of the community is the Stock Exchange itself, the lofty grey Colditz in Old Broad Street, which was opened in 1973 after Capel Court proved to be too small and inconvenient. It is a graceless piece of architecture, designed on the face of it to repel invaders. Narrow windows, small rooms, semicircular corridors – they give the impression of an indifferent government ministry that has spent too much money rather badly.

Nevertheless, it is the core of this important institution. The dealing floor is here and it is occupied exclusively by jobbers' pitches, hexagonal in shape, at which brokers inquire about prices and place orders for their clients. When dealing begins at 9.30 in the morning, there is a ritual rush of brokers on to the floor, but unless it is a very busy day this soon tails off into an unmomentous, purposeful trickle. Dealing brokers, as opposed to brokers who are salesmen or analysts, generally work from a network of their own 'boxes' just off the trading floor and can talk direct to salesmen at their firms' head offices through a walkie-talkie system. This means that when a broker is given a price, and it is not

177

the price the client had in mind, then he can talk to the salesman who will check on the phone whether the client will accept it. This happens in the case of big clients – a pension fund or an insurance company, for example – but it would be wrong to imagine that a small private client who invests just a few thousand a year gets the same treatment. He does not rank high on the list of most of the big brokers' priorities. Those priorities, basically, are to deal as much as possible with the big spenders – because that is where the large commissions are – and to give them a fast service. For a broking firm nothing succeeds like excess: the more excessive the investment – say £20 million – the bigger the commission. On the other hand, the private client *is* important to those brokers who have very little institutional business, since they depend on him to provide their commission revenue.

Size and People

It is an industry that deals in big numbers. In 1984 the total turnover of the Stock Exchange in UK government and industrial equities, that is the value of stocks bought and sold, was getting on for £365 billion – almost £80 billion more than the previous year. It is not surprising, therefore, that the organization of the Exchange reflects the turnover it is dealing with. While the whole industry employs about 16,000 people, roughly half of those are employees of no more than 16 or 17 firms. As there are some 220 broking and jobbing firms, ranging from small and isolated units in Cork in Ireland to Aberdeen in Scotland (the 'country' element accounts for some 25 per cent of all employees), it is easy to see that much of the financial power of the Exchange is concentrated in relatively few hands. Nor is it likely to slow down. Liquidations and mergers, combined with periods of economic uncertainty, have meant that the larger firms not only get bigger but they also get more of the available business. Many of the smaller firms consequently find they have a tougher row to hoe.

Given their size, it is quite logical that the large firms

have absorbed some of the characteristics of our industrial companies. These days they are organized along corporate lines with research, administration and finance departments, each headed by their own specialists. Almost all have their offices only a few hundred yards from the Exchange itself. Offices vary in style and comfort but they mostly favour large, open-plan rooms where forty or so staff sit in front of visual display units and computer terminals. There are few concessions to formality. Many brokers are rowdy, argumentative and opinionated. Clients are seen in conference rooms and entertained in considerable style in private dining rooms where, generally, middle-class girls with cordon-bleu training dispense hospitality. Money never seems to be short, but the number of really well-dressed brokers has declined over the years – probably because these things are no longer regarded as important. One senior partner wears suits from Marks and Spencer. Most London brokers have middle-class southern accents and if they don't come from public schools they give the impression they have. It derives, no doubt, from the fact that they work in an environment that is predominantly public school in behaviour, manner and outlook.

Schools

Where people go to school has not changed much. Cazenoves' two Senior Partners, John Kemp-Welch and Anthony Forbes, went to Winchester and Eton. The Senior Partner of Phillips & Drew, Bryce Cottrell, was head boy at Charterhouse while Jim Titcomb, Chairman of de Zoete & Bevan, was at Brighton College. Keith Heathcote of James Capel went to Downside. Gordon Pepper, one of the City's most cerebral brokers, is a Reptonian. Both Peter Wilmot-Sitwell, the Senior Partner of Rowe & Pitman, and Nigel Althaus, the Government Broker and Senior Partner of Mullens, are Etonians. Andrew Rutherford of Grieveson Grant went to King's, Taunton. Remarkably, John Robertson of Wedd Durlacher, Kemp-Welch of

Cazenove, Brian Peppiatt of Akroyds and Val Powell of Pinchin Denny were all contemporaries at Winchester.

Nepotism is Out

On the face of it, that pattern would seem to confirm the notion that firms favour public schoolboys, prefer Oxford and Cambridge to other universities and that the sons of partners enjoy the fruits of nepotism. There is a nugget of truth in some of it, but there are many partners who have never been near a public school except when they take their boys there. Nepotism is frowned on: there are a lot of firms now that make it a rule that sons of partners are not allowed to work under the same roof. The truth is that social patterns and preferences in the Stock Exchange are both less obvious and a good deal more subtle than they were in pre-war days when the charge of exclusivity was hard to counter. Self-interest is also a motivating factor. Public schoolboys' social and economic expectations are higher than those of their contemporaries who went to State schools and they are more money-minded; Etonians are said to think of little else.

The 'Stockbroker Belt'

Public school or not, all of them are supposed to live in something called the 'stockbroker belt', a leafy area of paddocks, pools and tennis courts where champagne and gin are dispensed liberally and where money is of no account. Some brokers and jobbers do live like that, but their geographical distribution does not show that they all do it in a preferred area where there is a community of social interest and behaviour. Just over half the members of the Stock Exchange (there are about 4,500) favour London, Essex, Surrey and Kent in that order as areas to live in. A quarter of them live in London and some of those inhabit the more distant provinces of Chingford and Leytonstone, scarcely addresses to impress a social climber. Essex narrowly heads off Surrey in popularity after London. Even so, Romford, Rayleigh and Hainault are not places that carry much social cachet and are certainly not identifiable as a 'belt'. If anywhere conforms to that idea then it must be Surrey where a big batch of brokers live in the area embraced by Dorking, Woking, Guildford, Farnham and Haslemere. Many brokers, especially the senior ones who have to spend many of their evenings across the dinner table from important clients, keep a flat or house in London and another in the country. But ostentatious displays of wealth – even when there is a lot of money – are infrequent.

Red Blood Rather than Blue

For connoisseurs of the social structure of City markets the Stock Exchange is surprisingly short of titles. It has only two marquesses (Ailesbury and Tavistock); two earls (Norbury, and Strathmore and Kinghorne); eleven barons, fourteen baronets and four knights – including the present Chairman of the Exchange, Sir Nicholas Goodison. Apart from the knighthoods, all the titles are hereditary.

Almost half the titled are Etonians and ten went to Oxbridge. The Marquess of Tavistock, heir to the Duke of Bedford, had a less formal education than most – Le Rosey in Switzerland, followed by Harvard. The best connected is the Earl of Strathmore and Kinghorne, a member of the Scottish unit of the Stock Exchange, who is a Bowes Lyon and related to the Queen. He lives at Glamis Castle in Forfar. Lord Faringdon seems to have more houses than most – a place in Holland Park, Buscot Park in Oxfordshire and Barnsley Park in Gloucestershire. Sir Edward Goschen, Bt (Eton and Trinity, Oxford), is a former Deputy Chairman of the Stock Exchange and Sir Edward Howard, Bt (another Le Rosey boy and Worcester, Oxford), is a former Lord Mayor of London. He lives in Croydon.

Titles, however, do not give an automatic entrée to the best jobs. Only six are senior partners, but of small to medium-sized firms; the rest are mostly partners. Nor is there an abundance of academic distinction. Among those men who have the best qualifications is Sir Christopher Larcom, Bt, Finance Partner of one of the biggest brokers, Grieveson

Grant, who was a Cambridge wrangler. The present Chairman of the Stock Exchange, Sir Nicholas Goodison, was a scholar of King's, Cambridge, and took a doctorate in architecture and history of art in 1981. Sir Kenneth Berrill, Chairman of Vickers da Costa, is a former Fellow and First Bursar of King's College, Cambridge.

Personality and Professionalism

Graduates

Firms on the whole do not place much emphasis on the importance of university degress. Most of the big ones recruit a handful of graduates each year and many of those will find their way into analysis and research. Phillips & Drew, one of the top twelve brokers, tend to be more 'academic' than most and have a liking for people with Firsts and good Seconds, with a leaning towards mathematics. Perhaps that is the reason why other brokers think Phillips & Drew are boring – too bad, they happen to be pretty good at what they do. There is a presumption that Firsts can have personality problems, while Seconds do not. Personality is one of the key ingredients of Stock Exchange man. He must be extrovert and personable. He can be clever and abrasive, but preferably not with clients. He must also show that he has a very strong interest in profit.

Professionalism

Just why brokers need to be keenly aware of profit and the importance of selling is amply illustrated by the development of trading in the last fifteen years. Brokers who depended on tips and inside information to keep their clients happy are a vanished breed. 'Insider' trading, for one thing, has been made illegal and the penalties are supposed to be harsh. But, more important, the institutions have been instrumental in destroying the 'gentlemen's club' and introducing professionalism into a community that not so many years ago was scarcely aware of analysis and research. The big pension funds and insurance companies

182

had funds running into billions of pounds and they wanted more service from brokers than they were getting. But research and analysis are immensely expensive. These days the big broking firms are churning out tons of glossy material, which thud on to the desks of every important investor in the country. The thrust of that research is aimed at the institutions with their enormous buying power and patronage. Institutional investment managers are constantly monitoring brokers' research, comparing one firm with another. They complain about the sheer volume of the stuff and often about its quality, but they are addicted to it and place large orders very often with brokers whose research has impressed them most. For their part, brokers have become locked into a service costing them a fortune but which they cannot afford to give up in case the institutions decide to abandon them.

Continental Illinois

For analysts, the rise of professionalism has proved to be a bonanza. They are busy people, constantly visiting firms in the market sector they specialize in, talking to management and assessing companies' prospects. James Capel take it so seriously that they have an early-morning session before dealing starts when analysts give them their latest news, hot from the presses as it were, so that the firm's salesmen can jump to their phones and start talking to clients. Twelve years ago, analysts got a further boost from the Continental Illinois Bank of Chicago. The bank decided to publish an annual rating of analysts' performance sector by sector, basing its information on the opinions of the institutions. The ratings make good copy for financial journalists, but brokers find them less amusing. Publicly, they tend to discount the Continental Illinois by pointing out that poor ratings have not affected their profits or that the annual survey has no bearing on their acknowledged expertise in certain fields. Privately, though, they fret over their positions and often take steps to improve their research by poaching analysts from other firms. The Continental Illinois has done much to improve the analysts' lot: good ones will make £60,000 a year; many are partners in their firms, which means, in good years, they will make substantially more than that.

Discretionary Clients

While the rise of professionalism may have done much to keep brokers on their toes in their new, tightly competitive environment, it has done very little for the private investor to whom the broking community has always paid lip-service without giving the service to go with it. The man in the street with just a few thousand pounds to invest will not get the same interest or service as the Prudential or the British Coal pension fund. He will probably be better served by the smaller brokers who are not stuck on the institutional treadmill of their bigger and hungrier brothers. Most of the big brokers have invented a useful device for dealing with their private clients: it is the 'discretionary' principle, whereby the client assigns the responsibility for the management of his portfolio to his broker. This is wonderfully convenient for brokers because they save thousands of man hours by *not* talking to clients on the phone. There are also substantial savings in administrative costs. Alternatively, the broker might suggest that the client's money goes into one of the firm's unit trusts – not a particularly good idea since brokers' trusts have an indifferent track record (with the exception of Framlington, run by Laurence Prust).

Institutions and Brokers

If surveys are anything to go by, institutions do not rate brokers highly. In 1983, only one broker managed to score more than 50 per cent for all-round ability, while the rest of the brokers in the sample scored anything from 29 per cent all the way down to 13 per cent. Institutions can, of course, be perverse in their judgement of brokers; indeed many are erratic. Nevertheless, the consensus on performance is a formidable one. If brokers cannot keep the institutions,

184

their most important clients, reasonably happy, there is no reason to believe that it is any better for the private client who has his money invested in funds managed by his broker.

Monopoly

It may be argued that if brokers do not remotely have the judgement of Solomon then there is no real reason for their existence – that the clearing banks, the merchant banks, the institutions and unit and investment trusts could all deal for themselves without using the Stock Exchange as an intermediary. But that would be to misunderstand the nature of the market. Its history shows that quite early on it established itself as a monopoly. It reinforced that monopoly with a rule book, part of which explicitly states that no one can deal in the Stock Exchange who is not a member. Banks are not members any more than institutions are. In other words, it is a market restricted to brokers and jobbers. It is also a market responsible only to itself. Occasionally, it receives some guidance from the Bank of England when it wants to see that the wheels of the National Debt are smoothly oiled, but interference is minimal or non-existent. In addition to its monopoly privileges, it is an industry where the power is concentrated in very few hands.

Who's Who

The lion's share of all dealings on the Exchange is handled by no more than twenty brokers. Although there are around 200 broking firms it is an illusion to imagine that they all prosper equally. They do not and it is difficult to believe that some scrape a living at all. There is another reality: twelve top broking firms dominate the market with more than 50 per cent of all business, while the top twenty scoop up just over three-quarters of all the commission revenue from trading in British equities, gilts and foreign equities. That does not leave much cream on the cake for the remaining firms, many of whom operate with minuscule staffs and are dependent for their living on a core of private clients who do not demand any sophisticated research or analysis.

The Top Twelve Brokers

Brokers will argue about the composition of the top twelve but in 1983 these were the front runners: Hoare Govett (the market leaders since 1978), Grieveson Grant, James Capel, Phillips & Drew, Scrimgeour Kemp-Gee (partly the result of a merger), Greenwell, Wood Mackenzie, Rowe & Pitman, Cazenove, de Zoete & Bevan, Messel and Mullens. Capel was founded in the 1770s and is probably the oldest firm in the Exchange. Mullens, which came a little later, has traditionally enjoyed the office of Government Broker since it was established in 1786 – a job that encompasses the timing and amounts of government debts issued to the market. Two other firms which go back to the eighteenth century are de Zoete & Bevan, Dutch in origin, and Cazenove, which was founded by Phillip Cazenove who was of French Huguenot descent. Cazenoves and de Zoetes still work in both firms; in fact, six senior de Zoete sons were senior partners in an unbroken line.

It's People Who Matter

But history has little to do with size or pre-eminence in the marketplace. That has usually been determined by competition and never more so than now. But the competition is not dramatic; firms do not come from nowhere to become market leaders. It is largely a war of attrition. Hoare Govett, for example, have hung on to their market lead for the last six years. But it took Grieveson Grant five years to move from third to second place in the pecking order and James Capel the same time to shift from seventh to third – as it did for Wood Mackenzie to make equal third in the league table.

But these shifts in rankings do not tell the whole story. It is people who make the running, both the hard-nosed and the toffee-nosed who enjoy the entrepreneurial challenge of pushing their firms ahead and increasing their personal earnings as profits rise. Wood Mackenzie is a shining

186

example of a tiny firm that made it to the top in little more than fifteen years. When John Chiene, the talkative and able Senior Partner, joined the firm in 1962 it employed only nine people. At that time it was based in Scotland and it was hampered by the rigid demarcation of separate stock exchanges throughout the country. It was in 1973, when they were all merged into a united exchange, that Woods was able to open an office in London. Since then, and under Chiene's direction, the firm has become pre-eminent in oil research, business publications and portfolio valuation for institutions – activities that account for some 30 per cent of its revenue.

James Capel is another firm that has moved ahead rapidly. In 1975 it had no real form as a broker, happy to trade for anyone on a day-to-day basis, anxious to please but without any real sense of direction. But under Keith Heathcote, the former Senior Partner, its reputation and rating have moved it into a powerful position in the market. Institutions now see it as one of the most able brokers overall and it has held a prime position in the Continental Illinois ratings for several years.

Cazenove, the Patricians

But the most singular of the broking firms is undoubtedly Cazenove. It is just in the top twelve by a short head, not that it would worry if it were not. Its reputation for research is poor and its share of commissions from the gilts market – a vital component of profit – is very low. The firm is often called blue-blooded by journalists who don't know another way of describing it, but even sophisticated brokers from other firms who have never worked there find it an enigma. Most of its partners went to the better-known public schools and many of them have private money – hence, no doubt, the inference that it's blue-blooded. But it has only one lord in the partnership, Lord Faringdon, so it can hardly be described as a privileged bastion of the aristocracy.

187

Money is 'Irrelevant'

The truth is that the firm takes a patrician view of the world. A former partner recalls that when he was offered a partnership he asked how much he could expect to earn. The answer was that money was 'irrelevant'. That complements perfectly the Cazenove premises in Tokenhouse Yard where the reception staff look like family retainers – many are second and third generation in the firm – who behave with old-world civility. Visitors are sometimes taken to the part-ners' room – an indifferent spot, to say the least – by 'the lift', a ramshackle contraption no larger than a coffin, which is the source of much innocent amusement among the retainers and brokers. The firm does not bother to impress anyone; it is people who should be impressed by the firm, that is the clear but unstated message.

Choosing Partners

It is said that after the Second World War there was a meeting of Cazenove Partners that was so disastrous that there has never been a full Partners' meeting since. It may account for the way Cazenove chooses its Partners, unknown among other firms, which practise a kind of cor-porate democracy. John Kemp-Welch, the Senior Partner, decides alone who shall be invited to become a Partner. He is wary about the consultation process after that but he cannot remember a time when the Senior Partner did not make that kind of decision more or less by himself. Kemp-Welch is a Wykhamist who looks as if he should be in an Oxford senior common room. Anthony Forbes, also a Senior Partner but an Etonian, is an agreeable extrovert who says of the Partners that a majority come from public schools 'and a majority of that majority come from Eton and Win-chester'. It is a laborious way of describing the social struc-ture but at least the intonation is clear.

'House-training'

The firm also has a patriarchal flavour, a language of its own. 'We see it as part of our job to look after our private clients, whether they've got millions or pennies,' Kemp-Welch says. 'If your tailor retires with £4,000, that's something you can't get wrong. But we don't study the size of our private clients with any great keenness.' In a community where brokers talk percentages, know the price of everything and argue about who is top dog, the Cazenove approach has a refreshing appeal. Forbes says that 'New recruits have got to be house-trained, they should be ambassadors to ourselves.' That sums up the Cazenove view of itself – a wealthy, enlightened monarchy surrounded by vocal republics.

The Corporate Leader

The style, however, conceals the firm's success. It may not be the size of Hoare Govett or Grieveson Grant, but Cazenove is far and away the leading corporate broker in the City, with an enviable client list that includes Barclays Bank, Great Universal Stores, Standard Chartered Bank, Wellcome Foundation and Schroders. It is also the leading broker in new issues and has raised more capital on the market for companies than any other broker. In recent years it has acted as broker to some very large foreign share placings in London and from Tokenhouse Yard it has established offices in the United States, Tokyo, Hong Kong and Australia. In 1967 it became the first British member of an American stock exchange when it bought a seat on the Pacific Coast Stock Exchange.

Cazenove has never felt a need to explain itself. Competitors are perplexed and frequently annoyed by what seems to be the firm's easy superiority and its indifference towards the modern tools of stockbroking. But its connections with the merchant banks are impeccable and that is where much of the firm's corporate business comes from – merchant banks, after all, are generally the first port of call when a company is looking for a quotation on the Stock Exchange and they dispense important financial patronage. Nor does Cazenove compete with the banks in fund management, a growing trend among the big brokers and one that the banks resent. The result is that when prospectuses for new issues are published the name of Cazenove is often there as broker to the issue.

Profits and Salaries

The big firms are obsessively secretive about their profits. As one chief executive put it: 'It would take major industrial espionage to find out what firms' profits are.' With few exceptions, they are not obliged to publish their profits because of their partnership status. It is something they take advantage of. Yet most senior partners of large firms claim that they are more profitable than their competitors and consistently do so without being prepared to reveal their figures. In fact, profits among the big brokers vary enormously – from £15 million (before tax and before distribution to partners) at the top end down to £9 or £10 million.

The secrecy is puzzling. Partners do change firms and they take a good deal of valuable information with them. In many instances, the figure for profits cannot be excluded. In any case, sophisticated brokers must have a very good idea of what the competition is making, otherwise they would scarcely deserve to be where they are. Closer examination shows that the reason for secrecy is both simplistic and remarkably English. It is not really the revelation of profits that matters so much as the fact that it's quite easy to deduce partners' earnings from the profit figure. It is that which matters, the age-old discretion surrounding personal earnings. It does not seem to matter that the salaries of most top industrialists are widely known and are often the subject of comment. Richard Giordano, who runs the British Oxygen Company, earned £750,000 in 1984, dwarfing the salaries of the Chairmen of Shell or British Petroleum. Yet brokers and jobbers remain intensely shy about profits and take-home pay. They argue that solicitors' and accountants' earnings are not common knowledge so why should stockbrokers' be. Another reason, even more quaint, is that the Stock Exchange Council is composed of brokers who come from both large and small firms. It would not be right if a small broker on the Council knew that the man he was sitting next to was earning four or five times as much as he was; he would be inclined to defer to the big broker's opinions. That is palpable nonsense because small brokers have a very good idea of what their bigger brethren earn; it would be very curious if they didn't.

Partnerships

However, it is important to get brokers' earnings in perspective. Figures were bandied about by the press that in the boom years of 1982–3 a handful of brokers were earning a million pounds or more each. That would be true of America but it is very wide of the mark in Britain. In good years a senior partner will probably make £400,000, roughly 20 per cent more than a man in a similar position in a large accountancy or solicitors' practice. Some senior partners will probably make more, perhaps another £100,000 at the outside, depending on the size of their shareholdings in their firms. Share of profits is dependent entirely on what percentage of the equity a partner holds.

Partnerships, therefore, are the way to financial self-improvement. While a good broker might earn £60,000 a year as an ordinary and valued member of his firm, he can't expect to make as much as a partner does. The arrangements for taking a broker into partnership vary a good deal but most firms practise a tenuous form of corporate democracy. Ability, not age, is the most important criterion. A man's name will be put forward to the whole partnership, probably by the senior partner, and 'soundings' will be taken. Sometimes a name is put forward by the executive committee of the firm and then put to the whole partnership.

There is no set Stock Exchange practice. Wood Mackenzie's partners disappear to the country for a whole weekend in November – the last two years to Gleneagles – when they discuss everything under the sun about the firm, including the new partners. Senior partners, or chairmen as some

191

firms like to call them, are generally elected by consensus or formal vote and are by no means chosen on the basis that the next senior man to the retiring senior partner gets the job.

A Partner's Equity

Since a new partner will have to buy equity or shares in his firm he will have to put up some capital. The entry fee is normally around £25,000 but not all promising men have that sum readily available. A few firms help out with loans; others steer them in the direction of friendly banks; others, like Cazenove, consider the matter so private they can't discuss it. But it is probably the best career investment a man in his thirties or forties is likely to make, short of being a very lucky speculator. His earnings should be substantially larger than those of a merchant banker, assumed erroneously to be enormous, and he will have a good pension when he retires.

Patronage

But his livelihood, like that of all brokers, will always be coloured and dominated by the enormous patronage dispensed by the institutions. A large institution will probably deal with as many as thirty brokers – one told me that it used no fewer than a hundred. There does not seem to be much logic in such a scatter-gun technique; twelve or fifteen brokers would do just as well. It seems to be based on the notion that once in a while a small broker will come up with an idea that an institution finds attractive. One effect of the system is to spread commissions rather than bunch them. The latter, of course, would soon sort out the wheat from the chaff: small brokers would find the going very tough indeed. The bigger brokers also have commissions allocated to them by institutions, the percentage depending on the value of the firm to the institution. But a broker is unlikely to get more than 7½ per cent of all commissions allocated by an institution in any one year, however good the firm's performance might be.

192

Institutional Views of Brokers

The competitive picture becomes even more clouded when an institution does not deal with a particular leading broker at all, perhaps because they have never got round to having a relationship or because the institution does not like the people it has met from the firm. One merchant bank, when asked by a big broker why they didn't use them, could not find a satisfactory explanation. But when asked, if they had only five brokers to deal with and not thirty, whether the bank would then use them, the answer was yes. A recent survey showed that institutions are not nearly so incisive in their judgements as people suppose them to be when it comes to assessing brokers. One top broker, perceived as one of the best, was criticized for being undermanned by a fund manager of a merchant bank and overmanned by a fund manager of an insurance company. One institution found the firm's staff personable; another said it had personality problems. Criticized for being too complacent by one insurance company, it was found to be too aggressive by another company.

Jobbers

In this climate of value judgements, patronage, uncertainty and competition the jobbers at least have a clear run. The beauty of jobbing is that it is a simple, uncluttered sculpture – not the collage of diverse fragments that constitute the broking world. Jobbers, for one thing, deal only with brokers. They are not much concerned with research. They have nothing to do with portfolio management or any of the 'investment arts', which are the province of brokers and institutions. They merely make prices in government stock, corporate bonds, industrial and foreign equities and hope to make a profit when they deal with brokers.

Bid and Offer

They are, on the other hand, principals. They deal on their own account and for their own profit, using their capital in the process. They hold shares on their books and hope to make a 'turn', or profit, when they deal with a broker. Let's suppose that a client has instructed his broker to buy him a thousand GEC at not more than 660 pence. The broker goes into the 'House', the trade name for the Exchange, and goes to that part of the trading floor where jobbers deal in the industrial market. The broker will ask the jobber, 'What price GEC?' The jobber has no idea whether the broker is a buyer or seller, but he will give him two prices. The first is the buying price, the price the jobber is prepared to buy at. The second is the selling price, the price he's prepared to sell at. They are called 'bid' and 'offer'. So the jobber might say, 'Fifty-seven to sixty', indicating that he's willing to buy at 657 and sell at 660 pence. The offer price is exactly what the client was prepared to pay but the broker might not necessarily leave it there. He could well tackle one or two other jobbers to see if he can save his client some money by getting a lower price. On the other hand, he may well stay with the first jobber and endeavour to get a narrower price, that is a smaller difference between the buying and selling price. So he says, 'Can't you come closer?' or, 'Is there nothing inside?' The jobber ponders and then says, 'I'll make fifty-eight fifty-nine', indicating that he's willing to buy at 658 and sell at 659. The broker buys at 659, saving his client a penny a share.

Evening Up the 'Book'

That deal was for perhaps 1,000 shares. But a larger deal, say 10,000 shares, might pose problems for the jobber. Having sold 10,000 GEC he may have very few left on his book; he could well be 'short of them', which means he has sold more than he has got. In which case he will have to buy them from somewhere before settling day. In any case, he will continue to quote GEC at 658–659. He will probably make his buying price more attractive to brokers who want to sell and his selling price less so. So he will quote 659–661 in the hope that he'll get more stock on to his book and warn off the buyers. If he succeeds, he will have bought GEC stock at the same price he sold them to the broker and 'evened up' his book without profit or loss. On the other hand, if he had previously bought GEC at 658, and so had the stock on his book, he will have made a profit. Generally speaking, jobbers usually make good profits on a rising or 'bull' market and more often than not will lose on a falling or 'bear' market.

Jobbers quite often protect themselves in times of uncertainty by 'widening' their quotations – so that GEC could be quoted at 655–660, thus discouraging both buyers and sellers. The only protection against that is competition in the market where, supposedly, not all jobbers will be doing exactly the same thing at the same time.

There are now only seventeen jobbers in the Stock Exchange, five of which dominate the market: Akroyd & Smithers, Wedd Durlacher (the two largest), Pinchin Denny, Smith Brothers and Bisgood Bishop. Akroyd & Smithers is a public company, while Wedd Durlacher is still private. They are the two dominant firms and the figures they deal in are astronomical. They account for 80 per cent of all dealings in British government securities, or about £167 billion in a year like 1983.

Profits

It might be thought that their profits are correspondingly enormous, but the gross profit margins are minuscule – somewhere in the region of 0.11 per cent on equities and a meagre 0.018 per cent on gilts or government securities. Translated into profit, Akroyds made £23.9 million in 1982 but that was before tax. The net profit was £12.6 million.

Earnings

Partners in jobbing firms do not do as well as brokers but they do not starve either. In the 1983 boom market Smith Brothers, which is not remotely the size of Akroyds or Wedd Durlacher, was able to pay its Chairman £105,000, which was an increase of £70,000 on the previous year. Eight other Directors (partners and directors are synonymous in the

Stock Exchange) earned between £95,000 and £100,000. Akroyds' Joint Chairmen, Brian Peppiatt and Tim Jones, earned roughly the same, but their personal stakes in Akroyds were worth a good deal more than their salaries. Jones's shareholding in November 1983 was valued at £1.25 million and Peppiatt's at £530,000.

Liquidity

Jobbers are content to believe that they provide sufficient competition for the market to stay as it is. Nevertheless, the present system means that the investor is landed with a number of costs: the broker's commission, Stamp Duty, VAT and the jobber's turn, or profit. The answer to that is that jobbers are able to provide liquidity (shares for cash and vice versa) for investors of all shapes and sizes. Furthermore, the risk positions they carry to provide that liquidity run into several hundreds of millions of pounds at any one time. But it also means that they have to resort frequently to banks and moneybrokers (the six Stock Exchange firms authorized by the Bank of England to act as the Exchange's money-brokers) to provide them with shares they do not hold or cash they do not have. The frequency of these transactions suggests that jobbers are undercapitalized – an argument that John Robertson of Wedd Durlacher rejects. It was, however, one of the main reasons why Akroyds decided to become a public company.

The Gilt-edged Market

Jobbers and brokers would not be where they are today without gilts, or gilt-edged government stock, which account for so much of the Stock Exchange's turnover. The growth of the National Debt has been amply illustrated throughout the history of the Exchange and without govern-ment borrowing the industry would be a fraction of the size it is today. With the two world wars of this century and government spending on defence, social welfare, health and nationalized industries, the National Debt has shot up by leaps and bounds. By the end of 1983, the face value of all quoted government stocks had reached almost £110 billion. It is the constant preoccupation of governments who want to prevent it rising. When a government cannot finance its expenditure wholly out of taxation it resorts to issuing gilt-edged stock to make up the difference. Critics call this 'printing' money; governments call it necessary financing. That, of course, is not the whole story: gilts are also issued to finance the interest governments have to pay on previous and existing borrowings. It is a treadmill and a very long way from the days when there were Commissioners for the Reduction of the National Debt; now there are just the National Debt Commissioners, an admission that public debt, like the poor, is always with us.

'Shorts', 'Mediums' and 'Longs'

Gilts come in convenient packages and with guarantees that were not a feature of government borrowing in the seventeenth century. There are 'shorts', which have lives of up to five years; 'mediums', five to fifteen years; and 'longs', anything over that; and there are index-linked. There are also a handful of irredeemable stocks, which the government will probably never buy back, such as 3½ per cent War Loan.

'Lives' and 'Maturities'

'Lives' have nothing to do with the quality of the stock. They simply show how long stocks have to run after their date of issue until they are redeemed by the government. Each stock has a 'coupon', which is the interest the stock pays to an investor over a year. Nearly all stock has a nominal or par value of £100, which means that any gilt, in spite of price fluctuations during its life, is redeemed at that figure when it comes to maturity. Payment is guaranteed by the government on the due date. Gilts generally carry the names 'Treasury' or 'Exchequer' followed by the coupon. But there are one or two quirks, such as Electric or Gas, which denote the stock paid as compensation to private investors in these industries when they were

197

nationalized. However, they are all part of the government or National Debt.

Coupons

A glance at the share information pages of the *Financial Times* shows the gilts that have been issued and the variety of coupons they carry. Broadly speaking high-coupon stock – anything from 10 to 14 per cent – stands at a premium over its par value of £100, while low coupons are well under £100. However, they are all redeemed at £100 on maturity, whatever their price was before redemption date.

Some gilts are redeemable not in a given year but during a period of two, three or four years – such as Treasury 11½ per cent or Exchequer 12 per cent. They are designed to give the government more flexibility. It will redeem at the first date if it's advantageous – in other words it can raise money less expensively by doing so; otherwise it will usually redeem at the last date. Stocks standing above par, indicating that current interest rates are lower than the stock's coupon, will probably be redeemed at the first date – because there is no point in continuing to pay high interest when market rates are lower.

Methods of Issuing Gilts

On the whole, governments will issue stock with a coupon that they think they can get away with. There is no point in paying more for money when a percentage point or two lower will still get investors into the market to soak up the supply of a gilt issue. New stock is usually offered to investors through a prospectus and application form published in the national newspapers – in much the same way that companies offer shares to the public. In the last few years, however, methods of issue have changed a good deal – largely because the Bank of England, the issuing authority on behalf of the government, was accused of selling stock too cheaply.

Previously, new stock used to be offered at a fixed price and the investor paid for it in full on application. The price of the stock was pitched in line with comparable stocks but in volatile markets the issue price could well be out of line by the time the application lists closed, even though a period of less than a week was involved. There were several cases of heavy oversubscription when the public wanted more stock than was available, an indication that it was too cheap.

Tendering

The authorities decided to even out the disparity between supply and demand by introducing the method of tendering. The Bank still lays down a minimum price for the stock but investors can offer above that price if they think it's worth it. All that happens then is that the Bank uses a scale of preferences: the people who bid highest get a full allotment of what they asked for and so on down the range of tenders until there comes the moment when partial allotments only can be made. When an issue is undersubscribed then all the applicants receive what they applied for, paying only the minimum tender price. The tender system simply means that the virtuous are rewarded and those who try to cut corners on price are penalized.

The 'Tap'

When an issue of government stock is not fully subscribed the balance is taken up internally by government departments, awaiting the day when there's sufficient demand in the market to issue it on 'tap'. Jobbers wait until sufficient demand for the stock has developed and then approach the Government Broker for a further supply.

As so much importance attaches to the business of funding the government debt, it is not surprising that the government gives its own stock financial advantages that the ordinary equity market doesn't enjoy. There is no Stamp Duty on transfers of stock, for example, and profits are exempt from capital gains tax if gilts are held for more than a year. Vast sums of money can be invested and realized within twenty-four hours – unlike shares, which have to go through the rigmarole of being settled or paid for either fortnightly or in a 3-week period, depending on the length of the 'Account' and how the calendar is working.

Bulls and Bears

It is not, therefore, much of a market for the speculator because he has to pay cash on the nail. The true speculator tries to use the Account as a period of credit during which he hopes shares will either rise or fall, depending on whether he is a bull or a bear.

The Bull

A typical bull will tell his broker to buy shares for him either at the beginning of a new Account, or during it, in the hope they will go up during the Account period and before he has to pay for them on settling day. If he is lucky, he will be able to take his capital gain and his broker will send him a cheque. The bull has not spent a penny, but he must pay commission.

The Bear

The typical bear, on the other hand, will sell shares he has not got hoping that they will go down during the Account period and before he has to deliver them. If, for example, he sells shares at £5 and they go down by £1 during the Account he has made a profit and his broker sends him a cheque for the difference. But the bear will, of course, have bought in the shares at the lower price so that he can deliver them to the buyer. The bull will also take delivery of the shares he's bought so that they can be resold at the higher price.

'Contango'

In practice, neither bull nor bear ever sees a share certificate if their speculations go to plan. They will just receive contract notes from their brokers. The shares will pass on. But if things do not work out during the Account period the bull can always resort to what is called a 'contango'. He can 'carry over' his purchase, without paying for it, into the next Account period and the following settling day. But it will cost him money. A jobber will have to 'take in' his shares, or buy them, and charge him interest for the privilege at current market rates. The bull could well make a profit by doing so anyway because the shares have gone up meanwhile. The definition of contango is 'the rate of interest for carrying forward a transaction from one settlement day to the next'. It is just like having a very short-term overdraft. But in the end he will have to pay up if he doesn't make his expected profit.

The bear is a different creature in the contango game. He has sold shares that he has not got and if he wants to carry over his bargain he has to find someone who's got the shares and will lend them to him so that he can deliver to the buyer. This does not amount to a physical hunt for the buyer – it will be arranged by the broker through the jobber, who has the capacity to match bargains of this kind. In normal circumstances, the bear does not pay for being accommodated in this way; on the contrary, he receives a rate of interest that corresponds to the contango rate paid by the bull. This is because in an active market there will generally be both creatures at work, bulls and bears. The bull cannot pay for his shares, or he does not want to if he can avoid it, and so he's happy if someone can be found who has sold the same shares and does not want to deliver them.

'Backwardation'

If there are more bears than bulls, on the other hand, then it is quite possible that the bear will be called on to pay for the shares he's sold but has not paid for. It is then he who is in the business of paying interest – a backward contango, or 'backwardation', the percentage paid by a seller of stock for the privilege of postponing delivery till the next Account or to any other future day.

It is not nearly as complicated as it looks. The main thing about the system is that it is merely a method of credit that carries a penalty, whether the speculator is on the winning or losing side of the deal. In fact, contango business these days is infrequent among ordinary clients. A much commoner practice is 'cash and new', where speculative purchases are sold in the Account and repurchased for 'new time' – that is, for settlement in the next Account. Bulls should not be confused with 'stags', although both have the same object in mind. A stag is a speculator who applies for a new issue hoping that when dealings begin he'll be able to sell his allotment at a premium before he has to put up more cash than the small application money.

None of this applies to the gilts market where cash has to be paid within twenty-four hours. Gilts have become very technical – unlike industrial equities, which are measured by crude factors such as whether companies are making profits or losses, the likelihood of recovery in a depressed economy and whether there are takeovers in the offing. Gilts, however, are affected by trends in interest rates not just in Britain but worldwide and by how the economy and the money supply are behaving. They are a huge market and it is not surprising that big brokers pay so much attention to them. The turnover in British government funds in 1984 was £268 billion; in industrial equities it was only £73 billion. There is no moral to be drawn from the figures, just the stark fact that brokers who want to get on and get ahead must have good positions as dealers in gilts. In 1983, Greenwell's penetration of the gilts market was a good 6 per cent ahead of its nearest rival, Phillips & Drew, and 10 per cent ahead of Hoare Govett. Mullens, which has 10 per cent of all commissions derived from trading in gilts, lay equal fourth with Scrimgeour Kemp-Gee. Probably the biggest improvement since these ratings were examined in 1978 came from Wood Mackenzie, whose market penetration in gilts jumped from thirty-seventh to fourteenth place.

The Stock Exchange Council

While brokers jostle for bigger profits and better places in the league table, they are being watched and supervised by the

Stock Exchange Council – the supreme soviet of the exchange. The days of proprietors and managers have long gone; they have been merged into a single body, the Council, which has fifty-two members. Forty-six, including the Chairman, are elected from the ranks of brokers and jobbers: the Government Broker is an ex-officio member and there are five lay members. The Council takes all the important decisions: it makes and amends rules – some of the most detailed ever put between two covers; it decides on expulsions and hammerings, suspensions of share dealings and anything of importance that affects the conduct of the Exchange, its reputation and policy.

The Council operates mainly through a number of committees, which deal with matters like membership, discipline, firms' accounts and quotations. They are all backed up by a staff of permanent officials, 1,000 in all, who do the leg work. Member firms do not get these services for nothing. In 1983–4 they contributed just over £5 million towards upkeep, administration and technical services and the Exchange pulled in another £16 million from quotation charges – the charges made to companies seeking a listing or quotation – as well as from rents and other sources. The Exchange's land, buildings and plant are valued at almost £116 million. It is a pretty large going concern.

The Inspectorate

The Council's main job is regulation of the market and the conduct of firms and members. It is not enshrined in law, except where the Companies Act has a bearing on the Exchange's activities, but it is a product of its perceptions of how member firms should be financially prudent, both in the conduct of their own affairs and in their relations with clients. Fraud is something the Exchange fears: it rattles public confidence and leaves a bad smell. In October 1981 the Council set up an Inspectorate, under Bob Wilkinson, a former Chairman of the Accounts Committee. It was prompted by a number of irregularities among firms but the case that caused the most trouble was Halliday Simpson, a Manchester-based broker, a scandal with which Sir Trevor Dawson was closely identified. Dawson was the investment boss of the bankers Arbuthnot Latham and later committed suicide when the scandal came to a head.

How It Was Done

The fraud rested on the use of an 'open account'. When shares were bought, either by Sir Trevor for his firm or by other people acting with him, they were booked to this account. When the price of the shares rose they were put back through the market and booked to one of the funds administered by Arbuthnot Latham at a price higher than the one prevailing in the market. This meant that the open account had manufactured a profit. The profit was then transferred to Dawson's wife, friends of Dawson or companies of which he was a director.

This is not the kind of thing over which the Exchange shrugs its shoulders. Six members were expelled from the Exchange, two suspended from trading for six months, one for three months and another member was censured. The case went to the Fraud Squad, but the Director of Public Prosecutions decided to take the matter no further.

Inspections without Warning

Wilkinson's Inspectorate is concerned with looking not only at firms' accounts but at every aspect of the way in which they deal. He is empowered to call on a firm at any time without warning to look at its books. Some visits last as long as two weeks, others half a day. On his appointment, Wilkinson told the press that the Stock Exchange could no longer operate like a gentlemen's club:

> One partner in about the third firm we went to had the quote pinned on the firm's notice board. He told me, 'I assume you think we're not gentlemen.' I said, 'Quite obviously that's not the case. I'm simply saying that an industry the size this one has become can't operate on that basis.'

Compensation Fund

Nevertheless, the Inspectorate has the approval of member firms. And with good reason. While the Exchange has an open-ended compensation fund to deal with frauds and failures, however many millions they might run to, no member wants to put his hand into his pocket. He would prefer people like Wilkinson or the Accounts Committee to get to the problem while it can be stopped. Wilkinson believes that the common factor in fraud is greed:

> There's a misguided belief that because people are handling large sums of money that somehow or other they have the right to a percentage of the money going through their hands. In a number of cases I'm sure they didn't think they were doing anything wrong – by their own standards. The fact they're paid a salary doesn't *appear* to cross their minds.

The Problem of Detecting Fraud

The Inspectorate is, of course, a useful addition to the Exchange's system of self-regulation. But it is bound to have flaws. Purists – mostly politicians who don't understand markets – somehow imagine that there must be a way of detecting fraudsters, or people who are acting against the best interests of clients, during the act of commission. If the Exchange were very lucky it might just be able to do that, either by detecting irregular and unexplained price movements or by lighting on a broker's accounts and books at exactly the right moment. It might even hear something on the grapevine. But on the whole frauds don't work like that. And neither the Fraud Squad nor the Department of Trade has yet devised a system of prevention rather than cure. It is a certain bet they never will. The best that institutions can hope for are safeguards and penalties that make fraud harder to commit and more unappealing in consequence. Expulsion from the Stock Exchange, often followed by prosecution in the courts, is a harsh penalty. For some people a year or two in prison may not be harsh enough, but that is a matter for the law. But at least, and after all else fails, the Stock Exchange has a compensation fund for investors who have become victims of malpractice. That much cannot be said for many other markets in the City.

The Quotations Committee

The Quotations Committee is a powerful regulatory filter as well. It has two functions. The first is to ensure that companies that apply for a quotation in the market are the kind of organizations in which investors can have confidence. This is an extraordinarily rigorous, not to say expensive, process, which involves the companies, their merchant banks and brokers in a great deal of detailed work. But it does not, and never will, eliminate the element of risk. If that were the case, investment would not be an 'art' but a certainty. No one can account for changing economic circumstances, the effects of competition or bad business decisions. All that the Quotations Committee can do is satisfy itself that companies are in good health when they come to market and that their prospects look sound.

Occasionally it slips up. Early in 1984, the stamp firm Stanley Gibbons went for a placing of shares on the market. Simon & Coates, the brokers, issued a prospectus that on the face of it declared all the material facts. It did not declare, however, that some years earlier the Chairman, Clive Feigenbaum, had been expelled from the Philatelic Traders Society, the trade association of the stamp business. Nor did it explain that he had been engaged in promoting issues through his private company that even the Stanley Gibbons Catalogue called 'bogus' or 'phantom' stamps. If a Sunday newspaper had not called attention to these facts the placing would have gone ahead the next day. Alerted, the Committee stopped the placing.

Price Movements

The second function of the Committee is to monitor price movements. Sudden and dramatic movements in the prices of companies' shares arise for a variety of reasons. There may be a takeover bid in the offing, often signalled by heavy buying by the company about to make a bid. It may be due to an element of insider trading, when an individual or group of people may have privileged information not available to brokers and investors. Or it may be due simply to the fact that the market has taken a view of a company and its forthcoming financial results.

Monitoring Prices

Whatever it is, the Committee makes it its business to find out. Initially, it does so in a quite primitive way. A group of people in the Quotations Department sits watching TV monitors on which all share prices are displayed through the Exchange's price-information system, called Topic. Prices are updated every minute so that any major changes can be seen very quickly. If sudden changes cannot be related to movements, say, in the price of oil, or to something the Chancellor of the Exchequer has said, then the Department begins to investigate. Its first port of call will probably be the company's broker who should usually know what's happening. If the Quotations Committee is satisfied that all is not well it will go to the Council and recommend a suspension of the company's shares until the situation is clarified. No further dealings can take place until the suspension is lifted. Of course, a jobber who unaccountably loses money on his book through the price vagaries of a particular share may be just as likely to raise the matter with the Committee.

Incompetence

This, again, is part of self-regulation. There is no reason to suppose that it is not done properly or without professionalism. What the Committee cannot do – nor the Stock Exchange as a whole for that matter – is protect the investor against an incompetent broker. This is not a question of regulation but one of professionalism. Investors, especially when they have handed over the total responsibility of portfolio management to their brokers, are not protected if the custodians of their capital decimate it by taking all the wrong investment decisions. It is generally conceded that it is rather more difficult to chose bad shares consistently than it is to choose good ones. A portfolio that is composed entirely of 'blue chips' – high-quality shares like ICI and Shell – is a good deal safer than small, speculative companies. But disasters sometimes happen. The same might be said of doctors who make the wrong diagnosis but are never challenged. There are people, however, who care more about their money than their health. For them the outlook is bleak if they fall into the wrong hands. Doctors can often put people right who have been badly treated, but brokers cannot do so if an investor's capital has been flushed down the drain.

Amalgamation of Stock Exchanges ·

In the same year the Stock Exchange moved into its new building in Old Broad Street, 1973, there were a number of important changes in the structure of the industry. The first was the amalgamation of seven stock exchanges into one. These were London, Belfast, Irish, Northern, Midlands and Western, Provincial and Scottish. It is extraordinary to think that only ten years earlier, in 1963, there were no fewer than twenty-four stock exchanges in the United Kingdom and Ireland.

The Jenkins Committee

There were a number of pressures for the amalgamation. The main thrust came from the Jenkins Committee on Company Law in 1962, which noted that only six stock exchanges

> have established funds which are available to meet defalcations by their members. So far as we are aware the other recognized stock exchanges have no such compensation funds. We have received no evidence that the operations of these small stock exchanges have led to serious troubles or difficulties. But it seems to us improbable that they can perform, as adequately as the

large exchanges, the two important functions of discip-
lining their members and scrutinizing applications for
quotations.

The Committee concluded that the time had now come for
the rationalization of the existing exchanges with a view to
reducing their number and increasing their size. The Committee also said that as a condition of their recognition
suitable arrangements would have to be made 'for the compensation of investors who suffer loss as a result of default
by members'.

These were not particularly onerous conditions and
brokers themselves could see the financial advantages of
rationalization by amalgamating with each other in the
same region. The larger units also made it possible for staff
to specialize more and reduce the duplication of effort. Outside London there are now three trading floors – in Glasgow,
Liverpool and Birmingham – as well as one in Dublin.

Dublin

Dublin has no jobbers, unlike the other three, so it operates
a 'Callover' system, an anomaly that has persisted over the
years. The 'Callover' applies to Irish stocks only, including
Irish government securities, and as the name of each
security is read out by an Exchange official brokers deal
among each other until dealings in that particular stock or
share are exhausted. The next security is then called. There
are two 'Callovers' each day. So much for Irish stocks. But
when an Irish broker wants to deal in quoted shares on the
London Stock Exchange he deals directly with jobbers on
the floor in London from his own office or he may use a
dealing agent – another broking firm.

Women Cause a Fuss

It is quite probable that if the provincial stock exchanges
had not been merged with London into what is now called
the United Stock Exchange, women would still be denied
membership. Membership is acquired by examination, not

terribly testing, after a qualifying period of three years' working for a firm. The 'country' units already admitted women but London held out. The debate – most of it absurd, chauvinistic and entertaining – began after a *Times* leader in June 1971, which attacked both the Baltic Exchange and the Stock Exchange for not admitting women to membership. 'These are not private men's clubs going about their own private activities,' *The Times* said.

> They are business institutions which exist to perform a public service and they are institutions which have an efective monopoly in their respective fields. There is therefore a public interest in this question in two quite separate respects. The first is that the exclusion of women from membership of these bodies imposes a barrier against the development of their personal careers in these professions.

The paper concluded that it was an indefensible restrictive practice and if they didn't amend their rules they should be reported to the Monopolies Commission:

> This ridiculous situation has been allowed to continue for far too long already.

'Overstatement'

Two days later that leader prompted a vigorous but extraordinary riposte from Graham Greenwell, an engaging but crusty partner of the broking firm, W. Greenwell:

> I suppose *The Times* still has a nuisance value of some sort, but in the pursuit of grounds for disruptive attacks on other and perhaps more important institutions such as the Stock Exchange and the Baltic, it might be wise to avoid the sort of overstatement in your leading article 'Irritating and Out of Date'.
>
> There is nothing anomalous in the rules governing the entry of women members; they embody the present wishes and past experience of members, and no pompous diktat from the press is likely to change them.
>
> In essence, both the Stock Exchange and the Baltic

are private men's clubs, and not business institutions, and wish to remain so, and are more confirmed in their views by the growing awareness that the philosophy of private enterprise is beginning to erode the socialist doctrine of the last fifty years.

The Stock Exchange is not an institution which exists to perform a public service, nor does it have an effective monopoly; both statements are red herrings, created by you, Sir, to deceive the ignorant.

No public interest is involved, any more than in preventing women from enlisting in the Guards to play in the band. Women could, I imagine, bang drums and blow pipes as well as many men, and I believe do so in some backward countries during presidential elections.

You denounce these rules or customs as a form of discrimination, and what of it. I don't expect the National Union of Boilermakers or Journalists to admit stockbrokers, though both these bodies would probably benefit by a breath of fresh air from the Stock Exchange.

The final paragraph of your leading article, suggesting that Mr John Davies (then Secretary of State for Trade) should order an amendment to the Rules of the Stock Exchange, or else, seems to betray the type of mind behind your outburst: to be specific the mind of a doctrinaire don, possibly of the female sex, from which our country has been suffering too long.

This was not a parody of a gouty reactionary written by a satirist. Greenwell meant every word of it and it was to damage his few remaining years in the Stock Exchange irreparably. As one correspondent pointed out, Greenwell had been elected a member of the Exchange almost fifty years earlier – in other words, he was living in the past. It also provoked a reply from Greenwell's son, Philip, a member of the same firm, who said it was an example of resistance to change 'only too prevalent in this country today' and he added that if the Stock Exchange was a private men's club he had yet to find either the dining room or the card room.

A Public Service

The gravest charge against Greenwell was his declaration that the Stock Exchange was not 'an institution which exists to perform a public service'. If it was not there for that purpose, then what on earth was it there for? Even Martin Wilkinson, the Stock Exchange Chairman at the time and no controversialist by nature, recognized the danger of Greenwell's heresy. He was alarmed by the reference to clubs but carefully avoided the main issue – the admission of women. 'It is totally untrue', he told *The Times*, 'for Mr Greenwell to allege that the Stock Exchange regards itself as a "private men's club". Furthermore, whether or not the Stock Exchange "exists" to perform a public service, it certainly does so.'

Ellen Winser

If Wilkinson thought that was the end of the matter, he was wrong. Although in favour of women members himself, he was in no position to railroad a membership that was hopelessly ambivalent about admission into accepting the proposition. Ellen Winser, now a partner of James Capel, was a graduate who had passed her Stock Exchange examinations but under the rules had no chance of being a member. She recalls she was very interested in the case of the woman who sued the Jockey Club for refusing her membership and won. 'If the Jockey Club was an organization of national importance, then the Stock Exchange was as well and would wish to be classed as such.'

Together with her husband, who is also a broker, she went to see Wilkinson to press her case: 'I thought I would put him on notice that I was quite prepared to see the matter through. As far as I could make out, I stood a good chance of winning.' Wilkinson asked her to give him a year: 'You're only 29, you can afford to give me a year.'

As it turned out, there was no litigation. The Stock Exchange Council was saved by the amalgamation of all the exchanges, which meant that London had to accept women if it was not to be accused of rank discrimination. It went through, as Wilkinson had predicted, within a year of Mrs Winser seeing him.

Women Members

There are now fifty-two women members, thirteen of whom are partners. Both Mrs Winser and Miss Haruko Fukuda are partners of James Capel. Wood Mackenzie has a woman partner, so has Sheppards & Chase, but they are comparatively rare in the big firms. James Capel, according to Mrs Winser, does not regard women as exceptions in a male world and she has never had trouble with sexual discrimination. But that, of course, depends as much on a firm's perception of women as it does on a woman's perception of her own role in the stockbroking community. Some women remark that men do practise discrimination. It generally takes the form of male archness, the raised eyebrow that suggests that they might be out of place or that they do well on the private client side precisely because they are women – as if there were some special allure that gives them an advantage. But that does not seem to be the case. Some women find that many male clients feel awkward talking to a woman broker; they find it much easier to strike up a quick working relationship with a man.

It is doubtful if women are likely to become senior partners of broking firms. Even those who are partners in the bigger firms still have a good way to rise in the hierarchy. They don't expect to undertake the task of running a large and sophisticated operation. These days senior partners find much of their time is taken in troubleshooting, thinking about the competition and finding niches in the market where their firms might get the upper hand. In any case, the pressure of competition among broking firms requires senior partners of a tough disposition who are able to handle their partnerships in a way that men would never give women credit for. However, there is little doubt that women members of the exchange are far better paid than their counterparts in industry and that on the whole they are, and have to be, a good deal more competitive, even

213

though their career horizons are prescribed by a male community.

The Unlisted Securities Market

In November 1980 the Stock Exchange celebrated an important event – the opening of the Unlisted Securities Market, a halfway house to the grander business of getting a full listing on the Stock Exchange. The snag with full listing for a private company is that it's expensive and laborious and requires a proven financial record going back at least five years. The idea of the USM was to give smaller companies with good prospects the chance of selling shares to the public without jumping through all the hoops held out by the Stock Exchange Quotations Committee. The USM requires only a 3-year trading history but, unusually, admission can be granted to companies with no trading record at all provided they have projects and products that have been fully researched and costed. Eleven companies have entered the USM in this way.

Requirements

That does not mean to say that a USM listing is easy going. A company normally has to show that its pretax profits for the last financial year were at least £200,000 and preferably more; and at least 10 per cent of its equity capital has to be in public hands already, whereas a full listing requires 25 per cent. Not least, it has to be able to bear the cost of a USM listing. This can vary enormously depending on the method of flotation. A recent survey showed that costs ranged from £3,000 to £1.1 million – a staggering variation that doesn't make much sense even if the costs of flotation are usually met from the proceeds of new shares issued. More than a quarter of companies found that total expenses significantly exceeded the sponsors' (merchant banks and brokers) original estimates and that sponsors sometimes gave estimates that did not include the fees of other professionals involved, such as lawyers and accountants.

Time and Preparation

What no one can put a figure on is the hidden cost to companies when they're involved in months of preparation. Most of them are not flush with management, and key directors, who are probably founders of the business anyway, find much of their time is consumed by preparing documentation. Rapidly expanding businesses often find that their trading progress is temporarily set back by meetings with sponsors, accountants and lawyers – a process that generally takes up to six months before a listing is granted.

Status

It might be thought that companies go to the USM entirely to raise capital for expansion. Yet 42 per cent of those companies which had obtained a listing between 1980 and 1983 thought the most important factor was that it enhanced the status of their businesses. It impresses customers and suppliers, whether at home or overseas, because their listing appears to make them more substantial. And it also provides USM companies with a firmer base for advertising the company and its products. Equally important, companies thought that a quotation would help improve their prospects of growth through the acquisition of other businesses: it puts a value on their companies, which can then be used in the complex trade-off of cash and shares that occurs in takeovers.

Sponsors

Sponsors, whether they are merchant banks or brokers or perhaps both, are obviously crucial to any company wanting a USM listing; certainly the Stock Exchange would not look at a company that did not have impressive backing from the market. Sponsors are a form of guarantee because their reputation and judgement are at stake. But the traffic isn't all one way: sponsors can expect to make money out of flotations. Although brokers keep their fees relatively low, they expect to benefit from subsequent share dealings (the 'after market') as well as from fees for future corporate activities.

A Tiny Number of Failures

Although 4 of the 300 companies that have come to the USM since 1980 have gone out of business, the new market has been a success. The USM probably has a total market value of more than £2.5 billion and it has created at least 180 paper millionaires – certainly one of them has shares worth £11 million. It's enabled many 'sunrise' or technology companies to find a place in the public eye and it's proved attractive to punters who find it a reasonable speculative risk.

Ratings

The ratings of share prices, however, have probably been too high. That is partly a reflection of a bull market, when investors tend to be overcome by euphoria, and partly because the weight of institutional money that has been invested in the market has pushed up prices anyway. It is quite likely that in bear conditions prices will overreact downwards and some fingers will be burned. No one can predict with any accuracy just how a USM company is likely to fare when the going gets tough. Most of them have short trading histories and many are in businesses that have seen a gap in the market that could easily be filled by new competitors. However, the USM has provided fresh capital for many companies whose prospects are good and given them that curious gloss of 'status', which they believe is so important.

No one would have thought eight years ago that the Stock Exchange was sufficiently innovative to produce a new market. It was settled and secure. It had invented its own technology to make trading and settlement easier and quicker. It was indispensable to funding the government debt. It provided a service of a kind to the private investor. No one could see the prospect of any fundamental changes.

Upheaval

They were wrong. The market is now going through the biggest structural upheaval that has ever been seen in the City. And it owes it entirely to one man – Sir Gordon Borrie, Director General of the Office of Fair Trading. The Big Bang, as it is now known, which takes place on 27 October 1986, has arisen because Borrie had concluded that the Exchange was riddled with restrictive practices. The shake-up that has been going on for the past two years has changed almost everything to do with the Stock Exchange: its affiliation, people, conduct and, above all, its market practices.

THE BALTIC EXCHANGE

St Mary Axe in the City is a narrow, rather indifferent street that does not have much to recommend it. Yet it is the home of the 'Baltic', the nerve centre of London's shipping community and the world's only international shipping exchange. A matter for some satisfaction, one would would have thought, yet it is possible to walk straight past the place without realizing it is there. Cross the street, however, take a pace back, and there is a very substantial edifice – brown marble columns, broad steps, glass doors. A large City club, perhaps, certainly not a major market. The lettering above the doors – BALTIC EXCHANGE – smacks of arcane practices somewhere off the Skaggerak and Kattegatt, but not much more. It is pretty much in tune with the general outlook of the exchange: 'You either know the Baltic or you are taken by a member – there's no need for the public to know where we are.'

In the days of the coffee houses, however, everyone knew where they were – they were at the Virginia and Baltick, a favourite haunt of shipping people who traded to the New World and Baltic countries. But only the Baltic has survived in name and given its title to the present Exchange.

Old-fashioned, perhaps, a little aloof, yes, but it is also a hefty contributor to Britain's invisible earnings from abroad (£250 million net in 1983).

'A Cross between the Commons' Lobby and a Cathedral'

The interior of the building has considerable pretension. It is substantial, with high domes, marbled pillars, stained-glass windows and an ecclesiastical aura, which was aptly summed up by a visitor: 'It looks and feels like a cross between the lobby of the House of Commons and a cathedral – dignified with uncanny echoes.'

Mutual Search

But the work of this market is a good deal less lofty. There are no side chapels around the edges of the 'Floor' (the main business area), just the tools of the trade: information boards with maps of world shipping lanes, the latest exchange rates, weather reports and confidential, up-to-date shipping information. There are also the daily papers, shipping registers and airline timetables. In the centre of the floor there is a pulpit-style podium equipped with a microphone from which a uniformed messenger acts as a traffic controller, putting members in touch with each other. This is a much more useful function than it sounds. When the Floor has filled up with the principals of the Baltic's 750 member companies – generally about 12.30 pm – they engage themselves in the business of 'mutual search' and the messenger can be extremely helpful. Shipbrokers, for example, are scouring the world's markets on behalf of the ship owners they represent, while charterers' agents are looking for the right ships to transport their principals' goods. The commodity could be wool from Sydney to Liverpool, eventually carried in a Hong Kong-based vessel flying a Panamanian flag (with all the tax dodges to go with it), or Canadian wheat bound for Tilbury docks in a Greek 'tween-decker.

219

The Baltic's Business

The Baltic deals mainly with the transport of bulk cargoes –
ores, coal, grain, bauxite and phosphate rock. But iron ore and
coal, once the backbone of the dry-cargo market, have lost much
of their importance because of the world economic recession.
Tanker chartering, which is concerned with oil and liquefied
petroleum products, is rarely conducted on the Baltic. It is done
from office desks, using telephones, telex and the latest electronic equipment to provide up-to-the minute market sum-
maries, lists of available tonnage and cargo inquiries. In
addition to the main dry-cargo market, there are also ship
brokers dealing in short-sea cargoes and vessels – transport,
perhaps, for a scrap-metal cargo from East Anglia to Italy with
homeward pumice stone from Lipari to Shoreham. Others
specialize in container shipping or heavy and awkward cargoes.
Whatever the speciality, anyone concerned with chartering has
to be aware of the latest state of the market and be in communi-
cation with other people involved in his line of business.

Market Intelligence

The Baltic, therefore, is not simply a marketplace where deals
are fixed. Whatever the role of a member is – a broker acting for
a ship owner, for example, or a charterer's agent acting for
merchants, or the ship owners and merchants themselves – he
cannot do business without being in possession of the latest
market information. So the Exchange is also an intelligence
centre that provides an intricate web of information not only
about which ships and cargoes are available at what price and
where, but also about the current political and economic situation in different parts of the world. 'We are directly concerned
here with world events, be they wars, famines, booms or slumps
... that's what affects the market,' says a former Chairman of
the Exchange.

Voyage and Time Chartering

It is factors such as these that any ship broker has to take into
account when he is looking for a profitable cargo. Nor are deals

concluded at the drop of a hat. He may have to go round twenty or thirty people, sometimes as many as fifty, before he can begin to negotiate. Today there are two main kinds of chartering: voyage chartering, when a ship is chartered for a particular voyage with a specific cargo; and time chartering, when a ship is chartered for a specific length of time for a variety of cargoes. Once a merchant or charterer's agent has got a 'feel' of the market, he will make a preliminary approach to a ship owner or broker who will give him a quote for the charter he wants. Quote in hand, he will look for other brokers or owners to see if he can get a more competitive rate.

But there is more to it than meets the eye. In the case of time chartering, for example, it is not just the basic chartering rate that is haggled over – there are the terms as well, perhaps fifty or eighty clauses, which have to be agreed. Nor does it end there. It has to be decided who is going to pay for the bunker costs, port dues, pilotage, tugs and so on. Usually the ship owner pays these bills during a voyage charter, but the charterer picks up the expenses for a time charter. It is up to the individual charterer to decide the kind of contract he wants. A merchant chartering half-a-dozen ships could well use a mix of voyage and time charters. He will do whatever is economically sensible at the time.

The Fixture

Once a deal has been agreed, it will be closed with the words, 'It's a fixture.' Although the written contract may not have been finally drawn up, at this stage there is no getting out of the deal, not even changing the terms. The penalty is instant expulsion from the Exchange – a sanction that has been used very rarely. But that does not eliminate disputes. The agreement, after all, has been drawn up by two people who represent other parties and it is the latter who could well create difficulties. 'I know our motto is "Our word is our bond",' says a member,

> but that's between two individuals. If the chap you're dealing with is working for a dud, then it's not going to do you much good. One of the advantages of the Baltic is that you try and pick somebody who doesn't pull out of a time

charter and leave you holding the baby. Mostly people doing that sort of thing avoid the Baltic. With personal contact you know who you can rely on.

The Charter Party

The formal, final contract between the principals is known as a charter party, derived from the Latin *carta partita*, meaning the division of the paper into two parts – one for the ship owner and one for the charterer. But the Exchange does a lot of business and inevitably disputes do arise over the legal interpretation of the charter party and so on. These are not the direct concern of the Baltic and the bulk of them are settled by the London Maritime Arbitrators' Association.

Matching Charters

These days the market is much more complex than it used to be. Until a few years ago, most bulk cargoes were carried in two kinds of vessel: cargo liners, which ploughed a regular route on a regular service; and tramp ships, which would go anywhere at any time. There are not nearly so many cargo liners around today and much more business is done by tramp ships. These charters demand very complicated matching – ideally suited, one would have thought, for the technology of the computer. But tradition dies hard in the Baltic and, according to the members, for very good reasons:

> There are far too many imponderables and variables and ifs and buts. Only a human brain can weigh up, for example, bunkering and victualling costs in one port as against waiting at $10,000 a day in another; consider the loading and unloading equipment – antiquated or the latest there is – in another; set the suitability of one ship, or port, for a particular cargo against the cost of waiting till just the right ship is available. Then there are factors like climate; dockers' bloody-mindedness in a particular port; the chance of political unrest in one country measured against the

efficiency of its port authority. That's just to mention some of the problems.

The Members

Who, then, are these people who have to pit their wits against time, money, shipping availability, industrial and political unrest and slumps and booms? Some members have sea-going experience, an advantage but not essential. Most of them probably came ashore before they had any real responsibility. It might be helpful to know how ships operate, but it is by no means crucial. One broker, who is typical of the market, takes an agnostic view of these qualifications: 'I doubt whether I or many of my colleagues know the blunt end of a ship from the sharp one.' But university graduates are much more common than they used to be. 'At one time,' says one of the largest shipping firms in the business,

> we used to recruit A-level leavers, but now we find that the bright, young extrovert people we want go to university or polytechnic. We also like the ones who have travelled round the world with a pack on their backs and enjoyed it. They've got the initiative, adventurous spirit, and above all they're likely to be good at getting on with very dissimilar types of people. That quality is absolutely essential in shipbroking. If new entrants know that Greeks are friendly and cheerful and like being chatted up, and that the Japanese are conventional and expect a conservative approach (and clothes), well, that saves us training time.

Green Badges

Prospective new members from member companies spend a year on the floor and can be identified by their green lapel badges, which they have to wear all the time. Women were admitted to the Baltic only in 1974. There are about 45 of them entitled to trade on the Baltic – that is out of a total membership of around 2,300. Feminism has not exactly got the Baltic by the throat. The Exchange expects high standards of dress and appearance from members and anyone found breaking the unwritten, but strict, rules is likely to be in trouble. Occasionally, it may be necessary to get rid of a member:

> Of course, some members quietly go away. They have to. We have a convenient arrangement whereby every member is considered every year. Most members don't realize this, but they are, and it's possible not to send out an invitation to renew their membership. In other words, if a member doesn't get an invitation to renew, it could be rather more than just a case of it getting lost in the post.

Shareholders

Unlike many other City institutions, the Baltic is an unquoted public company – the Baltic Exchange Ltd – owned by its members, who are all required to be shareholders. There is a board of directors, which elects the chairman. The directors are in turn elected by the shareholders, or members. The board decides who becomes a member and it can keep someone out indefinitely. On rare occasions, it actually expels a member.

The Air Market

Although the ship freight market is the main business of the Baltic, there are a number of other markets under the same roof. What was probably the original air charter party was signed in February 1928 to cover a two-way flight of cargo between Croydon and Cologne. But it was ten years before the Exchange considered setting up an air section and by then World War II was on the horizon. Although it held up the venture, the war at least showed the immense potential of aircraft transportation. The immediate post-war period saw a boom in air charter work, with former RAF pilots like Freddie Laker at its centre, because there was a shortage of shipping. Air charter companies mushroomed and in 1948 a committee was formed to foster the development of the

young but flourishing Baltic Exchange Air Market. The
market was quite active until a few years ago, but now there
are only five or six companies that do business on the
Exchange and their activities do not feature prominently in
the life of the Baltic.

Nevertheless, there are still charterers' agents, representing the business on offer, and owners' brokers, who
represent the aircraft operators. Many brokers act in both
capacities, but unlike their ship-broking colleagues they do
not actually work on the Floor of the Exchange. Telephones
and telexes are their *métier*. One of the main jobs of the air
broker is to fill 'empty legs' of a round trip – the return
journey of an aircraft chartered for a one-way flight that
would otherwise return empty to its base, loaded down with
costs but no cargo or passengers. In the early days of the
Exchange, the principal loads were perishable foodstuffs.
Later, air chartering was increasingly used for passenger
transport (many package-tour deals are struck on the Baltic) and for bulky cargo consignments.

London Grain Futures Market

The air market makes sense because, in one way or another,
it is tied up with freight. Yet there are corners of the Baltic,
one or two of them a little forlorn, that are devoted to commodity and futures markets. In the north-east corner, for
example, there is the ring of the London Grain Futures
Market, which is run by the Grain and Feed Trade Association. It enables farmers, shippers, merchants and users to
hedge their commodity deals against heavy losses should
there be wild price fluctuations. Like other futures markets,
it operates an 'open outcry' system – bids and offers are
shouted across the ring so that all traders are aware of price
changes. Prices of all business done are marked on two
boards and are then relayed immediately by the brokers on
the Floor to their clients by telephone and telex. A Reuters
video master shows dealers what is happening in Chicago
and in other London markets. Bids and offers in the London

Grain Futures Market go through the same process – through Reuters they are flashed up on screens around the world.

Potato Futures

Then there is the Potato Futures Market, which began trading in June 1980. Its purpose is to stabilize prices and enable growers and processors to plan in advance. Only a few yards from potatoes, there is the new Meat Futures Market, which was opened in 1984 by the Duke of Edinburgh. So far it deals only in pig-meat futures and its trading members represent farmers, wholesale meat traders, processors and speculators. It is the element of speculation in all these markets that does not have the whole-hearted approval of all the Baltic's shipping members. They did not open their arms to the introduction of futures trading on 'their' Exchange. There is no comparison between centuries of ship-broking and the new, smart markets where people can speculate in potatoes or the *Financial Times* Index. When the Soya Bean Futures Market was opened in the Baltic in 1984, the ship-brokers must have wondered what was coming next – futures, perhaps, for radishes and lettuce.

Freight Futures

What did come next, in fact, was the Baltic's own freight futures market, which was introduced in the middle of 1985 and which is known as BIFFEX, the Baltic International Freight Futures Exchange. The market comprises some twenty-five to forty members, who have the sole rights to trade on the Floor of the Exchange. Each member was required to demonstrate a minimum net asset worth of £250,000 and had to be approved by the International Commodities Clearing House. BIFFEX was a very complicated concept in futures trading and hedging because it set out to accommodate both American and Far Eastern interests, giving them a chance to use BIFFEX in their own time frames. The market is still in its infancy, but if most other futures markets are anything to go by it will settle down to a healthy and profitable life.

HARD AND SOFT COMMODITIES

In October 1985 the City faced its worst crisis since the Johnson Matthey banking collapse: the London Metal Exchange, the world's biggest and oldest metal market, was plunged into turmoil by the failure of the International Tin Agreement. In the ensuing months the whole market itself looked as if it might not survive.

Rigging the Market
The International Tin Agreement – there have been six since World War II – effectively rigged the world market price of tin so that producing countries, mainly in the developing world, would benefit from artificially high prices. It was boasted about as the great success of the international commodity agreements supported by the United Nations Conference on Trade and Development (UNCTAD). In the end, the boast was a disastrous illusion.

The Buffer Stock
The twenty-two members of the Agreement – the International Tin Council, which included the UK – supported the price pact in exactly the same way that the EEC

228

finances its beef or grain mountains: when members of the
ITC produced too much tin, a regular occurrence, they
simply bought back the surplus production at prices they
themselves had artificially inflated and put the tin into a
buffer stock. The agreement depended for its smooth running on the financial rectitude of the ITC's members. But on
24 October the buffer stock manager ran out of money. The
ITC's members had dishonoured their debts. These
amounted to £900 million and were owed to banks and
metal traders. There were 85,000 tonnes of tin in the
stockpile, with a 'market' price of £8,140 a tonne.

No Agreement for Rescue

The London Metal Exchange put forward a plan to refinance
the ITC with money from banks, brokers and member
governments but it foundered on opposition from Indonesia
and Thailand who claimed that it was too expensive. The tin
market had by then been suspended for almost four months;
the banks were clamouring for their money and traders
faced large losses. The LME had two options: it could reopen
trading with the frightening prospect of the tin price plummeting to a catastrophic £4,000 a tonne, or it could impose a
'ring-out' on trading companies through which they would
settle their ITC contracts at the LME price of £6,250 a
tonne. The LME chose the latter, demanding that all debts
should be paid by noon on 12 March 1986.

The Consequences

The 'ring-out' worked, but the consequences of the crisis
were immensely painful. The Exchange's decision was challenged in the High Court by Shearson Lehman, a member of
the LME, while Standard Chartered Bank and the Arab
Banking Corporation began court actions against the International Tin Council. One company went into liquidation,
MMC Metals, a subsidiary of the Malaysian Mining Corporation. Philipp and Lion, the metal trader headed by Jac-
ques Lion, Chairman of the LME, resigned its ring-dealing
membership – he said that the tin crisis had been 'the last

229

straw'. Rudolph Wolff, one of the LME's founder members, took a loss of £16.6 million while the total loss incurred by the thirteen ring-dealing members involved in ITC contracts ran to £140 million. A further eleven non-LME trading companies showed an additional loss of £40 million. But there were no immediate bankruptcies.

Cornish Tin

The Cornish tin-mining industry, whose production costs were much higher than elsewhere, was under threat: Geevor Tin Mines, the only independent company, suspended its operations early in April and laid off most of its 358 workers. It decided, however, to retain 50 people to keep the mine and treatment plant in working order while it continued to press the government for cash aid. The three other Cornish tin mines, which belonged to the Rio Tinto-Zinc natural resources group, continued to run normally but with the world price of tin against them it was not likely that they could survive for long.

Reform

Inevitably, the crisis not only raised questions about the way the LME conducted its business but there were demands for early reform of the market. Even before the crisis, the LME authorities were under pressure to change, both from some member companies and from the Securities and Investments Board, the agency set up to oversee the regulation of the City's markets. The feeling was that the LME needed to follow other London exchanges, and virtually every other commodities market in the world, by setting up a clearing house. LME ring-dealing members dealt directly with each other as principals. In a clearing-house system everybody deals through a settlement company, which is designed to prevent the collapse of one trader from bringing down others.

'Governments Don't Welsh'

Had the LME operated through a clearing house, with cash or securities to cover its members' liabilities, the crisis would probably not have occurred. The LME's brokers made the

cardinal error of lending money to the International Tin
Council (as did the banks – no less than £280 million) in
the mistaken belief that governments do not renege on
their debts or would not dare to shatter the entire system.
Worse, the ITC's creditors did not even insist on those pre-
cautions which the ITC was obliged by law to accept – such
as arbitration clauses. In the spring of 1986 the tin contract was suspended altogether and the metal was freely
traded on world markets at prices 50 per cent below the
ITC's rigged price.

The crisis amply illustrated the fundamental difference
between the hard and soft commodities markets in the City
and the way they work. The markets are divided into two
quite distinct entities with their own premises and staff.
The London Metal Exchange has the most complicated
market procedures of all the London exchanges, a *mystique*
of its own, which make the London Commodity Exchange's
trading look comparatively simple. We will begin with the
LME because much, but by no means all, of what happens
there is repeated in the London Commodity Exchange.

The London Metal Exchange

Fenchurch Street is one of the more agreeable thoroughfares in the City. Unlike Lombard Street or Cornhill or
even Threadneedle Street it has a bustling, active life
which is not concerned solely with the purposeful task of
shuffling bits of paper around to make money. There are
shops, pubs and sandwich bars and people going about
their business in a way that is not to be found in many
other City streets. It is a pleasant, natural mixture of shop-
keeping and commerce.

Yet it houses, albeit discreetly, a City market that
doesn't catch the headlines like the Stock Exchange or the
Financial Times Share Index in a buoyant or depressed
mood. The names who deal here are known only to a small
circle, but what they do is reported every day under the
heading of 'Commodity Prices' and it is these prices which

eventually feed their way into manufacturers' costs and ultimately affect what the public pays.

The Metals

Enter the elaborate portals of Plantation House, walk a few yards, and there on the left can be found the London Metal Exchange. At first sight it gives the impression of a small, modern museum: there are glass cases containing lumps of metal. They are there to remind people that the business of the Exchange is concentrated into seven metals – copper, tin (no longer), lead, zinc, silver, aluminium and nickel. Off this main room there are one or two sitting areas where 'ring dealers' relax between dealing sessions to talk and smoke. (Smoking in the dealing ring, incidentally, carries a stiff fine.) The dealers are mostly young, don't have cut-glass accents and seem impervious to the pressures of their trade. But like foreign-exchange dealers they have short, well-paid lives which won't kill them physically but which won't get them to the top of the ladder; not, that is, until they give up the job of dealing while they are still young enough to make commodity trading a serious profession. A harsh judgement, perhaps, but like most things in the City excitement and pressure are no guarantee of a solid career.

The visitor who looks down on the dealing ring from the gallery couldn't hope to understand the arcane tumult below. But the bedlam sets not only the world price for the metals the Exchange deals in, but it also provides a market in physical metal for producers and consumers. All the observer will see is a circular ring of red leather benches occupied by the dealers from the LME's twenty-eight ring-member companies. It is not a cartel: anyone can join who can show his net worth is £1 million or more.

Open Outcry

Behind the dealers stand their clerks and behind the clerks there are banks of telephones manned by young men who are in touch with their companies. Until quite recently the clerks used to get the prices from the ring and then run to the telephone. That was changed by a young clerk who joined the Exchange from a bookmaking firm. He quickly imported the tick-tack system and gave training classes to his colleagues. Now one sees the clerks peering over their dealers' shoulders and passing back information by hand signals to the men at their telephones. The distance is no more than a few feet but to the bookie it was a few feet too many.

So much for the set-up. Acoustically, the place verges on bedlam at peak times with lulls of variable loudness. This is because the LME employs the system of 'open outcry' where all the ring members can hear each others' bids and offers. Secrecy doesn't come into it. Dealing begins promptly at 11.45 a.m., starting with options. All trading times are in periods of five minutes. So at 11.50 the market moves on to silver for five minutes, then aluminium, followed by copper, tin, lead, zinc and nickel. There's a pause of five minutes at 12.25, followed by a further bout of dealing in the same metals, but in a different order. Trading for the morning session ends at 1.10 p.m. and that is followed by twenty minutes or so of 'kerb dealings'. The kerb is designed for members to complete dealings that may have been interrupted by the bell in the official sessions. A ring member, for example, may have been on the point of closing a tin deal when the bell went to indicate that dealings in lead were to begin.

The afternoon market begins at 3.20 p.m. and ends at 4.40 p.m., again followed by the 'kerb' – considerably more comfortable these days than the old tradition of dealing on the kerb outside the LME. Yet the Exchange, in its modern guise, has had its moments. In 1961 it dealt in the rain and in 1974 it dealt in the dark. The first occasion was in its old premises in Whittington Avenue, a building graced by a dome, which the Exchange decided to remove to make way for offices. The day the dome came off it poured with rain and all ring members dealt under umbrellas. In 1974 Edward Heath's 3-day week produced a power cut, so the Exchange had to deal in the dark – not so formidable as it

233

sounds since the system of open outcry meant that everyone knew everyone else's voice.

If the market looks eccentric, its purpose is deeply practical. Its roots lie in the early 1800s when the United Kingdom turned from being a net exporter of metals to become a large importer. This caused problems for consumers and merchants. Shipments were irregular and consequently prices fluctuated wildly. When communications improved, and people knew when shipments were arriving, merchants were able to offer metals with established delivery dates. However, that did not solve the problem of surplus supplies and what was to be done with them. Where there is a need for a market the City generally obliges and in 1877 the London Metal Exchange was set up in Lombard Court, the first of only three premises it has occupied in more than 100 years.

Setting the World Price

The LME has three basic functions. The first is that it sets the official world prices every day for the metals it deals in. These are announced at the end of the morning session and are decided by a 'Quotations Committee' of three members. These prices are watched by traders all over the world and they form the basis of contracts for the purchase and sale of metals wherever they occur. The London price can justifiably be called the world price.

The Physical Market

It is also a physical market, which means simply that metals can be bought and sold at any time in the LME. The buyer gets guaranteed delivery and absolute assurance as to the quality of the metal he's buying; while the seller has a guaranteed market where he can dispose of any amount of metal he wants to. None of that may sound exceptional, but it is not at all like buying or selling consignments of baked beans when many of the tins could be dubious. When the Exchange says it guarantees the quality of the metal, it means it. For example, all sales of cash metal that are due

for delivery the next day have to be backed by warehouse
warrants – the warehouses listed by the LME (ten in Britain
and eleven on the Continent) ensure that when the metal is
called 'good delivery' it has gone through a rigorous process
of analysis and assaying.

The Forward Market

But the LME has one other, extremely important function.
Its main business is the arrangement of forward contracts
for its clients, the producers or consumers of metals. A
producer, for example, may agree to provide 1,000 tonnes of
copper at a certain price three months ahead. But if the
price of copper rises in the meantime he will have lost on the
deal. So he will 'cover' his contract by buying the same
amount of copper three months forward. If, in three months'
time, the copper price has risen he will make a profit on his
'futures' copper even if he has taken a loss on the original
contract. One deal, therefore, should compensate for the
other. His futures contract is a 'hedge' against a possible loss
and the process is called 'hedging'.

Hedging

It operates in the same way for a manufacturer. Suppose he
buys 100 tonnes of tin. His next worry is that the price of tin
may have fallen by the time he comes to sell his product. So
he sells 100 tonnes of tin forward as a hedge at, say, £8,640 a
tonne. When his product is ready for sale he finds that tin
has moved up to £8,700 a tonne – a difference against him of
£6,000 on his hedge. He now has to buy back 100 tonnes of
tin at the new price of £8,700 and incur that £6,000 loss. But
his original purchase of tin was made at a price cheaper
than the prevailing one, so he has made a profit on his
product and the deal has roughly evened out. If, on the other
hand, tin had fallen in price since he bought it then he
would have made a profit on his 'hedge', but a loss on his
product. The bulk of trading in the Exchange – around 65
per cent – is in futures while the rest consists of cash or spot
contracts.

There's a great deal of money tied up in metal. At the peak in 1983 there was £48 billion worth of metals in the LME's listed warehouses, some of it belonging to the ring-dealing companies but the bulk of it owned by merchant banks and others that bought and sold it for future delivery – probably making rather more out of the investment than they would on 90-day Treasury bills. Anyone who uses the Exchange's ring dealers will, of course, have to pay for the services they give him. For an industrial customer brokerage would be around 1/16 of 1 per cent on the value of the purchase. For a speculator, on the other hand, the charge would probably be double.

The Big Members

The market is not controlled by the British. It is a cosmopolitan mixture and more than 60 per cent of the ring-dealing members are owned by overseas companies. The biggest are Metallgesellschaft of Germany; Billiton-Enthoven Metals, which is owned by Shell; Brandeis Goldschmidt, whose parent is Pechiney of France, and Triland Metals, which is owned by the giant Japanese conglomerate, Mitsubishi.

Small Fish in a Big Pond

But while the London Metal Exchange is by far the most important market in the world for the metals in which it deals, it has only just emerged from a very long period during which it was regarded as a second-class citizen in the City. Phillip Smith, a former Chairman of the LME and a metallurgist by training, says it was always looked down on by the City:

> The City was the Stock Exchange, the Baltic, Lloyd's and the banks. The commodity markets were always something down Mark Lane; they never had a corporate entity – which we're now trying to build up.

These days it has become much more respectable, due very largely to Smith's efforts in the post-war period to get the personalities of the Exchange better known in City circles.

We started to be invited to the Bankers' Dinner at the Mansion House and the Lord Mayor's banquet. But even that only became thinkable in the 1960s. Our forefathers were largely responsible. They wanted to go home at night; they didn't want to get involved in all that kind of thing.

There was some discussion that the LME should have its own livery company, but Smith says it was turned down by a large majority of the Exchange: 'They said it wasn't their kind of life.' Even now, only three members of the LME are members of livery companies.

Graduates

But graduates are beginning to take an interest in commodities as a career and as that momentum increases so, no doubt, the image of the Exchange will change. As far as dealing is concerned, the LME is remarkably open to newcomers. Young men can start dealing on the floor at the age of 21, after a probationary period of a few months and an examination in market practice and regulations. Some will earn £40,000 or £50,000 a year in their late thirties and early forties, but the average seems to be about £30,000. Like most market dealers who work in an atmosphere of frenzied activity they burn out early and Smith bluntly says that it's hard to know what to do with them after that.

The market has its traditions, of course. My favourite one is the Exchange's penchant for kümmel as a *digestif*. Legend has it that two of the Exchange's most prominent members of the golf association before World War II, Freddie Wolfe and Phillip Smith, popularized the drink through the happy conjunction of their taste and names, Wolfschmidt Kümmel. All golfing members of the Exchange – and there are hundreds of them – rarely drink anything else as a liqueur. But then most of them can afford to.

The London Commodity Exchange

The London Commodity in Mark Lane is a different kettle of fish. While all the LME's dealings in different metals are done in the same room by the same traders, the London Commodity Exchange has different markets for each of its soft commodities. There are seven in all: cocoa, coffee, sugar, wool, rubber, soya bean and – the most recent – oil.

Each commodity has its own Terminal Market Association. The floor members elect directors to serve on their association's management commitee, which sets the rules and regulations for its own market. Each management committee has a chairman and he in turn sits on the board of the London Commodity Exchange. The LCE provides each market with its premises, secretariat and a telecommunications network, as well as a real-time video price-reporting system. Like the LME, all trading is done by open outcry.

The International Commodities Clearing House

It is a futures market and these are traded in exactly the same way as they are in any futures market. Tens of thousands of contracts are traded each day and they are worth millions of pounds. Crucial to this business is the role of the International Commodities Clearing House, a company independent of the LCE and owned by six major banks. What it does is to guarantee the fulfilment of contracts between its clearing members, but the guarantee applies solely to members. The clearing house produces for each member all the necessary documentation to show the registration, settlement and tendering of those contracts which have been cleared.

Guarantees

It has another equally important function. If it guarantees fulfilment of contracts, it has to be sure that members do not get themselves into a financial mess. The details of all deals, therefore, are made available within minutes on computer terminals in the clearing house and those of its members. It means that the clearing house can monitor the trading that is going on and see what impact it is having on a member's position. In fact, the clearing house has got itself well covered. Every member who has contracts registered in his name has to provide cash or security to cover his liability and the clearing house can make calls for more money if the market is rising or falling rapidly. In view of the tin crisis, which hit the LME so hard, it is a system that the LME could emulate with benefit.

Other Customers

The ICCH has a very good business. It provides much the same services to the London International Financial Futures Exchange, the London Gold Futures Market and the Sydney Futures Exchange, as well as managing the clearing for the traded stock options market for the Stock Exchange and processing the monitoring system for the London Metal Exchange.

The London Commodity Exchange has been doing well, too. In the ten years from 1970 to 1980, the volume of turnover has increased from £3 billion to £60 billion, and it contributes at least £300 million a year to Britain's invisible earnings.

LIFFE

There is a small champagne bar in the Royal Exchange Buildings called the Greenhouse, where City people congregate for bubbly and smoked salmon sandwiches. It is always crowded and noisy. Among the dark suits there's always a peppering of young men in bizarre blazers who look as if they've just dropped in from Butlins. The bar couldn't be better placed since it's a stone's throw from the London International Financial Futures Exchange (LIFFE) which has its home in the Royal Exchange Building. LIFFE's young dealers are a captive market. They don't even have to get wet to get a drink.

Trading Money

The young men and LIFFE owe their existence to Chicago where money managers believed that money could be treated like any other commodity that's traded in futures markets, whether it be pork bellies or frozen orange juice. It was the increasing volatility of exchange, interest and inflation rates in the 1970s that led them to accept the idea, put forward by leading economists such as Milton Friedman, that money could be traded in a futures market to minimize the risk to which the users of money were constantly exposed.

Chicago Made the Running

The Chicago Mercantile Exchange pioneered the first financial futures market – the International Monetary Market – which opened in 1972, offering futures contracts in Japanese yen and other foreign currencies. Three years later the rival Chicago Board of Trade introduced the first interest-rate futures contract, followed by other contracts for Treasury and bank bills, as well as exchange-rate futures. In just over a decade Chicago has become the hub of a network of financial futures markets around the world, which before long will probably take in not only London and New York, but also Hong Kong, Tokyo, Singapore and Sydney. Twenty-four-hour-a-day interest and exchange-rate risk management will then be possible. As one senior American executive put it, 'It's an insomniac's dream come true.'

The Contracts

When LIFFE opened in September 1982, equipped with modern electronic equipment, it began by offering three interest-rate contracts and four currency contracts. By May 1984, these had proved their value to such an extent, particularly the interest-rate futures, that two new contracts were introduced – another long-term interest-rate contract and a new stock-index contract. This is not an easy market to grasp, but perhaps the easiest way to understand financial futures and how they work is to look at the three different kinds of participant in futures trading.

The Hedger

First, there is the *hedger*. As a money manager in a bank or investment institution, or as the treasurer of a corporation or public body, he wants to minimize the negative effects on the funds he handles of an adverse price movement in interest or currency rates. He does this by taking a position in the futures market that is equal and opposite to the position he is taking or expects to take in the cash market. Financial futures are standardized contracts to buy or sell a financial instrument (such as government bonds or Eurodollars) or foreign currency at a stated price by a certain date.

For example, a fund manager may know that he will receive cash for long-term investment in three months' time. Rather than wait to see what the interest rate will be at that time, he can lock in to today's quoted lending rate by buying financial futures contracts for delivery of gilt-edged stock in three months' time. If the general level of yields then declines, the price the investor would have to pay for gilt-edged stock will be higher. However, the price of futures contracts will also have risen and the fund manager can sell his contracts at a higher price than he paid. This profit will enable him to pay the higher price of the stock, while preserving the return on his funds.

Its Use to Industry

Another example would be a corporate treasurer whose company needs to borrow £1 million for expansion in July, six months from now. The borrowing rate on 1 January is 12 per cent but he's worried that by the time he actually needs to raise the cash interest rates will have risen. He can guarantee the price of his borrowing at today's prices by *selling* September sterling deposit futures at the current futures rate of 11 per cent. As cash and futures prices generally move in parallel, he can offset a rise in interest rates in the cash market by *buying* in July the same amount of September sterling deposit futures as he previously sold. If the cash interest rate has risen to 16 per cent by July, when he wants his £1 million, and the futures interest rate to 15 per cent, the yield gain on his newly bought futures will equal the additional borrowing costs and enable him to meet the increased cost of borrowing.

242

Nothing is ever Perfect

But the financial futures markets have not taken all the
risks out of money management. Perfect hedges like the one
just illustrated can't always be achieved. Although cash and
futures prices for financial instruments tend to move in the
same direction, they don't necessarily move in strict parallel. The difference between the cash and futures price is
known as the *basis*: this can be either positive or negative,
but from a hedging point of view the most important feature
of basis is that it can change over time. Suppose in January
a bank expects to receive a $10 million loan repayment in
four months' time and it proposes to invest the money in
3-month Treasury bills. The bank believes that interest
rates are likely to decline and it therefore wants to lock in to
the current interest rate of 13 per cent. To hedge its position,
the bank might buy $10 million face value of June 3-month
Treasury bills at the current futures market rate of 13.5 per
cent. When the loan is repaid in May, the bank can sell its
$10 million futures Treasury bills at, say, 11.25 per cent (a
gain of 2.25 per cent) and go to the cash market to invest the
$10 million repayment. However, between January and
May the basis has changed and interest rates in the cash
market are 10.5 per cent (a loss of 2.5 per cent). This means
that while the bank will make a 2.25 per cent yield gain on
its futures transactions due to the interest-rate fall, the
yield loss in the cash market is 2.5 per cent, as the spread
between the spot Treasury bill rate and the futures rate has
widened from 0.5 per cent in January to 0.75 per cent in
May. In this case, the futures market gain has not offset all
the cash market loss. But if the basis had narrowed the
reverse would have happened and the bank would have
made a net gain. Sometimes changes in the basis can wipe
out the entire value of a hedge.

The Arbitrageur

This brings us to the role of the *arbitrageur*. He attempts to
detect and take advantage of small temporary anomalies in

the cash and futures prices of financial instruments, simultaneously buying and selling related contracts in both the cash and futures markets. Arbitrage activity benefits hedgers by keeping futures prices closely in line with spot market prices, thereby reducing the risk of adverse changes in the basis.

The Speculator

There is one other participant in this market – the *speculator* or trader, who's prepared to risk substantial amounts of capital for extravagant gains by buying or selling financial futures in anticipation of lower or higher interest rates. He's a much maligned character, generating unnecessarily large price fluctuations at the expense of other market participants. But that doesn't do justice to the importance of his role as a provider of market liquidity and a forecaster of future interest- and exchange-rate movements. Without the speculative trader the financial futures market would be unable to function efficiently.

Nevertheless, there are those who maintain that currency futures trading has exacerbated international exchange-rate instability. The London economist for Stratecon Corp, Arnold Simkin, believes that currency futures trading immediately affects the spot market, helping to set off a dollar rally or collapse that might not otherwise have happened. And a number of central bankers, particularly in Japan and Germany, are worried that speculation could lead to global market manipulation. Singapore and Hong Kong have ruled out futures contracts on their own controlled currencies, largely because they fear that futures trading could make local interest and exchange rates more volatile. Clayton K. Yuetter, president of the Chicago Merc, argues that the best defence against manipulation is larger and more liquid markets. The opening of futures exchanges in London and elsewhere has helped to enhance that prospect.

The Clearing House

In setting up LIFFE, its Chief Executive, Michael Jenkins, says, 'We really modelled ourselves on Chicago.' Like its American model, all LIFFE transactions are carried out by a clearing house, the International Commodities Clearing House Ltd, an independent body owned by leading UK banks. The Clearing House guarantees every transaction on the Exchange floor. It can do this only by requiring members to 'put up margin' on every futures contract that changes hands. When a deal has been struck both buyer and seller must pay, either in cash or collateral, a percentage of the face value of the contract to the Clearing House to provide a cushion against adverse movements of the futures contract. The minimum level of this 'initial margin', as it's called, is set by the Clearing House and reflects the volatility of the underlying financial instrument. Margin typically ranges from 0.2 to 3 per cent of the contract's face value. As prices fluctuate each day, the value of outstanding contracts will change, so the amount of each day's gain or loss – called the variation margin – is added to or subtracted from the margin account in order to maintain the initial margin intact.

That isn't the Clearing House's only role. It monitors the business of the Exchange closely and maintains a visible presence on the floor in the shape of two young ladies perched in raised boxes on the side of each pit. They keep a cool eye on the frantic scenes in the pits below where huge quantities of money are traded by 'open outcry' – the system whereby all the dealers bawl at each other. It's neither uplifting nor enlightening to the outsider and it requires a good deal of training. It's also a young man's business because the learning curve in middle age wouldn't stand the pace. But as the phenomenal success of Chicago has proved – and other markets in London have shown – it's a very effective way of transmitting information about money trading around the world in a matter of seconds. Orders to buy and sell flow into the Exchange through telephones and telexes from banks, from dealers and speculators overseas, and these are immediately passed on to the dealers in the pits. Prices churn dozens of times a minute and are speedily reflected on overhead screens. As one floor manager puts it, 'Eyeball to eyeball, there are no secrets in the pits.' If a major player, such as the West German Bundesbank (the central bank), intervenes agressively in the market, buying German Marks and selling dollars, it will be felt in Chicago and London within seconds. Alert traders around the world will quickly detect that a heavy buyer of Marks is on the scene and will try to cover their risks with futures contracts. A pit dealer may try to hide the size of an order by breaking it into smaller lots, but if trading is fast he'll often dump a whole order, bringing about an instant shift in price.

The Cost of a Seat

Only members who have bought a seat on the Exchange are allowed to deal in the pits. Of the 400 seats available when the Exchange began business, a total of 373 were bought up initially at prices ranging between £20,000 and £30,000. As the expected shake-out occurred, there was a brisk trade in seat sales and rentals with transfer prices ranging between £26,000 and £41,000. Banks are quite the biggest presence, representing 40 per cent of the original membership, and since opening day they've been picking up additional seats. Others have decided they're better off in the back office. Several stockjobbers and some stockbrokers who bought seats never quite geared up to the market and have since withdrawn. With a few notable exceptions, corporations have been slow to enter the market. While Treasury departments may be interested, the fact is that LIFFE has a casino image and deters boards of directors who are uncertain of the relative benefits and risks. One major difference between Chicago and LIFFE is the number of 'locals' – individual traders – operating in the market. When LIFFE was launched, the absence of large numbers of these traders was expected to restrict the market's liquidity. But John Barkshire, then LIFFE's Chairman, was more sanguine:

Chicago's market liquidity is built on the system of
individuals, the locals, the traders standing in their
own right on the floor. The liquidity in our market will
be provided by the professional trader, the banks, the
brokers, the commodity houses.

He's turned out to be right. In May 1984 the Exchange
reached its daily peak volume of 20,588 contracts, and in the
week ending 14 June it was trading on average 11,240
contracts a day. After seventeen months of business the
Exchange felt able to add two new contracts to its original
range – an indication that trading had reached a satisfactory level with an adequate pool of liquidity to enable the
market to function properly. Of the individual contracts
with a track record, the 3-month Eurodollar interest rate
has been the most active, with the long-dated gilt-edged
contract in second place and the 3-month sterling contract
in third. The four currency contracts, however, haven't been
a success. They're of no interest to the big banks, which have
access to the highly efficient forward foreign-exchange markets, nor to the large corporations on the same grounds. The
contract sizes are so small it's necessary to take out multiple
contracts to deal in any size. While there's been talk of
changing the structure of the contracts, perhaps adding a
'jumbo-sized' future to appeal to the banks, LIFFE doesn't
regard it as a priority.

Footsie's Contract

Much more important has been the launch of the new stock
index contract, based on the FT-SE 100 Index ('Footsie').
The same kind of contract was highly successful in the US
and it's expected to attract the big institutional investors in
Britain, particularly the pension funds and insurance companies. The insurance companies are already actively
involved in the market, and the pension funds are poised to
take part in significant numbers now their tax position has
been clarified as tax exempt. The second new contract – the
US dollar long-interest rate – takes as its blueprint the
successful Chicago Board of Trade T-bond futures contract.

There are more contracts on the drawing board. Two that have been talked about are a Eurobond contract and a short-dated gilt – the latter is already in the pipeline, ready to be launched when Footsie has been established and a bigger volume of trading has been built up in the gilt contract. There have also been discussions about links with the two Chicago exchanges, but there's some reluctance in London to tie LIFFE too closely to any one exchange on the lines of the relationship between the Chicago Merc and the new Singapore International Monetary Exchange.

In just over a decade financial futures have established themselves as an indispensable tool for asset management. John Barkshire predicts that they will be as important to the world over the next twenty years as Eurodollars have been over the past twenty years. Which means that the young men in the Greenhouse won't be short of the wherewithal to go on drinking champagne.

INSURANCE AND PENSIONS

LLOYD'S OF LONDON

No market in the City has been more bedevilled in recent years by scandal, fraud and failure than the major insurance market, Lloyd's of London. There is no other institution that begins to compare with Lloyd's in size and scope, nerve and brazen cheating, for a series of disasters that at one time threatened to bring this august insurance market to its knees. Paradoxically, they all occurred in an institution that uses 'utmost good faith' (and you cannot have more good faith than that) as the yardstick for its dealings and that also happens to be a club whose members are bonded together by their private wealth. For years, the rich, the landed and the upper middle classes have been prepared to put their money into Lloyd's in the expectation of a handsome return. Being a Name at Lloyd's carried with it presumptions of class, wealth and social attitude. The members were not, therefore, likely to acquiesce willingly when their money was put in jeopardy for all the wrong reasons. Members of the best clubs sometimes turn on their committees. It happened at Lloyd's but the row was not about the quality of the claret or port. It was about something much more important: money.

From Coffee House to Lime Street

To understand what went wrong, it is important to grasp what went right in Lloyd's and how the basic structure of the market works. Like many of the major institutions in the City, its origins were rooted in the coffee house – in this case, the coffee house of Edward Lloyd, which he opened in Tower Street some time before 1687. In 1691 Lloyd moved to better premises in Lombard Street, the centre of the banking community, to which he attracted a large clientele engaged in pretty well everything to do with shipping. (He had started a shipping newssheet, *Lloyd's News*, which lasted less than a year.) Here, it's believed, but not known for certain, that the first marine insurance was written by merchants who, in those days, undertook any business they could profit by. After Lloyd's death in 1713, the place changed hands several times, but it still remained the undisputed centre for marine underwriting. Premises were moved on a number of occasions until Lloyd's eventually settled in Lime Street – twice – where it opened a new building in May 1986.

The Lutine Bell and 'Boxes'

It's here that a visitor, provided he is accompanied by a member, can see how the place ticks. The nucleus of Lloyd's is the Room. To say it is commodious is an understatement, since it measures 220 feet by 150 feet and rises to a height of 300 feet. The ground floor accommodates the marine market, the senior market by age and size; the first and second galleries have a mixture of marine, aviation, motor and non-marine markets; and the third gallery is exclusively non-marine. In the centre of the Room there is the rostrum, manned by a red-robed Caller with a microphone who summons members who are wanted. In front of him sits the loss clerk, who looks after two books – the loss book and the missing and overdue book. And, inevitably, there is the *Lutine* bell, probably Lloyd's best-known symbol and a grim reminder of one of the largest losses Lloyd's ever had to pay out. HMS *Lutine* foundered off the Dutch coast in 1799, carrying a vast treasure of gold and silver bullion and coin.

It seems appropriate, therefore, that the bell should be the harbinger of disturbing news: two rings for an overdue ship, one for a loss.

Underwriters work from 'boxes', a euphemism for two rather uncomfortable pews facing each other, separated by a table. Down the centre of the table there are shelves containing marine manuals, rate books and the paraphernalia necessary to an underwriter's trade. Each box represents a syndicate, sometimes more than one, and syndicates are known by numbers rather than names. That does not mean to say that underwriters are anonymous. Far from it. Lloyd's has always had its star performers, whose names are known throughout the insurance community: among them Ian Posgate, the acknowledged superstar until his downfall; Sir Peter Green and Stephen Merrett. Many are the sons of famous underwriting fathers, like Green and Merrett, and some are selfmade men like Posgate – though none have had his golden touch, hence the soubriquet 'Goldfinger'.

Social Habits and Racy People

They are mostly upper middle class, expensively educated at the best schools and have distinctive life-styles, which are based on money and social preferences. They are to be seen at Newmarket and Ascot, on the grouse moors of Yorkshire, casting for salmon in Scotland and getting soaked on their ocean racers. Sir Peter Green, Chairman of Janson Green and former Chairman of Lloyd's from 1980 to 1982, lists his recreations as shooting, fishing and sailing, and his clubs as Royal Ocean Racing, Pratt's and the Royal Yacht Squadron. They go to good tailors, mix with pretty girls and even in lean years seem to have an enviable knack of enjoying the best. They are also a little racy, with just that touch of flamboyance that isn't to be found in other markets. It may have something to do with the fact that every day of their working lives they are risking their syndicates' money on insuring everything from supertankers to a stallion at stud to a satellite.

Qualifying Wealth

Their backgrounds are not dissimilar from that of the members they represent on their syndicates. To be a member of Lloyd's, or an 'outside Name', as opposed to an active or working underwriter, people have to 'show' wealth of £100,000. But it has to be unencumbered: there should be no claims on it from another source, such as a bank. If the assets are shares, the Name is not obliged to sell them to realize £100,000 in cash, only to lodge them with the syndicate in trust. In other words, those shares can continue to earn them income. Working Names do not have to 'show' as much wealth; foreign Names have to show more. But there is, of course, a catch. It lies in the principle of unlimited liability. If a syndicate is caught with a massive loss far in excess, say, of the total of each member's £100,000, then the Names on the syndicate may have to part with everything they own – houses, cars, even cuff-links – until they have met their liabilities in full. That is a prospect that is always on the cards and, as we shall see later, it is bitterly resented when it occurs.

A Slice of the Cake for Everyone

So Names have two clear objectives in mind when they join Lloyd's. The first is to make a profit. The second is to minimize the losses they might incur in a bad year. But this is not something that outside Names decide for themselves. Lloyd's has a pecking order, a way of managing its affairs that ensures that someone gets a slice of the action all the way along the line. Anyone wanting to join a syndicate, for example, can still do so for himself (a 'direct Name') but he would be well advised to be an insurance professional if he did. Most outside Names do not have that kind of expertise. Farmers, businessmen, gentlemen landowners, do not know the business. Most Names, therefore, use 'members' agents' who will place them with syndicates. Who the member's agent places them with is a matter of professional skill and judgement. A smart agent will place them with syndicates with a track record of profitability (people used to queue to join Posgate's syndicates) and he will do so for a very good reason: he stands to make money out of it. He will do this in two ways. When his Name makes a profit, he will take 20 per cent of it. He will split this with the managing agent, 5 per cent to himself and 15 per cent to the managing agent. Who, you might well ask, is this second agent? He is the man, or people, who manages the affairs of the syndicate or perhaps a group of syndicates. He keeps the syndicate's accounts, invests its premium income until it is needed to pay claims and he also pays the claims. But he does not render this service for nothing. He gets paid by underwriting commission deducted from the Names' accounts. This is known as an underwriting 'salary' and it is normally split 60 per cent to the managing agent or company and 40 per cent to the members' agents. So agents get two bites of the cherry and Names pay twice.

Once Names have been placed with one or more syndicates, they have effectively left their wealth in the hands of the active underwriters who write insurance for those syndicates. Most Names don't see their underwriters from one end of the year to the other and probably have little idea of what they get up to in their boxes. Yet the professional underwriters are accepting risks on their behalf and using their judgement to 'write' what they hope is profitable business. Outside Names will not know whether that business has been profitable or not for quite some time since the Lloyd's system of accounting is based on a 3-year period. The books for 1980, for example, won't have been closed until the end of 1983, by which time all claims will have been settled and the syndicate will know whether it has made a profit or loss. The settlement of claims is often a lengthy and sometimes litigious business, especially when fraud may be involved. It is up to underwriters to protect their Names' interests; by doing so, they are also protecting themselves because they share in the profit and loss of a syndicate.

Lloyd's Intelligence and the 'Slip'

Underwriters, however, have a pretty good idea of how their business is faring on a day-to-day basis because on the marine side Lloyd's has an elaborate and sophisticated system of worldwide intelligence based on its Intelligence Department. This is open day and night to collect and distribute the news provided by Lloyd's agents and sub-agents from all over the world. These agents not only collect and forward information of interest to members, they also negotiate claims certified as 'payable abroad', investigate damage to cargoes and ships and, when necessary, employ surveyors for independent assessments. Much of the information they supply is published daily in *Lloyd's List*.

The infrastructure of services Lloyd's provides to underwriters is undeniably important: it gives them information, background and the latest news. But it does not give them business. That is provided by Lloyd's brokers. In the same way that an investor cannot approach a jobber direct on the floor of the Stock Exchange (he has to use a stockbroker as an intermediary), members of the shipping or business community must place their insurance through a Lloyd's broker and not directly through the underwriter. Suppose a shipping firm wants to insure a 250,000 d.w.t. supertanker. It will approach a Lloyd's broker who will enter details of the insurance on a 'slip', at the head of which is the broker's name. He will then walk round to the Room at Lime Street and approach a marine underwriter sitting at his box. He may well have to queue. 'Lead' underwriters – the leading syndicates in their field – are always in demand and it's important for brokers to get a good 'leader' to the slip; it makes it easier for the broker to get other underwriters to insure the tanker. If he likes the risk, the leading underwriter sets the rate of premium, the broker's commission (which comes out of the premium) and the proportion of the risk he is prepared to accept. He then stamps the slip with the name and number of the syndicate he represents and writes his initials over it. By being the leading underwriter on the slip, he is also taking responsibility for settling any claims arising from the insurance or any negotiations with the broker that may be involved. The proportion of the risk he is prepared to accept depends on the nature of the risk: if it is small, he may take 100 per cent; if

LLOYD'S OF LONDON

it is a supertanker, he may take as little as ½ of 1 per cent.

Of course, the process is not always automatic. An underwriter may want to know a good deal more about the nature
of the risk he is taking a 'line' on and which may not be
apparent from the details supplied to him by the broker. He
could ask questions about the past history of the ship, its
previous record, the last time it was surveyed and its claims
record. He may cross-question the broker about the client,
whose name may not be familiar. But once the underwriter
has agreed to accept the risk, he has committed himself and
the Names in his syndicate – whether they're stalking deer
in Scotland or skiing at St Moritz – to everything they
possess. It is a sobering thought and, as we shall see, in
recent years it has sometimes taken the form of a
nightmare.

The Lloyd's Brokers

A big marine syndicate may have as many as 2,000 Names.
The redoubtable Ian Posgate, when he was at the height of
his form, was writing for four syndicates, representing
something like 6,000 Names. This was due partly to the
magnetic attraction he had in the market for making his
Names a lot of money and it was due partly to the presence
of Alexander Howden, a big Lloyd's broker, which owned
two syndicates, 126 and 127 under the name of 'Spalding',
for which Posgate also wrote. The large Lloyd's brokers have
sizeable stakes in underwriting agencies and in a number of
cases these syndicates have made substantial contributions
to brokers' overall profits. Howden was one of them – it
ranks roughly fourth in the Lloyd's league of top brokers.
Hogg Robinson was another – its underwriting agencies,
Janson Green and Gardner Mountain & Capel-Cure, contributed £3 million out of the group's total profits of £9
million in 1981. And J. H. Minet, sixth in the league table,
was also the beneficiary of profits made by its PCW underwriting agency.

There is a critical and intimate link, therefore, between
Lloyd's brokers and underwriters. It is strengthened by the

fact that the brokers bring underwriters their business. One feeds off the other. There was never any question that this cosy and profitable arrangement would be anything other than British-owned and controlled. Lloyd's was imperishably British. It could point to the substantial contribution it made to Britain's balance of payments through 'invisible earnings'. It could claim that 90 per cent of all insurance contracts on hulls and cargoes in the international maritime trade are placed at Lloyd's. What it could not aver was that all its premium income was generated by British brokers. Roughly half, in fact, is placed by American brokerage houses through Lloyd's brokers and then into Lloyd's syndicates. Lloyd's owes a great deal to this transatlantic link and the American houses were keenly aware of it – so much so that in the late seventies they hit the takeover trail leading to some of the biggest Lloyd's brokers. It was perfectly logical that they should do so. The domestic American insurance market had already had a surfeit of amalgamations, so that there was little more to take over or merge with. The rationalization process was virtually over. And the Americans were acutely aware that the commissions on the insurance they were selling to Lloyd's were being shared with Lloyd's brokers. If they took over some of the British majors, they would have to share nothing – it would be all theirs.

The Americans began stalking the British brokers at a time of particular vulnerability in the Lloyd's market. Although Lloyd's membership had been increasing very rapidly, due largely to a determined recruiting campaign to repair the damages of the mid-sixties when insurance losses had been appalling, there was a substantial amount of 'overwriting' in the market. Each Name, for example, is given a premium income by the Committee of Lloyd's and the Name is allowed to accept premiums up to that amount. (Effectively, it is all handled by the active underwriter.) In the late seventies there were big profits to be made and there were formidable temptations to write above premium limits. This led to a further recruiting drive for more Names, whose

capital would dilute the amount being written and therefore
bring syndicates within their limits. It happened at a bad
moment. Just when everything looked set fair, Syndicate
762 collapsed like a pack of cards.

Sasse and the Beginning of Trouble

Syndicate 762 was a small one, just 110 Names, a mixture of
people from business, the aristocracy and the arts. The
active underwriter was 'Tim' Sasse, a sociable character
who was a member of another syndicate, unconnected with
Lloyd's, which owned Rheingold, winner of the Prix de l'Arc
de Triomphe in 1973. After the race he was sold for £1
million. Sasse was not only overwriting, he was writing
some of the worst risks ever seen in a market that has
encountered some very dubious propositions in its time. The
whole affair was a blend of fraud, bad luck, incompetence
and litigation. The Committee of Lloyd's itself was not only
caught up in a barrage of writs, but it was made to look
negligent as well. As for the syndicate's Names, once they
had some idea of the losses they were facing they called for
their lawyers.

Binders

In 1979 the true position became known. The syndicate had
lost approximately £20 million, roughly half of which was
on computer leasing (computer leasing turned out to be a
tiger that many syndicates had by the tail), and half on
some shoddy property in the Bronx, which was high risk and
high claim. Sasse was unusual in his underwriting habits –
he preferred to underwrite from his office rather than his
box. For the Bronx insurance he had used what is known as
a 'binding authority', or 'binder', by which an underwriter
gives authority to a broker to write insurance in his name.
The practice has grown up because the volume of business
from the United States is too important to be ignored, so
that if someone in America can produce business on a
'binder' it will enhance a syndicate's premium income.
There are certain limitations: the underwriter sets a limit

on the amount that can be written and he specifies the risks and the area they apply to. The first binder was issued to an Englishman, Dennis Harrison, who lived in Florida, and subsequently two more names were added to it.

The details of the swindle are complex and intricate, but Harrison offered Lloyd's business to a man called Jack Goepfert, or at least one of his front men. Goepfert had an awesome pile of trashy insurance business on his book and saw in the Lloyd's binder a heaven-sent chance to stuff this business into Lloyd's while skimming off substantial amounts of premium through an assortment of crooked devices and companies he controlled. Harrison and Goepfert managed to divert the best part of $3 million of premium, the bulk of which belonged to the Sasse syndicate.

No Liability

However, matters were to get worse. Much of the insurance had been reinsured with IRB, the Brazilian State reinsurance company. The Names could reasonably expect that most of their losses would be covered by this facility, but the IRB fought shy of admitting any liability, convinced – rightly – that the business was crooked. Added to that, Stephen Merrett, who, under pressure from the Lloyd's Committee, had reluctantly agreed to try to sort out the mess in the Sasse syndicate, had discovered another binder (on Canadian fire insurance), which plunged the Names even further into financial distress.

The Names who were Caught

If Lloyd's is a club, it is distinguished from others that go by that name by the brutal fact that it's a club of self-interested people with money at stake. It is expensive to join and continued membership depends on the financial viability of its Names. The Names on 762 were extraordinarily varied, both socially and financially. There were the seventh Earl Fortescue, Lord Napier, Princess Margaret's Private Secretary and Major the Honourable Sir Francis Legh, Equerry to the Queen Mother. These were the well connected. From business, there were Murray Gordon, Chairman of Combined English Stores; Joe Benjamin, a property developer who enjoyed ocean racing; and Paddy Davies, who ran companies with trading interests in South America. From the arts, there was Nigel Douglas, the opera singer and brother of Robin Leigh-Pemberton, Governor of the Bank of England.

Murray Gordon faced a liability of £250,000. So did Paddy Davies, who told me that if he had to meet his liabilities he would be bankrupt: 'I've calculated that if I continued in Lloyd's, and it proved to be profitable all the time, I would have to live until the age of 160 before I wiped out the debt.' Murray Gordon was little short of furious. He heard the news with 'profound shock': 'In a very bad year you might expect to lose £20,000, but this was something quite different.'

These were Names, though, who were comparatively well off. For Douglas, a gentle and charming man with small children, the Sasse collapse was a terrible blow. Ironically, he had been a working Name in Lloyd's until he turned to music twenty-five years ago. There were no large assets at his disposal: a flat in Switzerland, which he had bought as a bachelor to be close to the international opera circuit and which he had planned to sell to pay for his children's education; and a modest family house in London. His income from Lloyd's was for his retirement. In early 1980, when news of the enormity of the crash had begun to filter through to horrified Names, he told me:

> I'm now in the position of accepting private charity. One good friend has given me a loan of £25,000, interest free, for as long as I need it. And others have come forward. My only chance of paying off these debts is staying a member of Lloyd's.

It was a long way from the sleek years of the early seventies when a Name showing £100,000, and writing twice that in premium income, could on average make £26,000 in a year – a combination of underwriting profit and investment income. And that took no account of any capital gains. No wonder there was anger and bitterness in the Sasse syndicate. Nor was it surprising that two groups of Names in 762, one led by Paddy Davies, the other by Murray Gordon, called their lawyers and prepared for a long legal fight. The Lloyd's club, however disparate or angry its members were, was not going to go down without a fight. The common bond of money was a good deal stronger than any social affiliations they might have had.

The Committee Draws the Fire

Oddly, it was not 'Tim Sasse' they had directly in their sights. It was the Committee of Lloyd's, which the syndicate blamed for not heeding the warning signals that had been flashing across the Atlantic from Lloyd's general counsel in New York, LeBoeuf, Lamb, Leiby & Macrae. They had telexed Lloyd's early in 1976 – twenty-one months before Sasse was suspended from doing business – that there were rumours about that Goepfert and an associate were involved in the affair. Later, the New York lawyers passed on even more damaging information – complaints from policy holders whose claims had not been paid. That, in particular, should have alerted Lloyd's officials that something had gone badly wrong. There could be no worse publicity than Lloyd's welshing on its policies, especially in America, which provided a vital flow of premium income to London. But the warnings went unheeded.

When action was taken in January 1977 it proved to be thoroughly unwelcome to the Sasse Names. Leslie Dew, Lloyd's Deputy Chairman, instructed that the Sasse binder issued to Dennis Harrison – and earlier cancelled by Sasse – should be signed and processed by the Lloyd's Policy Signing Office, thus giving it the official seal of approval. It was not only going against Sasse's own instructions to cancel contracts that had been improperly written, but as far as the Names were concerned, it was doing something much more damaging: it was committing them, down to their last penny, to a plethora of claims whose origins lay in fraud. While the Committee of Lloyd's could claim that it was vital to keep the good name of Lloyd's untarnished in the eyes of the American market, it was a moral and commercial stance that did not have much foundation.

There were other irregularities, too, which were going to have repercussions on the Committee. The first concerned the standing of 'binding authorities'. Lloyd's specifically forbids underwriting to take place outside the Room. The Harrison or 'Den-Har' binder, as it was known, was in breach of that rule because it gave Harrison authority to write insurance in the United States. But commercial pressures being what they are, especially when there's the opportunity of a good flow of business from the States, which could not be obtained without a binder, there are arrangements within Lloyd's for approval to be given for a binding authority provided it has been 'tribunalized' by a tribunal set up by the Lloyd's Non-Marine Underwriters' Association. No such tribunalization had taken place. Nor were the Names ever aware, or so it appeared, that a binder had been given to Harrison by Sasse.

The Committee Gives In

The Lloyd's hierarchy was simply asking for trouble and deservedly it got it. Altogether, there were too many irregularities, too many breaches of the rules and too little regard for the storm signals from across the Atlantic for the Committee to have much chance when the Names' lawyers got to work on the available evidence. Yet the Committee of Lloyd's doggedly persisted with its contention that the Sasse Names should pay. It was concerned only with Lloyd's reputation, not the equitable treatment of its members. After much delay, the Committee was finally persuaded that if the case went into court Lloyd's would lose. Just as bad, perhaps, the Committee would be savaged for the way it had acted. The good name of Lloyd's, 'utmost good faith', and a few other principles that the institution held dear would have been incalculably blemished. In fact, Lloyd's reputation in

America was already close to its nadir. A court case that went against the Committee would have been disastrous.

Even though Lloyd's settled out of court, the Sasse Names could scarcely claim a great victory. It was one of principle, but financially they still took a buffeting. They agreed to put up just over £6 million of the 1976 losses (£80,000 per Name, in other words), while the Corporation of Lloyd's put in £9 million and a further £7 million – the full amount – for the 1977 losses.

In effect, each member of Lloyd's had to put up a few hundred pounds for the Lloyd's contribution. Some of the Names complained to Nigel Douglas that they thought it was unfair: he had, after all, enjoyed good profits in his time. 'What they didn't realize', Douglas said, 'was that it was my first year of underwriting. I would have felt less badly if what they said had been true.'

When I spoke to him late in 1984, Douglas told me that the three years following the Sasse crash were the bleakest in his life:

> I couldn't afford to spend a penny. When we were asked to friends, one was painfully aware that they were looking at a man whom they probably thought was ruined. Financially, it was a dreadful time. Socially, it was very uncomfortable.

Incredibly, Douglas managed to survive and is still a Name. So, too, are most of the others who were caught in the Sasse crash.

The Americans Hit the Takeover Trail

The big American brokers, who were anxious to acquire a slice of the action in the London insurance market, did not seem to be put off by the Sasse scandal. Nor were they deterred by a major scandal in the marine market, the *Savonita* affair. The *Savonita* was a ship carrying Fiat cars to the United States. A fire broke out on board and Lloyd's was presented with an insurance claim. But some of the cars later turned up on the Italian market. In spite of that, the claim was finally paid amid a storm of recrimination and condemnation of the way Lloyd's had handled it. Nor were they scared off by the large shipping losses of the late seventies (many of them due to fraud) or the losses on computer leasing incurred through IBM introducing a new generation of computers, leaving the insured to collect on their policies, which were written to protect them against that kind of eventuality. They were not concerned about the claims, litigation or losses. But they probably welcomed the fact that, after the glare of publicity Lloyd's had been exposed to, the Committee at last decided to try to put its house in order by asking an eminent judge, Sir Henry Fisher, to inquire into self-regulation at Lloyd's.

In 1980, Marsh & McLennan, the biggest American broker, merged with C. T. Bowring of London. (Bowring then ranked number 2 in the Lloyd's league.) The merger was not uncontested. The Bowring board did not like the idea, although the whole of the London market was enthusiastic about the deal. Even the Committee of Lloyd's did not oppose it. Bowring, however, did not want to lose their independence; on the other hand, they did not want to lose all the comfortable business Marsh & McLennan was putting their way from America. John Regan, Marsh's shrewd Chairman, eventually outmanoeuvred the Bowring board with an offer for Bowring shares that was too sweet to resist.

At about the same time, Alexander & Alexander, another big American broker, was having talks with the largest of the Lloyd's brokers, the Sedgwick Group. They continued for two and a half years until they were broken off. Alexander & Alexander then renewed its courtship with Alexander Howden, the fourth largest of the Lloyd's brokers, whose underwriting star was Ian Posgate. The courtship was a whirlwind one. It took just six weeks to consummate and Alexander & Alexander acquired Howden for £150 million in cash and shares.

To understand the full significance of the merger and the scandal that followed it, it is necessary to go back to

January 1971, when Ian Posgate was very nearly kicked out of Lloyd's. In that month, the Committee of Lloyd's severely censured him. It had found that he had misapplied money belonging to Syndicate 128/9 and that he had not kept proper accounts. They imposed a number of penalties, but the important thing about the censure was that he was not banned from underwriting. He was able, therefore, to continue as the active underwriter for Howden.

Goldfinger's Troubles

If Sasse had been in trouble for overwriting, for Posgate the problem had been a continuing one. The difficulty for Posgate was that he was too successful. Business poured into his box, as brokers queued up to bring him their slips. The main reason for his popularity was that he was a rate-cutter. Normally, when there have been losses, say, in the marine market, rates will rise. Posgate's knack was to cut rates after they had risen. It was an offer no broker could refuse. Hence the high volume of business he attracted. But Lloyd's syndicates do not operate like supermarkets, where volume is the key to lower prices. Syndicates can do as much business as they like provided they do not exceed their premium income limits set by the Committee of Lloyd's. If a syndicate is writing a lot of business, it can do so only within its limits. There are two ways a syndicate can get round the problem: it can get more Names on to its books, thus raising its premium limits, or it can reinsure – or lay off – some of its premium income in the reinsurance market, thus bringing itself inside its limits. Posgate did a good deal of the latter; even so, he was often in trouble with the Committee. Late in 1974, it told Howden that it would remove it from its list of approved underwriting agencies unless it persuaded Posgate to obey the rules.

That was a very serious threat since the Posgate syndicates contributed substantially to Howden's profits. (By 1979, for example, its premium income was £80 million.) Posgate's genius was making Howden money hand over fist, yet his waywardness put it at risk of losing the lot.

Fortunately, the threat never materialized. Posgate slowly worked his way back into the Committee's good books until, in 1981, he was elected a member of the Committee itself. Considering that he had started underwriting only in 1965, and had negotiated some serious pitfalls in the intervening years, it was a remarkable step forward.

No sooner had he achieved this accolade than things began to go wrong once again. It was during this period that the Lloyd's Bill providing for effective – if such a thing were possible – self-regulation of the market was making its laborious passage through Parliament, many of its proposals based on the recommendations of Sir Henry Fisher. One of its provisions was for divestment – divestment, that is, of underwriting syndicates from the brokers who owned them. The received wisdom was that it was impossible for a syndicate to have an 'arm's length' relationship with a broker if that broker owned it. It might, for example, find itself obliged to write insurance it wouldn't otherwise undertake simply because the broker wanted the commission on the premium. It would be captive to the broker.

An Argument about Divestment

The two men who most strongly advocated and opposed divestment were not casual acquaintances. They were Posgate, who believed that divestment could do nothing but good; and Kenneth Grob, Chairman of Howden, the man who had the trying task of controlling Posgate's underwriting. Grob was passionately opposed to it. Both men employed counsel, at a cost of thousands of pounds, to argue their cases before a House of Commons Committee. Grob knew quite well that if he had to divest Howden of the Posgate syndicates, the group's loss of income would be extremely damaging. For one thing, the Posgate syndicates contributed at least 20 per cent to Howden's profits. But it did not end there. When Posgate reinsured premium income, it was Howden who placed more than half of it – mostly with insurance companies owned by the Howden group. It was a beautifully neat, interlocking relationship worth millions of pounds. Grob was desperate to keep the arrangement as it was and it is not difficult to see why.

Posgate, on the other hand, had strong financial and personal motives for wanting divestment. He had built up the Howden underwriting agencies over a period of ten years. He was the acknowledged star of the market, a magnetic draw who could be relied on to make large profits for his Names and, incidentally, for Howden. Here was a chance to break free of the Howden parent. The financial incentives were immediately apparent. He stood to profit enormously.

But Posgate was never able to take advantage of the Act when it was passed in July 1982. (The provision for divestment had been written in.) Something had cropped up meanwhile and it was to bring Posgate's career at Lloyd's to an abrupt, possibly permanent, end. Earlier that year, in March, Posgate had resigned from the Howden board (he was, incidentally, the group's major shareholder and profit earner), on the somewhat flimsy grounds that he had never been included in the negotiations with Alexander & Alexander. When the American parent assumed control, a number of skeletons began rattling in the Howden cupboard.

Millions Go Walkabout

It is not necessary to go into the exact nature of what Alexander & Alexander found, since the story is long and complicated. But, initially, they discovered that one of Howden's subsidiary companies was not only making surprisingly large losses, amounting to millions of pounds, but that those millions were ending up in the pockets of Kenneth Grob and three other Howden executives, Allan Page, John Carpenter and Ronald Comery. It is worth quoting the suit filed in the United Kingdom by Alexander & Alexander:

> The suit against the four former officers and Mr Posgate alleges that, through a series of Lichtenstein [sic] trusts and Panamanian corporations, the four former officers and directors named above own Southern International AG ('SRAG'), a Lichtenstein [sic] corporation engaged in the insurance business. Also, the four

individuals, along with Mr Posgate, owned interests in
New Southern RE Company SA ('NSR'), a Panamanian
corporation.

Beginning as early as 1975, funds totalling approximately $55 million, including payments purporting to
be insurance and reinsurance premiums from Howden
insurance companies and quota-share premiums from
Howden-managed insurance underwriting syndicates
of which Mr Posgate was the underwriter, were paid to
SRAG and Southern International RE Company SA
('SIR'), with SIR paying approximately $7 million to
NSR. The moneys taken in by these entities were used in
part for the personal benefit of the four individuals and
Mr Posgate.

  ... The funds paid by SIR to NSR were used on behalf
of the four and Mr Posgate to purchase a substantial
interest in the Banque du Rhône et de la Tamise SA from
Howden at a time when they and Mr Posgate were
directors of Howden. Neither the four nor Mr Posgate
disclosed their interests to Howden. These interests
were held in Liechtenstein trusts. Additionally, information developed by the Registrant (A & A) during its
inquiry indicates that certain bank loans to Mr Posgate,
totalling approximately $2.5 million, were partially
guaranteed by SIR.

In plain language, money belonging legitimately to the
Howden Group, and therefore Alexander & Alexander, had
been siphoned off into various trusts in which the four men
and Posgate had interests. Some of it had then been used for
their own benefit. It also transpired that a good deal of this
diverted money had been used to buy a magnificent villa for
Grob in the South of France, valued at £2 million; two
Pissarro paintings and one by Redon, worth several hundred
thousand dollars; and a block purchase of 1 million shares in
a petroleum company. One of the Pissarros was a 'gift' to
Posgate from Grob, or so Posgate claimed.

America Voices Concern

It was the last thing that Lloyd's needed. The Lloyd's Act
providing for effective self-regulation had just been passed.

The Sasse affair was over. The Augean stables looked as if they had been sanitized. Then this. Albert Lewis, the New York State Superintendent for Insurance and a persistent critic of Lloyd's, attacked Lloyd's for incompetent regulation:

> From the United States perspective, the idea of a handshake and good fellows making an international reinsurance agreement is archaic. It certainly doesn't work in today's modern world and we find that the credibility of Lloyd's and the London marketplace is being eroded by the number of scandals. The United States is a consumer and we use Lloyd's to support much of our licensed industry. We want to see better regulation and control.

Michael Meacher, the Labour MP who chaired the House of Commons Committee on Lloyd's, called for a full inquiry. The Department of Trade said it would investigate Howden's affairs under the Companies Act. Once again, Lloyd's had become the focus of a blazing row.

Posgate Fights Back

Litigation is a way of life at Lloyd's. Through their solicitors, the four men denied everything. So did Posgate. The Queen's Bench Divisional Court in January 1983 found that the Committee of Lloyd's had no power to suspend Posgate from his underwriting activities, but that if it required the syndicates managed by Howden and Posgate & Denby to suspend their underwriting until the Committee was satisfied, that would amount to the same thing. The Posgate syndicates are now managed by Alexander & Alexander Services but, typically, Posgate found his suspension and the probable loss of his career quite unacceptable. The Lloyd's Disciplinary Committee had recommended his expulsion from the market for life.

In May 1985 Posgate opted for a public hearing of his case at the National Liberal Club before Lord Wilberforce, the President of Lloyd's Appeals Tribunal. Robert Alexander QC (said to be the most expensive and successful counsel practising at the Bar) appeared for Posgate and argued that his client had been entitled to ask for and accept gifts from Grob in recognition of his valuable services to the Howden Group. The gifts were the Pissarro painting, valued at $90,000, and the Banque du Rhône shares, worth $750,000. Posgate had already been acquitted of all the serious charges against him – namely, of being a party to 'plundering, siphoning off funds and shuffling figures of the Alexander Howden Group for the personal benefit of himself and others' – but faced life expulsion on the charge that he had accepted the gifts knowing that they were intended to influence him to place reinsurance through the Howden Group.

For Posgate, the stakes were high. He had at one time been earning £700,000 a year from his underwriting and he faced a legal bill for his defence amounting to £400,000. Life exclusion would cost him a fortune in potential earnings. And there could be no doubt that if he gained readmittance to Lloyd's he would be welcomed back with open arms by thousands of Names.

Alexander argued that Posgate was being judged by the philosophy Lloyd's had adopted since the passage of the 1982 Lloyd's Act, which required total separation of broking and underwriting interests, rather than by the standards that had prevailed at the time. Inducing a successful underwriter like Posgate to stay with a group by giving him large rewards would not, by those standards, have been in any way improper. The pattern of Posgate's reinsurance business had not changed after he had received the gifts, nor had he ever obtained reinsurance other than on the best terms for the Names in the syndicates for which he acted.

Appeals at Lloyd's are cumbersome and drawn out and decisions have to be ratified by the ruling Council. But at least they have the merit of being final. The Council can reduce the awards by the Appeals Tribunal, but it cannot increase them. By the middle of June 1985 Lord Wilberforce had made his decision known to Posgate. The underwriter was suspended for six months, which meant that he was notionally back in business in January 1986 with a ready-made clientele only too anxious to invest in his expertise.

But Lloyd's had other ideas. While Posgate continued to write business on his own account for £1 million, Lloyd's were determined that he should not run any more syndicates. Posgate took the matter before Lord Wilberforce in June 1986, once again represented by Robert Alexander QC. Messrs Grob, Comery and Carpenter, however, were all expelled from Lloyd's.

The Howden Four

While Posgate was litigating over his career, Alexander & Alexander had its hands full trying to decide what to do about the funds siphoned off by the Howden four – Messrs Grob, Comery, Carpenter and Page. The American firm was advised by counsel that if it went to court to retrieve the assets it would be a lengthy and enormously expensive business. Accordingly, John Bogardus, Chairman of Alexander & Alexander, offered the four men a deal – a guarantee of immunity from prosecution by Alexander & Alexander, but not immunity from elsewhere, if they returned the assets. The deal never came off, largely because no one could agree on a valuation of the assets.

Peter Dixon and PCW

The trouble with Alexander & Alexander's probe into the affairs of Howden, now its subsidiary, was that it didn't end with Grob and his compatriots. Nothing is ever that simple at Lloyd's. There were other connections, it was to discover, that led back to the Howden four. While the American company was investigating the Banque du Rhône et de la Tamise, it discovered that two men – Peter Dixon and Peter Cameron-Webb – had owned 15 per cent of the bank between them. Peter Dixon was Chairman of two underwriting agencies, PCW and WMD, which was owned by the major Lloyd's broker, Minet Holdings. When Alexander & Alexander dug deeper into what was rapidly becoming a mire, it unearthed the fact that PCW and WMD had paid no less than $40 million in reinsurance premiums to offshore companies, which had yielded a profit of $25 million. That should have gone to the Names on both syndicates, but it didn't. Further investigation revealed that the reinsurance business had been placed by two firms – one called APEG, the other Zephyr. APEG was owned by Peter Dixon, Chairman of PCW and WMD, and Peter Cameron-Webb of PCW. Zephyr, on the other hand, was owned by Kenneth Grob and his chums in Howden. The wheel had swung full circle, but by this time there were quite a number of people strapped to it.

One was the Chairman of Minet, John Wallrock, a keen advocate of Lloyd's supervision but an opponent of divestment. He was to admit eventually that he had a clandestine interest in the PCW and WMD reinsurance business. He saw nothing wrong in it – it amounted to only 5 per cent, worth no more than $2 million. It was an astonishing admission. In all walks of life there are pirates, but perhaps the most brazen are those who support regulatory supervision of markets while at the same time regarding themselves above it. Wallrock resigned shortly afterwards. He was tried in private by Lloyd's at his own request but at the time of writing the disciplinary committee had not published its verdict.

The Green Connection

The other name was a good deal more important and therefore more embarrassing. He was Sir Peter Green who, as Chairman of Lloyd's, had a prime responsibility for seeing that the place behaved itself. He found no evidence of dishonesty in the way PCW and WMD had conducted their affairs – carelessness, yes, but no more than that. Green was an Establishment figure down to his boots, a bluff Harrovian capable of defending Lloyd's interests on television, though not with great conviction. Even while the market was in uproar, he managed to give the impression that he couldn't see what the fuss was about. It was not good public relations, any more than was his linkage – indirect – with Peter Cameron-Webb and Peter Dixon, both of whom had been associates of his father, Toby. Long ago, Toby Green had set up a company called the Imperial Insurance Company, which was later registered in the Cayman Islands. Sir Peter used Imperial to reinsure some of the risks accepted by his syndicates, of which he was the active underwriter. When he became Chairman of Lloyd's in 1980, he explained to the Council that he had tried to sell his shareholding in Imperial, but had not been able to find a buyer. So a discretionary charitable trust was formed to hold the shares, but the Green family was not to be a beneficiary. It appeared that a farm company owned by Sir Peter might benefit.

But Sir Peter had many interlocking interests in Lloyd's. He was a director of Hogg Robinson, the Lloyd's brokers. Both the Chairman and Deputy Chairman of Hogg Robinson were members of Sir Peter's syndicate. Hogg Robinson was also a major shareholder in Janine Services Ltd, an investment service company by which Sir Peter, as chairman, was paid £77,000 in 1981. Sir Peter's main syndicate was 932, whose members included Prince Michael of Kent, Princess Alexandra and several Peers. But up until the end of 1981, Sir Peter had a much smaller syndicate, 941. It was a 'baby' syndicate, whose few members included the chairman of Hogg Robinson (of which Sir Peter was a director), several members of Sir Peter's family and, not surprisingly, Sir Peter himself. It has now been wound up.

Baby Syndicates

A baby syndicate is pure gold. In the language of Lloyd's it is called 'preferred underwriting', which means that a chosen few are preferred over anyone else. The underwriter offers his 'preferred' Names the cream of the business at low risk and high premium. It is a club within a club, a cosy arrangement by which some of the most profitable business is split away from the main syndicate and placed with the baby. By its very nature, it creates two types of Names: first and second class, and it deprives the second class of the chance to earn larger profits. It was not only curious that a man who was Chairman of Lloyd's, and therefore something of a moral arbiter among his fellow members, should have been running these arrangements, it was also scandalous and a grave reflection on an institution that was supposedly in the process of cleaning itself up. For years Lloyd's has been happy to live with these anomalies, inequities and preferences without batting an eyelid. Outside Names have had their legitimate profits plundered by active underwriters who, with the spurious presumption of superiority, have been happy to ride roughshod over the people whose interests they were supposed to represent but who in reality were pawns in a game whose rules were made by the underwriters. In 1983 Sir Peter retired without completing his second term of office.

PCW, Minet and Beckett

The nadir of such unprincipled behaviour was reached in mid-1985 when Peter Cameron-Webb and Peter Dixon were revealed in their true colours. John Wallrock, then Chairman of Minet, was involved in the affair and so, indirectly, was the Howden Group. Cameron-Webb, a former business associate of Sir Peter Green, was a respected underwriter within the Lloyd's establishment and, according to some people, was one of 'the brains of the market'. Cameron-Webb, together with his partner Peter Dixon, had set up his own agency, PCW, and by 1973 the agency was an undoubted success. In that year Cameron-Webb decided to sell it to Minet in a deal that was extraordinarily preferential for the two partners. Cameron-Webb got £2 million for the agency but forced Wallrock to make a number of concessions, which gave Dixon and himself total autonomy in the running of PCW. The two men owned the voting shares in the agency, with Minet holding the non-voting equity. And Minet was allowed only one representative on the board. He was, of course, John Wallrock.

Given the run of the field, the two men went about their business untroubled for the next nine years, using the reinsurance market as the vehicle for siphoning funds into companies abroad. Reinsurance is used to lay off the risks of a syndicate with other insurance concerns, which are then expected to pay claims to the syndicate in the event of losses.

275

The syndicate pays the money in the form of premium to gain the necessary protection.

In the case of the PCW syndicates, the reinsurance premiums duly flowed out – ostensibly to cover the syndicates against losses – but not all of them ended up in their proper home: they were channelled to companies in Gibraltar owned by the interests of Cameron-Webb and Dixon. Some £40 million had gone missing, allegedly spent by Dixon and Cameron-Webb on a variety of pleasures and toys: yachts, executive jets, film production, oil and gas wells, and a French orange juice company. When Minet's Beckett agency (formed to take over the affairs of the PCW syndicates) began to unscramble the mess it found that £25 million of the missing funds were in Gibraltar. This money was eventually returned to the underwriting members and it was topped up by £13.14 million – a contribution by Minet and Alexander & Alexander, the parent company of Howden through which much of the missing money had been routed.

These arrangements were crucial for the syndicate members. They were facing claims (some £233,000 a head) arising from asbestosis insurance written in the US under the old PCW management, as well as claims arising from Agent Orange, the defoliant used during the Vietnam war. But there was worse, much worse, to come. The Beckett agency had to provide for future claims – asbestosis, for example, can take a long time to appear – and these were reckoned to amount to a staggering £130 million over a twenty- to thirty-year period. Underwriting members were asked to stump up £60 million as an immediate provision by 31 July 1985.

No 'Lifeboat'

If Hell hath no fury like a woman scorned, then Names who stand to lose their shirts must come a very close second. There were 1,525 of them (Lloyd's has 26,000 Names) and they included Jeffrey Archer, the best-selling novelist, the Duchess of Kent, the Duchess of Marlborough, Viscount Portman and the fabulously wealthy Saudi businessman, Adnan Khashoggi. But beneath this aristocratic and financial crust there were lawyers, farmers, accountants and insurance professionals who worked in the Lloyd's market itself. A handful faced losses of up to £500,000 each and many were likely to be bankrupted. When they met at the Royal Festival Hall in May 1985 they gave the professionals running the Beckett agency a very hard time.

Nor was it surprising. Minet, which owned the Richard Beckett agency, had just decided to close the agency down, leaving the Names without any management. It was improper and callous, but Minet had had enough. Furthermore, it was facing allegations from outraged members that its management of the Beckett agency was not up to scratch. The Names' affairs were later taken over by a Lloyd's Additional Underwriting Agency headed by Sir Ian Morrow. But while it was gratifying to know that they had not been totally abandoned, the Names had a far deeper concern. Back in the days of the Sasse affair, Lloyd's members had footed a substantial bill – though not on the scale of PCW – to bail out the stricken Sasse Names. They had not paid everything, but they had made a contribution. The PCW Names now looked to the Council of Lloyd's to provide a similar 'lifeboat'. It was not forthcoming. Peter Miller, the new Chairman of Lloyd's, invoked the principle of unlimited liability. 'The one thing the council cannot do', Miller told the representatives of the frantic Names, 'is to provide some sort of so-called financial lifeboat and depart from the principle that we each individually have to respond for our share of losses if, unhappily, they occur.'

It was the last thing that the Names wanted to hear. They had been given until 31 July 1985 to prove themselves solvent – another way of saying that if they didn't meet their liabilities by then they would be suspended from underwriting. Miller promised them another inquiry, this time into the way their syndicates had been run by Richard Beckett, the agency that had taken over the old PCW. But he stressed that 'there was no evidence of malfeasance on the part of the directors'. The Chairman also offered a few of them an olive branch. Some thirty members thought they were protected by stop-loss policies arranged for them by the former managers of PCW.

The policies, giving cover of about £7 million, turned out to be worthless. Miller said that Lloyd's would honour them.

The Beckett Names were quite unimpressed. They had every reason to be. The Department of Trade and Industry had been investigating PCW for nearly three years; the City of London Fraud Squad had put a nose into its affairs, and had conducted two inquiries – one of them a personal investigation by Sir Peter Green, which had studied only one insurance contract and concluded that there had been no dishonesty. The years had dragged by and nothing had happened – except a very real and traumatic demand for the Names to stump up £130 million. Ironically, one of the two men at the centre of the storm, Peter Cameron-Webb, was running an insurance outfit in Miami. The Names had every right to feel outraged.

Liability

By the beginning of July 1985, 400 Beckett Names, advised by Lord Goodman and Robert Alexander QC, decided to take action. They denied all liability if there had been fraud or misconduct in the handling of their affairs and they planned to take action against Richard Beckett Underwriting Agencies, Minet Holdings, Peter Dixon, Peter Cameron-Webb and the Corporation of Lloyd's itself. It was not a bad opening gambit. But there were additional complications. If the Names failed to meet their liabilities by the end of July, they would fall foul of the Lloyd's ruling Council. Initially, the Council would have to find the money to honour the defaulting members' liabilities. If these turned out to be the £130 million estimated by Richard Beckett, then there would not be much left of Lloyd's central fund of £167 million which can be used for meeting liabilities. The Council would also be obliged to sue the Names who had refused to pay.

Ian Hay Davison

The man who found himself in the middle of this financial and legal tangle was Ian Hay Davison, the chief executive of Lloyd's. Davison took on the new job late in 1983 when the

278

Governor of the Bank of England, Gordon (now Lord)
Richardson, decided that a tough outsider should be put into
Lloyd's to try to prevent any more major scandals erupting
and tarnishing the reputation of a market that already
looked terribly vulnerable. Davison took on the job for
£120,000 a year. Financially, he was superbly well equipped
for the task: he was previously senior partner of the major
accountancy firm, Arthur Andersen & Co.

> I took it on from a sense of duty. I thought that if the City
> couldn't provide a chief executive then it didn't say
> much for the City. But I can't say I find it an attractive
> job. My presence is resented, although most of the
> underwriters are well-mannered.

Lloyd's is a self-regulating body and Davison's job was to
see that self-regulation worked. He began by upgrading the
calibre of Lloyd's professional staff by importing a number of
accountants, lawyers and civil servants. 'I think one has to
realize,' Davison said, 'that underwriters know nothing
about management' – a reference to the fact that Lloyd's
administration has always been in the hands of the underwriters. Davison was a tough, shrewd operator backed by an
administration largely of his own making. However, even
under Davison, who was not the most self-effacing of men, the
administration managed to make a £22 million accounting
error in Lloyd's 1985 accounts. While Davison made substantial strides in establishing a new regulatory framework, his
relationship with the new Chairman of Lloyd's, Peter Miller
(whose family had been in Lloyd's for something like six
generations), was unsatisfactory. One of the terms of
Davison's appointment as chief executive of Lloyd's was that
he should be totally independent. Miller, he thought, was a
threat to his independence and consequently he tendered his
resignation in November 1985 and left the job at the end of
February 1986. He was succeeded by Alan Lord, a former
Treasury mandarin and Managing Director of Dunlop
Holdings.

Fundamentally Davison's power ceased at the point where

irregularity and fraud occur – namely, in the Room where insurance is written and reinsurance disposed. There are just two factors here that matter: the competence of the underwriting and the probity of the underwriters. Names cannot expect to make profits every year. What they do have a right to expect, however, is that their agents, who make a profitable and undemanding living, should monitor the quality of the insurance that their syndicates are writing and that they should ask awkward questions when they appear necessary. There is no reason to suppose that, just because people are wealthy and can afford to become Names, their money should be left to the whims of the avaricious, fraudulent and negligent. Some of the underwriting of recent years had bordered on the criminally irresponsible.

On the question of probity, Lloyd's has dragged its feet for too long. Its disciplinary procedures are lengthy and tedious and need to be tightened and speeded up. Some of the worst excesses of the market, such as binding authorities, have virtually been dealt with. But the rule on 'baby' syndicates turned out to be a bad joke. Lloyd's ruled that a 'baby' syndicate could exist only if it had fifty members or more. By the time such a syndicate has been filled up with wives, family, mistresses and staff it would not only reach the required fifty quite comfortably but it would still exclude the hundreds and thousands who have a legitimate claim to better treatment. Furthermore, the excesses of fraudulent behaviour that have tarnished this market for so long have mostly gone unpunished. Lloyd's must share some of the blame for that; so, too, must the State's legal departments whose inertia now gives the impression that fraud pays handsomely. Lloyd's is now undergoing another government investigation into its regulatory arrangements, conducted by Sir Patrick Neill QC, the distinguished lawyer. Sir Patrick was no fireball when he was Chairman of the Council for the Securities Industry and even less so when he was Chairman of the Press Council. He is an Establishment figure, which is the last thing Lloyd's needs for an inquiry. Lloyd's is no longer a gentlemen's market and its members should not be treated as gentlemen.

INSURANCE COMPANIES

While Lloyd's is essentially a private insurance market financed and serviced by its members, there is a much larger market outside Lime Street, which encompasses much of what Lloyd's does, such as marine and general insurance, and a good deal that Lloyd's doesn't do, such as pension and life funds. Both markets compete against each other for a lot of business, but they also do business with each other – for example, in reinsurance.

The Names

There are some very big names involved and they are familiar to almost every adult in Britain. Not just the Prudential, which operates from a vast, red Victorian building in Holborn, but the Pearl, the Legal & General, the Phoenix, the Norwich Union, General Accident, the Royal and a powerful contingent from over the border such as Scottish Widows, Scottish Life and Scottish Amicable, all of whom keep a London presence but prefer to make their decisions in that fine city, Edinburgh. It is said, not without reason, that some of the shrewdest and best investment minds are to be found in Scotland.

What They Insure

But what do these famous companies insure? Bricks and mortar, for one thing. No one who takes out a mortgage is allowed to do so without insuring their property, be it a house or flat. It may seem an unnecessary incubus for someone who already has the cost of a mortgage to bear, but at least it provides security for the building society or bank that has put up the money. Then there are industrial buildings, factories, machinery, offices, house contents – almost anything of value is generally insured. Motor insurance is a mandatory necessity, a motorist can be prosecuted if he does not have it. Most companies that undertake it lose money. Some have tended to compound their losses through the innovative use of insuring motorists against loss of their no-claims bonuses. The premiums are minimal, but the claims are extravagant.

It is upon such simple and natural fears as these that the insurance industry has been built. Its profits arise from one simple calculation: that the premiums it receives exceed the claims it pays out. Of course, there are numerous factors involved in arriving at that desirable result. High-risk motorists pay higher premiums because their records show that they are more likely to have an accident. People who live in expensive parts of London pay bigger premiums for their contents insurance because they are more likely to be burgled. Householders who go to the trouble and expense of protecting their premises with alarm systems will probably have to pay less than the going rate.

Probabilities

Insurance companies are mines of information about probability – the probability of this or that happening, a tanker sinking during hostilities in the Arabian Gulf or the odds on a heavy smoker dying of cancer or heart disease. That is why they carry large complements of actuaries, particularly in the life offices, who are paid to make calculations about life expectancy, illness and risks of one kind or another. Being mathematically inclined, they also play an important part in the investment policies of these companies.

282

Life Policies

In its entirety, it is a tremendously large business. But the eye-catching part of it is the life assurance and pensions industry. Lives are *assured*, not insured, and life assurance takes a number of forms: a whole-life policy, for example, which means that premiums are paid continuously until the day the assured dies (it is designed to leave the family a lump sum); an endowment policy, which entitles the assured to receive a lump sum at a certain age; 'with profits' life policies, which entitle beneficiaries to a lump sum together with a share of the profits earned by the company and which are attributable to that class of assurance. There are also 'without profits' policies (premiums are cheaper) which give just a lump sum.

Annuities

But there are other classes of business in which the life offices are very active. There is the annuity business, by which people can buy an annuity for a fixed sum, which entitles them to a given annual payment for the rest of their lives. It can be immediate or deferred, in which case payment does not start until a named future date. Deferred annuities are the bulwark of self-employed pension plans. A self-employed person may contribute regularly over a number of years to a scheme that will provide him with a guaranteed pension when he comes to retire – or sometimes more than the guaranteed sum, depending on how his fund has performed. He can take either the full pension, or a lower one plus a cash benefit. He can apply that cash to buying more annuities or, if he has sufficient money, to spending it in some other way.

Pensions are Big Business

But it is the 'group pension' and pension-fund business that has grown by leaps and bounds over the years. Group-pension business is generally derived from smaller employers who entrust the management of their contributions to an insurance company that runs a group pension

fund of its own. Then there are the very big pension funds –
like British Coal and British Rail in the public sector and
Shell, ICI, GEC and Courtaulds in the private sector. Some
funds are self-administered – that is, run by the companies
themselves – and some are run by insurance companies,
merchant banks, stockbrokers and sometimes a combination of all three.

£153 billion – and rising

The size of these funds is enormous. In 1984 they totalled
£153 billion – £110 billion of that was attributable to the
main pension-fund business and £43 billion to group-
pension funds. Together, they are growing at the rate of £15
billion a year. Some of that represents new money coming
into the funds and some is capital gain from investments.
The figures are dauntingly large. So, too, is the size of the
insurance companies' involvement. According to Ron Artus,
the Group Chief Investment Manager of the Prudential, if
all the Pru's equity shareholding were spread evenly
throughout the market,

> We would have between 3 and 3½ per cent of every
> company quoted on the Stock Exchange. Therefore, our
> stake in those companies in which we do hold shares is
> often substantial and we are frequently the biggest
> shareholders.

The market value of the British Coal pension fund's holding in UK property in 1983 was £1,000 million with £220
million overseas. Those figures may seem enormous, yet
according to Hugh Jenkins, British Coal's Director General
of Investments, the amount the fund has been investing in
property in the UK has actually been declining:

> In 1977, 30 per cent of the fund was invested in
> property, but in 1983 it was only 17.7 per cent. In the
> seventies there was a great deal of activity in real
> estate, but with the build-up of competition and the
> growing number of funds involved, there has been a
> decline in yields to 3½ per cent for shops, 4½ per cent

284

for offices and about 7 per cent for industrial properties.
We have not bought any completed or let property in
the UK for four years.

Yet Postel (the Post Office and Telecommunications Pension
Fund) had 30 per cent in property in 1983 because it was 'a
hedge against inflation'. BP had 30 per cent (about $450
million) invested in UK property – 10.5 hectares of Mayfair,
the Brompton Road past Harrods and a great deal of Cardiff.
Legal & General, with £8 billion under management, had
more than £2 billion invested in real estate. The Pru has
been in property from the early days of the company. 'Even
where there's a property glut,' Ron Artus says, 'one's hopes
may be delayed, but property does not go away or go
bankrupt.'

What They Hold

This view is broadly reflected in the insurance companies'
and pension funds' holdings of assets. Property accounts for
about 18 per cent, government securities around 21 per cent
and company equities very nearly 50 per cent. What is clear
about these large investments is that they are not made in a
hurry and they are not sold quickly. When the Pru takes a
large stake in a company it does so because it means to stay
there for some time, even if – as sometimes happens – it has
to put pressure on management to improve its performance.
The insurance companies and pension funds have such large
amounts of new money, investment income and capital
gains flowing into their coffers each year that they are not
obliged to hop around from investment to investment like a
small man with a few hundred pounds looking for a 'snip'.
They are long-term investors. Because of the nature of pensions, they are never under pressure to make quick profits.

Size and Influence

They also have very heavy investment commitments, which
tend to limit the mobility of their capital. British Coal's
pension fund, for example, is often the biggest shareholder
in some companies, with holdings ranging from £15 to £20

million. 'You cannot easily dump shares of that size in the market,' Hugh Jenkins says.

> So we have to ride with the fortunes of the companies we invest in. That means we have to have some participation in those companies. I and the Managing Director of our securities section will meet company chairmen and directors perhaps once or twice a year. They let us know of any major changes and we give them our feedback on their ideas. If it's necessary, these occaions can be an opportunity to express concern about a company's affairs.

Is It Only Pensioners Who Matter?

However, it is the size of the assets that they are using, the great concentration of wealth they are disposing of, which has caused their left-wing critics to attack pension funds for not investing in the long-term recovery of British industry. The funds, so the left-wingers said, were much more interested in property. The argument presupposes that British industry could recover in the long term if it received massive injections of capital from the investing institutions and that that is the only factor delaying the recovery. It takes no account of the quality of management, trade-union practices in the work place or whether those companies who could be identified as being in need of capital are producing the right products. The problem could be settled, so the argument goes, if a proportion of the funds' assets were placed in a National Investment Bank which could direct the money to where it was most needed. The economic wisdom of such a bank, assuming the wisdom was available (a dubious proposition, to say the least), would identify areas of need, expansion and competition.

The Counter-Argument

The pension funds argue – and will have to go on arguing while a left wing exists – that their duty lies to their pensioners and policy-holders. To debate that proposition would be sterile since that is the sole purpose of pension funds – to provide pensions. Moreover, there does not seem to have been any shortage of capital for those who need it. The Wilson Committee found that to be the case. Companies with good track records have been able to raise money from the market. The inhibiting factor has been that many companies did not want to do so because they lacked confidence in themselves. 'The responsiveness of industry to the available money has not been great,' says the Pru's Artus.

> This is because the UK's underlying competitive weakness in the marketplace had led to cautiousness in many companies about expansion. But a company with an established pattern of long-term growth will not usually have too much difficulty in raising funds.

Movement of Capital Overseas

Since the abolition of exchange controls in October 1979 the pension funds have been able to move their capital freely overseas, thereby giving rise to the accusation that they are taking money out of the country at the expense of British industry by depressing levels of physical investment, output and employment, while strengthening rival industries and undermining Britain's efforts to meet international competition. Artus believes that the linkage between institutions investing in industrial securities and industrial companies then investing in plant and equipment is a tenuous one:

> Even if institutional investors were to concentrate on the primary, or new-issue, markets, increased investment is unlikely to be translated into increased physical investment on any significant scale. As the Wilson Committee found – and as business surveys have continued to confirm – what is holding back industrial investment is not so much a shortage of finance as a shortage of attractive investment opportunities.

Pension funds are so sensitive to the charge of starving British industry of cash that some of them have done something about it. British Coal's fund has notionally committed

15 per cent of its cash flow to project funding for quoted and unquoted companies, but this target has never been reached and it has never exceeded £30 million in any year. Hugh Jenkins maintains that it underlines the fact that capital is freely available. In 1975, he started a scheme for funding new projects in companies in which the fund had large stakes. Part of the risk was borne by the fund and the idea was that it should take a percentage of the through-put, rather like a royalty payment: 'Because we take a long-term view, it was as good a risk as long-dated gilts.'

Unquoted Companies

The Prudential – together with the Midland Bank and the British Gas pension fund – set up Moracrest to look at investment opportunites in smaller, unquoted companies. It was not a resounding success. Artus says:

> One found that that one was looking at a relatively small number of proposals which hawked themselves around the various interested bodies. Money did not go out all that fast and the scope and scale of the operation never expanded much. We did not get involved in new technology fields. We found that investments were just not coming forward. I would say that Moracrest has had an unexciting but acceptable track record.

With Prutech, the Prudential did tackle new technology. The potential for above-average rates of return had been reduced in other industries and the company recognized that the risk–reward ratios for entering promising fields was favourable – if it could only learn how to do it properly. Artus again:

> There have been the inevitable trials and tribul-ations, but with hope of eventual reward. I would say that we are on course, but there are problems – as we expected.

There is nothing about any of these modest attempts in the venture-capital field to suggest that the pension funds are indifferent to investment in British industry. Many of them are heavily involved in the bright, new companies that emerge into the light of day on the Unlisted Securities Market. But it is extremely difficult for them to raise the veil that covers small unquoted companies and that could well conceal some hidden gems. In the first place, insurance companies do not have the resources for that kind of work. Second, hidden gems do not remain concealed for very long: they come to market, become quoted and, if all goes well, make their proprietors a lot of money.

Perhaps their energies could be more usefully devoted to doing something to improve the quality of British management. It is a contentious area. Some companies, like the Pru, and some pension funds, like the Post Office Superannuation Fund and British Coal, have from time to time told companies in which they have large investments to improve their performance. Some observers – and there are pension funds among them – do not regard this as a function of the pension-fund industry. It is argued that it does not have the skills to tell companies what to do; the insurance companies are supposed to know about investment, not about management. That is a gross over-simplification. There is not an abundance of first-class managers in Britain, but most people have a good idea where they are. It is merely a question of tempting them, with the right offer, into special company situations where their skills can be put to work.

A Bigger Role

But the pension funds have always been conservative. They were hostile to the government's proposals for portable and personal pensions. They do not like change and their natural disposition is to oppose it. When it comes to improving the performance of British management, and hence the performance of their own investments, they are the only people who have the money to do it. The expertise can be easily acquired.

THE BIG BANG

Sir Gordon Borrie is the mild-mannered but hard-headed
Director General of the Office of Fair Trading. It is
primarily a consumer organization but its remit extends
well beyond the role of organizations such as the National
Consumer Council. The OFT can take people to court, call
for changes in the law and exert considerable pressure on
organizations and companies to alter their trading practices so that they are fair and competitive. But the
distinction between fairness and competition is often blur-
red and in practice they frequently overlap. The law, for
example, is a profession riddled with uncompetitive and
restrictive practices. Solicitors cannot practise advocacy in
the higher courts and barristers cannot do the work of
solicitors. It is a single-capacity system, each capacity
jealously guarded by its practitioners. But it is arguable
whether it benefits a litigant, who pays two bills and talks
to two separate entities engaged in the same enterprise. If
the solicitor prepares the brief, why should he not be able
to argue it in court as well? He is not allowed to compete
with a barrister even though he may be able to do the job
equally well for a lower price. It is not strictly fair to the

client because the system binds him to the conventions of historical practice.

Fixed Commissions

Not even Borrie could crack that one, the law is too well entrenched. But commercial practices are a different matter. Borrie identified in the Stock Exchange a whole raft of restrictive practices, embodied in its immensely complex rule book, which militated against investors' interests. Minimum commissions were just one example: there was no earthly reason why investors, whether private or institutional, should pay fixed commissions for the equities or gilts they bought. Resale price maintenance in the retail market had been abandoned long ago, but here was a major institution clinging rigidly to an out-dated notion that it was desirable. It was not merely restrictive, it was uncompetitive in the sense that it did not allow brokers to compete against each other by offering variable commissions and, by definition, did not enable investors to seek out the best deals on offer.

Single Capacity

That was one point. The separation between broker and jobber was another. The system of single capacity, which was enshrined just before World War I, ensured that only a broker could deal with a jobber. The broker, in turn, acted for the investor, trying to secure the best price he could from the jobber and being paid by his client in the form of fixed commission. Single capacity, so the Stock Exchange thought, protected the investor from rigged prices. The clear separation of functions, with the jobbers making markets in equities and gilts and the brokers acting for clients without fear or favour, kept the market sanitized and above suspicion. There were no conflicts of interest, no cosy deals between jobbers and brokers that were not in the interests of the investor.

But the jobbing system was already under strain. The number of jobbers had declined, reducing competition. Some stocks were dealt in by only one jobber. Occasionally, two jobbers ran their business together as a 'joint book' and sometimes they agreed on the 'spread' – the difference between the buying and selling price. Large institutional deals did not help the jobbers either. Brokers often bypassed jobbers, matching big institutional sellers with buyers ('put-throughs'). Foreign banks and brokers had also skirted round jobbers in the search for business. Although jobbers had always argued that they did not suffer from a shortage of liquidity (capital to make markets in a wide variety of equities and gilts), they had resorted to the money market through the Exchange's money brokers for longer periods of borrowing than they cared to admit. The Americans abandoned single capacity in 1975. Firms made markets in equities and also dealt for clients, combining the dual roles of broker and jobber. As a result, prices were supposed to be more competitive.

Xenophobia

There was one restrictive practice, however, that was shamelessly protective of Stock Exchange members. It was the rule that prevented overseas brokers from becoming members. It excluded the big players of Wall Street – Goldman Sachs, Salomon Brothers, Merrill Lynch, Morgan Stanley – from dealing on the Stock Exchange floor and thereby creating a more competitive environment. The Americans are mammoths by comparison with English firms, greedy competitors with bottomless pockets who would not have been welcomed by the Old Broad Street community snugly cocooned in its rule book. The rule simply said that no outsider could buy more than 29.9 per cent of any British broker or jobber. And that went for British banks as well or any financial institution that wanted to break into the Stock Exchange.

Rule books are by definition restrictive. Once an institution creates barriers to membership, dictates codes of dealing, rates of commission and a host of other practices, it can be accused freely of anti-competitive practices that are not in the interest of the investor or consumer. That was certainly how Borrie and the OFT saw the Stock Exchange rule book. It was clearly a case for the Restrictive Practices Court – a case, incidentally, that would have established precedents for other kinds of commercial practice. But, above all, it was a case that tackled head on one of the City's most hallowed institutions. It was a piece of bold effrontery that was much too near the knuckle for the Stock Exchange's comfort. It had to be fought.

The Government's Deal with the Exchange

The out-of-court costs of the case had already reached around £1 million when relief came to the Stock Exchange in the shape of Cecil Parkinson, then the Scretary of State for Trade. One day in June 1983 Borrie was visited by officials from Parkinson's department who told him that the government had decided to offer the Stock Exchange a deal. Parkinson confirmed the decision to Borrie a few days later. The Director General was taken aback, in his own words 'stunned'. It was not the fact that a plum had been snatched from him at the last moment. What worried him was the nature of the deal.

He was not the only one: every City commentator expressed alarm at a lost opportunity to shake up Old Broad Street. The supposition already existed that the Stock Exchange deserved what it got from the OFT and that the Restrictive Practices Court was the place to do it. The government was condemned on two counts: it lacked courage; and the whole arrangement stank of a capitalist conspiracy. In other words, the can of worms, if there was one, was to remain firmly shut.

Pressure for Reform

The criticisms turned out to be wholly groundless. The government proved to be a good deal more pragmatic than people gave it credit for. The 'deal' was a simple one: in return for blocking the OFT case, the government expected the Stock Exchange to reform itself. It made it clear that the

Exchange should bring forward reforms abolishing the minimum commission structure which ruled out price competition between stockbrokers. And it expected the Exchange to make it easier for outsiders to become members of the Old Broad Street club. On the question of single capacity, Cecil Parkinson remained agnostic. 'It is by no means clear whether you can abolish minimum commissions and keep the current single capacity system,' he said. 'There are differing views. I do not know the answer yet and neither does the Stock Exchange.' In fact, all member firms will be able to operate in single or dual capacity from the date of the Big Bang on 27 October 1986. If anyone believed that there was a capitalist conspiracy it was obvious that the government was not part of it.

The effect of the government's decision was to start the ball rolling a good deal more quickly than if the case had gone through the cumbersome procedure of the Restrictive Practices Court. The Stock Exchange was faced with a government insisting on reform and which said that it would not hesitate to intervene if there was deadlock or the pace of reform was too slow. It was a *fait accompli* in all but name. For Sir Nicholas Goodison, the Exchange's Chairman, and his Council, the problem was to persuade members of the importance of speed and the structural changes in the market that were likely to be involved. The abolition of minimum commissions, in theory set for the Big Bang, would mean radical changes in the financial viability of all firms, particularly those which were not in the big league.

How the Bank of England Saw the New Market

Whatever the fears of brokers and jobbers were, and they had much to be fearful of, the pressure for change was unremitting and no one had given much thought to the future structure of the market and how it was likely to affect firms and individuals. The Bank of England, on the other hand, had thought about it a great deal. Its main concern was that the Stock Exchange had been losing a lot of business to other international markets, particularly Wall

Street. A prime City market, technically proficient and admired for its skills, had been unable to stop the haemorrhage of business abroad. The amount of outward portfolio investment in the five years to 1984 (that is, money from Britain invested overseas) had amounted to around £20 billion, of which only 5 per cent had gone through British intermediaries; the lion's share was handled by overseas brokers and investment banks. At the end of 1984, 24 per cent of ICI equity was held in New York and it enjoyed four times the turnover of the remaining 76 per cent held in the United Kingdom. The Bank saw the shake-up as an opportunity to revitalize the Stock Exchange and make London a prominent securities market. Another opportunity might not occur.

The logical way to do that was to create much larger financial units, or conglomerates, which would not only be substantially bigger than the major broking and jobbing firms, but which would have a wider spread of financially related services. The Bank actively sold and promoted the idea, urging brokers to merge with clearing banks, merchant banks and any relevant institutions that would give the new conglomerates a firm capital base. It was promoted, of course, on two broad assumptions: that single capacity would disappear and that the Stock Exchange would be obliged eventually to open its doors to outsiders. The disappearance of single capacity would involve broking firms in the dual roles of making markets in equities and gilts as well as continuing their traditional business of acting for institutional and private clients. Market making requires substantial amounts of capital. Making a 'book' in large parcels of shares, just as jobbers do, cannot be done without adequate capital resources. It would be a new role for stockbrokers who, while profitable, have never had large reserves. The source of this money would be the banking institutions, clearers or merchant banks, which would provide the financial muscle. Size, too, was important. Come the day when the 'Thundering Herd', in the shape of Merrill Lynch, came stampeding through the doors of the Stock

Exchange, then the new conglomerates would be big enough
to defend their pitches in the O.K. Corral.

On the Way to the Altar

With change an established fact, and with the Bank of
England actively promoting conglomeration, it was not surprising that there were a series of shot-gun engagements.
Some brokers were worried that if they did not find a
suitable partner quickly they would be left out in the cold in
the rush to get engaged. By August 1984, only fourteen
months after the government reached its deal with the
Stock Exchange, twelve brokers – the most prominent of
whom were Grieveson Grant, W. Greenwell, De Zoete &
Bevan and Rowe & Pitman – had pledged themselves to a
diversity of partners, ranging from the merchant bankers
Hill Samuel, Samuel Montagu and Kleinwort Benson to
Barclays, NatWest and the American giants, Citicorp and
American Express. Under Stock Exchange rules, of course,
none of the banks could buy more than 29.9 per cent of any
of these brokers. Consummation, total merger, could be
achieved only when the Stock Exchange scrapped its rule on
membership. Until then, everyone would have to live in sin.
The Exchange later agreed a date, 1 March 1986, when
everyone could merge totally. Five weeks later Citicorp
completed its acquisition of Scrimgeour Vickers (the merged
entity of stockbrokers Scrimgeour Kemp-Gee and Vickers
Da Costa) which became a wholly owned subsidiary of
Citicorp Investment Bank. Shearson Lehman, itself a subsidiary of American Express, took total control of L. Messel,
the 113-year-old London stockbroker. Samuel Montagu, the
merchant bank subsidiary of the Midland Bank, took over
the whole of W. Greenwell to become Greenwell Montagu.
Merchant bankers Kleinwort Benson stumped up the
balance of £44 million, plus £10 million of working capital,
for Grieveson Grant, the brokers. The new company became
Kleinwort Grieveson. And the planned merger of the merchant bank S. G. Warburg, the stockbrokers Rowe & Pitman and Mullens & Co., together with the jobbers Akroyd &

Smithers, was completed to form Mercury International Group.

Golden Handcuffs

What, precisely, did the first wave of brokers think they had achieved? They had done a deal, of course, which is what stockbroking is all about. Some of the deals were so success-ful in financial terms that many partners were substantially richer than they could ever hope to have been had they continued to the end of their working lives as their old, unconglomerated selves. Indeed, there were critics who argued that the banks in some instances had paid dowries that were well over the odds. But the banks were not that easily taken in: many of the arrangements were designed to ensure that partners who held the largest chunks of equity in their firms would not take their money and run. While the initial valuations of the big brokers varied between £40 and £55 million, delivering to some partners a bonus of several million, the broking firms had their hands tied financially. There was no question of dishing out large cheques to partners when consummation occurred. Most of the deals were done by converting the broking firms' equity into the equity of the buying firm. This would then stand at a discount for five years or so, thus discouraging the part-ners from selling before their 'golden handcuffs' were unlocked. The mix of deals between brokers and bankers was both complicated and varied and it was impossible to find a single senior partner who did not claim that his was the best.

Big Money and Golden Hellos

In terms of morale, however, things were much less happy. For broking partners, the people who held the equity, it would be simple enough at some stage to convert their 'paper' into hard cash. But for those at the level just below them, what became known as the 'marzipan set', and where no one held any equity, there were bound to be feelings of envy and resentment. They had literally been deprived by a year or two of the substantial financial benefits enjoyed by their seniors. But the market was quick to compensate them. The hunger for good people with market-making skills (the jobber and his book) and for brokers with specialist expertise meant that many conglomerates couldn't afford not to buy the available talent that was around. Large cheques were written simply to persuade people to change firms, often at double their old salary. 'Golden hellos' of £100,000, and sometimes much more, were changing hands like so much confetti. Mrs Thatcher, for once in tune with the Labour Party, expressed her distaste for the large sums that were being paid. By the end of 1985 it was estimated that at least twenty people were receiving salaries, commissions and bonuses of £1 million each. The impetus for higher remuneration went through every level of the market. Analysts, some not particularly good, were crossing the road for salaries of £100,000 to £120,000. Eurobond dealers in their mid-twenties were commanding pay packets of £60,000 to £100,000. The Big Bang was exploding beneficially in everyone's pockets well before the magic day, 27 October 1986, had arrived.

Alarmed by the new, high level of remuneration City types were getting, people forgot two important things: competition will be fierce after the Big Bang and the price of many financial services will fall. Firms will need to prune their costs, not increase them. They will be able to afford high salaries only if business expands; otherwise some of them will go bust. While it is true to say that City pay is coming more into line with Wall Street – abetted by Wall Street firms and banks in the City that don't blink at handing out large sums – it is equally true that City men enjoy many perks that go along with their salaries: generous pension and redundancy provisions, company cars and sick-pay and health schemes. These add enormously to firms' overheads. Wall Streeters get fewer of these frills and employers are merciless on those who don't bring home the bacon; they are on the street within hours without any severance pay. If City firms used the same rigorous standards they would benefit in two ways: they would have a better chance of surviving a downturn in business and they would attract only those people who were prepared to take a risk – far fewer than those who at present enjoy a comfortable, secure existence. In such circumstances City pay might be even bigger than it is now, but with reward more closely matched by risk there would not be a need to justify what appear to be excessively large remuneration packages. It would also help to fill a gap in the industrial market for young executives. Many able graduates head for the City after leaving university, attracted by rewards that industry cannot hope to match.

There was another thorny issue, again concerned with money. It was how to remunerate a man of senior-partner status, who was earning perhaps £500,000 a year in his broking firm, when a chairman of a bank was getting well under half that figure. Bankers, when I spoke to them, admitted that it was not only a problem; they had no intention of being paid less than their broking counterparts. They argued, pragmatically enough, that when some partners were being made millionaires in cash, shares or a mixture of both, having their earnings cut in half would be no hardship in the twilight of their working years. One chairman told me that the disparities in earnings between brokers and bankers was an opportunity to increase the most important peoples' earnings to a level more commensurate with remuneration on Wall Street. Apart from these important financial disparities, there were also cultural differences between the broking and banking community. One senior partner said that the bank with whom he had merged was a 'bureaucracy', thus illustrating the gulf between the broking community's entrepreneurial instincts and preferences and the formalized structure of the banking system, which has its balance sheets and shareholders to worry about.

Liquidity and Competition

No doubt the differences in culture, earnings and outlook will be ironed out once the initial suspicions engendered among

people who act and think differently have been broken down
because of the urgency of corporate strategy and endeavour.
If they are not, by the time of the Big Bang, then the whole
idea of conglomeration will have failed dismally and the
City will have demonstrated a serious flaw quite alien to its
psychology – that self-interest, the bond common to everyone working in the Square Mile, has come apart at the
seams. If that does not happen, what matters most is
whether these fledgling conglomerates will emerge from the
nest after the Big Bang fully feathered and capable of sustained flight. The cult words in the British market are
'liquidity' and 'capitalization'. They stand for the same
thing: money, and in the present context they mean sufficient money for firms to make markets in gilts and equities
without resorting to borrowing. Capital is crucial. The
assumption was that when a broker merged with a merchant bank the bank's capital would be available for
market-making. It is not the availability that is questionable (if it were, there would be no point in mergers at all), it
is the *amount* of capital available and whether it is sufficient. Merchant banks are admired for many things, but
their capital resources are limited: under-capitalization, for
example, is endemic in those banks where family interests
still remain dominant. The gain in liquidity in some of the
new groupings could well be insufficient to cope with the
competitive pressures of making markets.

If that is put into the context of the brave new world after
1986, problems begin to arise. If the American firms decide
to take the British market seriously (and the evidence is
that they are, to judge by the money they're spending on
dealing rooms and offices), they could cause serious distress
to under-capitalized domestic conglomerates. In 1985, for
example, Salomon Brothers made net profits of $557 mil-
lion, Merrill Lynch $224 million and Morgan Stanley $106
million. They probably doubled the aggregated profits of
brokers, jobbers and merchant banks in the UK in the same
year. The two largest British merchant banks, Kleinwort
Benson and Warburg, netted $53 million and $35 million

respectively. Once the American giants start playing seriously in the British market the competition will be formidable. One broker made this analogy:

> In London we've been playing cricket for centuries. When the Big Bang comes we're going to be asked to play baseball, which is difficult enough to cope with anyway. But our first match will be against the world champions.

He did not include the Japanese in his analogy. Nomura (net profits in 1985 of $398 million, nearly double those of Merrill Lynch) is already a Stock Exchange member and it cannot be long before it will be joined by other big players from Tokyo once 'reciprocity' (the right of British market makers to join the Tokyo exchange and vice versa) has been agreed between Britain and Japan.

Against that kind of competition, only the largest and best capitalized of the British conglomerates would be likely to survive. At a guess, these would include James Capel, with the enormous liquidity of the Hong Kong and Shanghai Banking Corporation behind it; de Zoete & Bevan and Wedd Durlacher (one of the two top jobbers), backed by Barclays Merchant Bank; Scrimgeour Vickers, supported by the American banking giant, Citicorp; Phillips & Drew, backed by the Union Bank of Switzerland, the biggest of the Swiss banks with assets of nearly £40 billion; Laurie, Milbank and Simon & Coates, supported by Chase Manhattan, the third largest bank in the US; Hoare Govett, in which Security Pacific held 29.9 per cent – a deal that was at least a year ahead of the rest of the market; Bisgood Bishop, the jobbers, taken over by NatWest; and a curious relationship between Deutsche Bank, West Germany's largest bank and the merchant bankers Morgan Grenfell. Deutsche took just 5 per cent of Morgan, which in turn paid £31 million for Pinchin Denny, the jobbers, and Pember & Boyle, the gilts brokers.

Some of these conglomerations have more significance than others in that a few of the banks made it clear from the beginning that they were prepared to compete at pretty well any level. Union Bank of Switzerland, for example, said that sufficient lines of credit would be made available to Phillips & Drew so that it could 'grow and participate in new markets'. Initial projections suggested that P. & D. would need capital in excess of £40 million. Chase Manhattan (Laurie, Milbank and Simon & Coates) said that it would put up whatever capital its UK securities venture needed. These seem to be the only public pronouncements about the intentions of bankers in relation to their new but expensive fiancées. One suspects that there was a good deal of caution about, the traditional reticence of banking men whose prudential instincts would not allow them to make a commitment in advance of the way the market was likely to behave. But their new partners will need capital, a lot of it, and they will need even more should the Americans come plunging into the market, greedy for business and prepared to cut prices to the bone. All the banks, except the merchant banks, in these new conglomerates have large amounts of capital, but the real question is how much of it they are prepared to put at risk once international competition begins to hot up. The Bank of England has probably underestimated the strength of that competition and the market has probably underestimated the size of conglomerates needed to compete effectively. It is quite likely that if American competition really begins to bite the British conglomerates will have to merge into much larger units.

Nor were the early mergers completely thought through. While some banks bought early stakes in brokers, they did not seem to give a thought to buying jobbers – a crucial consideration if a conglomerate is to become a fully formed market maker; jobbers know how to make books in equities, something brokers are ignorant of. Warburg did not make that mistake; it quickly acquired Akroyd & Smithers. Barclays Bank, too, ensured that it was covered by buying Wedd Durlacher. But there were plenty of big players who were left with a gap in their armoury – among them Hong Kong and Shanghai who, though they had a valuable investment in James Capel, were left without a jobber. So, too, were

Kleinwort Benson who picked up Grieveson Grant, but there was no jobber to accompany the deal. Kleinwort solved the problem by poaching but at enormous cost. In July 1985 they lured eight senior men away from Wedd Durlacher who by then were cosily ensconced with Barclays and de Zoete & Bevan. It's thought that the Wedd eight moved for a transfer fee of £1 million and annual salaries totalling more than £2 million. Wedd had already made up forty people to partner level to avoid defections, having seen the danger when they lost a senior man to Merrill Lynch, the American giants, as well as their entire European market-making staff, which crossed the road to Savory Milln's international dealership. This is bound to be a continuing process as conglomerates try to beef up their market making. It will be enriching for those who are being courted, but increasingly expensive for those who are the courtiers.

Primary Dealerships

When this major City revolution began, the air was full of talk about protecting the small investor. No one doubted that the major institutions, such as the insurance companies, could not look after themselves; the concern was for the private client who was likely to prove vulnerable in a new environment where commissions were no longer fixed but negotiable. His importance will be enhanced because the new market will be divided into two distinct parts. The first is what the Bank of England calls primary dealerships in gilts. To become primary dealers, the conglomerates had to 'dedicate' capital – a lot of it – to separate dealing subsidiaries. The Bank of England eventually awarded twenty-nine primary dealerships (the number quickly dropped to twenty-eight) and all the big players were included. Their aggregate capital was around £600 million. None of them expected to make a profit because there were too many of them. One senior partner, one of the most experienced men in gilts, said: 'I think we only did it for the prestige. Certainly there won't be any money in it.' A very different story from the palmy days when the top gilts brokers could always

306

be sure of a handsome return. It is very likely that this dedicated market, designed by the Bank to protect government funding, will end up with ten or a dozen dealerships at most. Prominent among those awarded dealerships were a muscular American contingent: Goldman Sachs, Shearson Lehman/American Express, Prudential-Bache, Salomon Brothers and Merrill Lynch, which is already a broking member of the Stock Exchange. These Americans will no doubt join the Stock Exchange a few weeks before the Big Bang.

Abuses

The second source of Stock Exchange activity is the equity market, which is open, of course, to institutional and private investors. But if market makers become less profitable in gilts they will not only want more private clients, they will want to make more profit out of them – a legitimate enough aspiration, but one that could lead to abuses.

The institutional investors can be expected to look after themselves (if they can't, there is not much to be said for their expertise), but the private investor is a different animal. He has no investment advisers (except his broker); his knowledge of market practice is limited and he cannot be expected to know – unless he is a semi-professional – what constitutes a good price to the nearest couple of pence. By the time of the Big Bang the Stock Exchange will have in place a piece of electronic equipment known as SEAQ (Stock Exchange Automated Quotation System) which, the Exchange believes, will prevent an abuse that everyone fears: a broker rigging prices against his private clients. The core of SEAQ is composed of two screens, Level 1 and Level 2. Level 1 will show the best bid and offer price for any particular security and the name of the market maker. Level 2 will show all bid and offer prices, with the keenest ones highlighted. Due to its cost, SEAQ will be limited to members of the Stock Exchange and the institutions. The private client, therefore, will not be privy to this information and will be dependent solely on his broker to get him the best prices. And that is where the snag lies: the client will have no way of knowing whether that has happened or whether his broker has adjusted prices to suit his own pocket. If, for example, a client buys 10,000 shares at 201 pence each – when the sharpest price was 199 pence – the client will have lost £200 and the broker will have gained by the same amount.

Under SEAQ, the Stock Exchange proposes that no such thing will happen. Every bargain made between broker and client will be time-stamped. By looking at the *Stock Exchange Official List* the client will be able to check the price he paid against the price of the security that was quoted in the market at approximately that time. This makes the assumption that investors are diligent enough to get hold of the *Official List* and do the detective work. Most of them are not. The Exchange's surveillance people, however, will also be doing 'audit trails' on specimen contracts and if they find that a broker has been guilty of rigging prices he will be out on the street. The penalty should be a sufficient deterrent to malpractice, but markets are ingenious by nature and can be extraordinarily innovative if there's money to be made. To be fair to the Stock Exchange, its claims to fair pricing can be tested only after the Big Bang when the system is up and running.

For private clients, however, there is one Stock Exchange innovation that could save them much time, money and trouble. Within a year of the Big Bang, the Exchange will introduce a system called the SEAQ automatic execution facility (SAEF). Forty per cent of the Exchange's bargains are for orders of 1,000 shares or less. The execution system will enable a broker, or a share shop in the high street, to punch in an order for up to 1,000 shares on a simple terminal. The system will then hunt through SEAQ for the best price, execute the order and pass the details to Talisman, which will arrange for the share certificate to be sent to the client through the Company Registrar. The dealer later receives a computerized confirmation of the bargain and the market maker receives confirmation of the execution. The trade is also published on SEAQ screens and passed to the Exchange's surveillance computer. It will effectively stop the broker, or agent, from fiddling the price. It is also faster and cheaper than dealing outside the system. In time, the system will be extended to orders of up to 5,000 shares, which account for 80 per cent of the Exchange's transactions.

Commission

But what the private client will have to face, even when such execution systems are in place, is a jungle of commissions and supplementary charges. As the Exchange is pledged to abolish minimum or fixed commissions and make them all negotiable, clients will be obliged to use the telephone extensively while they shop around brokers to find one charging the least commission or not making supplementary charges for items like 'research'. It is not a problem for the institutions, which tend to buy shares in large parcels and have consequently been accustomed to negotiating prices and commissions. That practice will continue. But the small man will have to be very diligent indeed if he is to minimize the dealing costs of buying and selling shares. Nor is life likely to be any simpler if, and when, the market moves to a system of 'net prices' where the share price and the commission will be wrapped into one price.

The Independent Broker

The private client may, in fact, be better off using a broker who is an agent and not a principal as well. Much depends on what happens to those brokers who are not part of the big conglomerates. No one seems to doubt that the medium-sized brokers will disappear from the scene: they never had the capital to become primary dealers in gilts and they do not have enough private or institutional clients to keep them in business. However, small brokers in the provinces – and some in London – are totally dependent on private clients and have built up client loyalties that will not be that easy for the big conglomerates to break. Many investors prefer personal advice and contact to the discipline and impersonality the big brokers have tended to impose on their private clients. This gives the small broker an advantage, but it is probably one that will have to be shored up by a range of services that most of them do not offer at the moment.

Research is one of them. Its cost is punitive, but that need not prevent groups of small brokers funding some kind of central research service that they can all use. Rapid portfolio valuation is another. It is dependent on computer support, which is not to be found in most small brokers. But at least one institution has suggested to small brokers that it will provide them with an on-line computer service for such things as portfolio valuations. With that kind of back-up, small broker services may turn out to be viable and profitable. The private client will have to pay, of course, either through a commission system or perhaps a flat fee, but at least he will know that he is getting a personal service without the risks attendant on dealing with big market makers.

There is also another problem concerning the Big Bang – potentially more intractable than that of the private client. The government realized it when it set up the Securities and Investments Board in 1985 for the purpose of investor protection at all levels, whether private or institutional. While market makers may theoretically be confined to buying and selling securities, they will also be part of a conglomerate which has other functions: managing and investing funds belonging to pension funds as well as their own investment companies. This role immediately produces a conflict of interest in the sense that a market maker, holding shares on its own account and anxious to make a profit from them, may try to influence the decisions of an investment company within the same conglomerate. In simple terms, a market maker may attempt to sell shares to its investment arm, knowing that the deal looks good in its own books (e.g. selling shares for more than their market worth) while it is detrimental to shareholders in the investment company.

The government recognized the problem, but had no answer to it. The market makers acknowledged the problem, but in the end assumed that their own probity was the safeguard. It will probably be the most difficult area of investor protection that the Securities and Investments Board has to supervise.

Regulation

The SIB entered 1986 with a batch of rules to which it has been adding ever since; it will continue to do so as different market practices begin to emerge after the Big Bang. Clustered around the SIB are a number of self-regulatory organizations (SROs), chief of which is the Stock Exchange itself, which are responsible for different areas of the market. The government's White Paper of January 1985 envisaged that the SIB would recognize these SROs and have authority over their rules and practices. The SROs would have to show their ability to regulate the admission and conduct of their members and would also have to demonstrate that their rules were equivalent in standard to those of the SIB itself. The government saw this arrangement as 'self-regulation within a statutory framework' but reserved the right to get rid of the Board if it ceased to conform to the legislation's criteria – another way of saying that if self-regulation did not work then there would have to be statutory regulation, a view taken by a growing body of market practitioners which at one time thought the idea of government control over the market was unthinkable. It can fairly be assumed that the market needs only one major scandal to show that self-regulation is unworkable and that there has to be a statutory alternative.

The Exchange Tries to Keep Total Control

One effect of the Big Bang has been to concentrate the Stock Exchange's mind on trying to ensure that every market comes within its aegis, that it does not lose control of its function as a central market. There was one market, in particular, which concerned it: it was the one that traded in international securities. This accounted for 20 to 30 per cent of the Exchange's total turnover, but trading took place outside the Exchange. It was represented by the International Securities Regulatory Organization (ISRO), whose members were most of the leading banks and investment houses. It encompassed the huge Eurobond market and all the leading international securities. International securities are shares in which there is an active liquid market in a country other than their own. Beecham, Glaxo, ICI and British Telecom are typical British examples of international securities.

In the spring of 1986 ISRO and the Stock Exchange had virtually reached agreement on the formation of a recognized investment exchange to govern trading in these securities and there was little reason why one should not be set up. The two bodies were also considering a merger of the Stock Exchange and ISRO into a single self-regulatory organization that would govern their combined areas of activity.

The Third Market

The Stock Exchange also staked its claim to control over the unofficial, over-the-counter market (OTC) in shares of small unlisted companies. The OTC was operated by independent firms, which, with one exception, were not members of the Stock Exchange. They were, however, licensed to deal in securities and their regulatory body was the National Association of Security Dealers and Investment Managers (NASDIM) which later merged with another SRO. A few years earlier the Stock Exchange would not have countenanced recognition of the OTC market. Some of the dealers on the OTC were 'beyond the pale'. They dealt in highly speculative companies – including dubious North American stocks – and their settlement 'systems' (if they could be called that) were ramshackle. There were one or two that NASDIM refused to recognize – including Harvard Securities, the largest of the OTC traders.

By creating a third market, the Stock Exchange acted

with a good deal of guile. It argued that there was a place for
very small unlisted companies, even for those who had as
little as one year's financial record. (The Unlisted Securities
Market requires three years.) But if these companies were
to be brought into the third market they would have to be
sponsored by a broker who was a member of the Stock
Exchange. That did not exclude OTC traders, which would
be welcomed as members provided they could put up the
money for membership (as little as £10,000 at the bottom
end) and provided they passed the test of being 'fit and
proper' people to conduct investment business – a standard
laid down by the Securities and Investment Board. There
were, of course, one or two small snags – such as the rule
that to be dealers in the Exchange people had to pass the
Stock Exchange's examinations. That, of course, was not
insurmountable: OTC traders could easily buy people who
were already members of the Exchange if, and it was a
pretty large if, they were prepared to move from established
firms. The 'fit and proper' test, however, depended on value
judgements used by the Exchange to decide who should be
admitted, a much more subtle yardstick not unlike the system of blackballing used by London clubs. With adroit application of this test, the Stock Exchange will no doubt find
good reasons for excluding some OTC traders.

However, the attraction of a third market for OTC traders
is obvious: it will give both a higher profile to small companies and it should increase trading volumes in their
shares. Those, in turn, should enlarge the turnover and
profits of OTC traders. It is unlikely, however, to eliminate
the OTC market altogether. There will be some traders who
will not want to upgrade themselves to the third market,
either because they cannot or because they don't want to.

Opening Hours

In April 1986 the Stock Exchange took the decision to open
its doors for trading at 9 a.m. instead of the traditional time
of 9.30 a.m. Much of the pressure for earlier opening came
from the London International Financial Futures

313

Exchange, which found that it was missing out on a good deal of gilt-edged business that was being done with Europe and the Far East before 9.30 a.m. LIFFE had held back from opening its gilts contracts before that time because the Exchange was not officially open. Had LIFFE taken the decision unilaterally it would have been unpopular with the Stock Exchange, and probably with the Bank of England, because it could have accelerated a move away from trading through the Stock Exchange floor. It was yet another example of the Exchange's and the Bank of England's anxiety to keep Old Broad Street as the central market. So the Exchange decided to open the entire London trading floor for gilts, equities and options from 9 a.m., beginning on 28 April 1986.

The Exchange's grip on the market, however, is never likely to be total. In the first place, trading in gilts and equities has always taken place off the floor at any time after official hours. And second, the Exchange's desire to be the dominant market will generally be determined by the quality of the technology it can offer to members. It will always be threatened by telephone or screen-based markets unless it can provide adequate, competitive trading mechanisms. The trading floor of the Exchange is traditionally important but not vital in practical terms. When most market makers and brokers will be using SEAQ and its ancillary systems for prices and dealing, the floor will really be useful only when dealers want to trade in very large parcels of equities where the price will be negotiable and when there have to be discussions between dealer and broker. It is probable that when market makers (former jobbers) start to make prices after the Big Bang they will not let the habits of a lifetime die that easily and will continue to use the floor for the 'market feel' they have always found so important through face-to-face dealings. But in time, when they have acclimatized to technology, it is difficult to imagine that they will find the floor essential.

Internal Changes on the Exchange

The Stock Exchange has always been the doyen of the self-regulatory bodies. It has now come under the jurisdiction of the Securities and Investments Board, which is a blow to its prestige. In the spring of 1986 it was discussing ways of reducing its cumbersome Council of fifty-two to a manageable size, perhaps sixteen plus eight outside or lay members. The transition from club to public service organization is not an easy one, but the Exchange has always been very conscious of its public responsibilities, even though there have been embarrassments in the past. Quite its hardest task after the Big Bang will be to stop its standards being eroded by the pressures of the new market environment.

These will be much more formidable than in the past. No one doubts that the competitive battlefield after the Big Bang will not have its casualties, many of whom will be British rather than foreign. There will always be a desire on the part of some firms to reduce standards or change the goal posts simply to stay in business. That is a heavy onus for the Exchange to bear. Up to now the administrators at Old Broad Street have moved with commendable speed to get the new market into shape for the Big Bang. From now on they have the difficult job of seeing that it is not distorted by players who are not fussy about the rules of the game.

The City's Survival

If the revolution in the City has been caused by the abolition of the Exchange's restrictive practices, its main purpose has turned out to be a bold attempt to restore to the Square Mile its former pre-eminence as a financial centre. But it demands the question that has always been uppermost in the minds of the City's severest critics: 'Can the City itself survive?' Short of a substitute for capitalism, by which the free world's financial markets live, the answer has to be 'Yes'. The City will survive; it will change; it may get smaller or larger but it will not disappear.

On the question of whether the Big Bang will attain its

main objective, that is quite another matter. The City has always maintained that it welcomes competition and that it can match it. That was an easy claim. As long as people in the Square Mile could make a handsome living, there was never anything much to be worried about. From time to time a few firms would disappear to be replaced by others, but the even tenor of City life has managed to remain remarkably unruffled in spite of the occasional crisis. If things go badly wrong after the Big Bang, then it has only itself to blame. It has, after all, always claimed that it has the ability to keep abreast of change, to initiate change and to be flexible. In that sense, what is happening now in the City will determine whether it will be *primus inter pares* in the financial world or be relegated to the second division.

INDEX